The New European Community

The New European Community

Decisionmaking and Institutional Change

EDITED BY

Robert O. Keohane and Stanley Hoffmann

HARVARD UNIVERSITY

Westview Press

BOULDER • SAN FRANCISCO • OXFORD

Copyright © 1991 by Westview Press, Inc.

Published in 1991 in the United States of America by Westview Press, Inc., 5500 Central Avenue, Boulder, Colorado 80301, and in the United Kingdom by Westview Press, Inc., 36 Lonsdale Road, Summertown, Oxford OX2 7EW

Library of Congress Cataloging-in-Publication Data
The New European community : decisionmaking and institutional change /
   edited by Robert O. Keohane and Stanley Hoffmann.
   p.   cm.
Includes bibliographical references and index.
ISBN 0-8133-8270-X — ISBN 0-8133-8271-8 (pbk.)
   1. European Communities.   2. Commission of the European
Communities.   3. Council of the European Communities.   4. European
Economic Community.   I. Keohane, Robert O. (Robert Owen), 1941–
II. Hoffmann, Stanley.
JN15.N49   1991
341.24′2—dc20   91-15478
                                                                          CIP

Printed and bound in the United States of America

 The paper used in this publication meets the requirements of the American National Standard for Permanence of Paper for Printed Library Materials Z39.48-1984.

10   9   8   7   6   5   4   3   2   1

Contents

Preface

Because to both of us good conversation is one of the highest forms of pleasure, it is appropriate that this volume had its origins in conversations with colleagues, friends, and one another. Its beginnings can be dated to a luncheon conversation in June 1988 between Andrew Moravcsik, then a graduate student in the Harvard Department of Government, and Robert Keohane. Moravcsik had just been in Europe, scouting out Ph.D. dissertation topics; Keohane had been in California, working on theories of institutions and paying little attention to current events in the European Community.

Moravcsik's enthusiastic description of the opportunities for research that the Single European Act presented induced Keohane to approach Stanley Hoffmann about jointly chairing a seminar series on the European Community, in conjunction with the Harvard-MIT seminar on international institutions, funded by the Ford Foundation. With alacrity Hoffmann agreed, and as a result, a series of well-attended seminars, sponsored by the Center for European Studies and the Center for International Affairs, took place in spring 1989. At one of these sessions Peter Ludlow delivered a brilliant talk on the European Monetary System.

After the seminar series had been planned, but before it had started up, another important conversation took place, not in Harvard Square but in Berkeley, California, at a conference convened by John Zysman in January 1989. Keohane attended the meeting in order to learn enough not to be embarrassed at the Harvard seminar series that he was about to co-chair. Between sessions, Helen Wallace of Chatham House (Royal Institute of International Affairs, London) conveyed to Keohane an offer from William Wallace, also of Chatham House, to write a paper giving a U.S. perspective on the European Community for a project on "the dynamics of European integration." One of the appealing aspects of the invitation was that a conference was planned for Florence in September 1989.

Keohane immediately said that he was not enough of a European expert to write such a paper on his own, but that he would see whether

Stanley Hoffmann might be interested in writing one with him. Once again, Hoffmann's response was enthusiastic. Several lunches in spring and summer 1989 yielded what seemed to be some promising ideas, and with the able research assistance of Victoria Gerus, then a second-year graduate student in the government department, they wrote a paper on institutional change in the European Community, which they delivered in Florence. This paper formed the basis for their contribution to the present volume. The argument of both versions is the same, although the chapter here has been reorganized, revised, and updated.

During the academic year 1989–1990, the joint seminar on the European Community continued, this time with a more definite theme: European institutions and their evolution. The papers in this volume by G. Federico Mancini, Andrew Moravcsik, and Shirley Williams, and the paper by Keohane and Hoffmann, were presented in this series. Wolfgang Wessels would also have presented a paper had his schedule permitted. When we planned this seminar, we had not thought of creating an edited volume until, in her inimitable way, Shirley Williams urged us to do so. This discussion led to further conversations with Susan McEachern and Jennifer Knerr of Westview Press, and then to our joint decision to go ahead. To ensure that this volume would examine all four major European institutions, we asked Peter Ludlow to write a paper on the Commission, and he kindly obliged, even without the enticement (if such it is) of another trip to Cambridge.

For each author, love of scholarship and the desire to present ideas to a wide audience provided the principal motivations for writing. Whatever royalties pertain to this project will be shared among the authors and editors—a rather uncertain and probably insubstantial monetary reward for their labors.

We dedicate this volume to our students, whom we expect to contribute greatly to our understanding of European institutions during the next several years. We hope they enjoy the scholarly inquiry, and the attendant conversations, as much as we have relished the activities involved in creating this book.

Robert O. Keohane
Stanley Hoffmann

1

Institutional Change in Europe in the 1980s

Robert O. Keohane and
Stanley Hoffmann

Since the revolutions in Eastern Europe in 1989, the position of Europe in world politics has been transformed. No longer do Soviet troops occupy the eastern portion of a divided Germany. The limitations on German sovereignty resulting from the rights in Germany of the four occupying powers, which persisted for forty-five years, came to a formal end in September 1990. The European Community (EC) is coordinating Western aid to the incipient democracies of Czechoslovakia, Hungary, and Poland and, more cautiously, to Bulgaria, Romania, and Yugoslavia. No longer is it meaningful to speak of "Western Europe" and "Eastern Europe" as distinct entities; for the first time since World War II, "Europe" is a political as well as geographical reality.

This Europe, however, is very different from the Europe of 1938. The most important institutional difference is that in the 1990s, much European policy is made not in national capitals but in Brussels, capital of the European Community. As of 1990, the EC comprised twelve countries with a joint population of about 340 million people and a gross domestic product of over $5,000 billion. The progressive elimination of trade barriers within the Community had created the world's largest market. It also meant that between 1970 and 1989, while EC countries' exports to the rest of the world grew ten times (in nominal terms), their exports to each other grew fifteen times, so that by 1989, 60 percent of these countries' exports went to each other.[1]

Not only have European Community rules prevailed in internal trade, its members have given up national trade policies to the Community,

FIGURE 1.1   The New Europe

which has negotiated international trade rules with the United States, Japan, and other external trade partners. Furthermore, between 1984 and early 1987, EC members agreed on the Single European Act (SEA), which reformed Community decisionmaking and mandated the creation of an internal market, without internal barriers or discrimination, by the end of 1992. By fall 1990, the successful implementation of these plans for an internal market seemed all but assured, and EC members were planning to extend the Community's powers in two respects: toward economic and monetary union (EMU) and by making far-reaching constitutional changes. It was expected that these constitutional reforms, discussed at the Intergovernmental Conference (IGC) beginning in December 1990, would help to define European citizenship, strengthen security cooperation, and, in particular, expedite European decision-making and make it more democratically accountable.

The success of the SEA was indeed a surprise. In the years immediately before the signing of the SEA in February 1986, few observers foresaw more than halting progress, and many expected stagnation or even decay of European movement toward regional centralization of decisionmaking. In his skeptical analysis of European decisionmaking during the 1970s, published in 1983, Paul Taylor stressed the limits imposed by states on European integration, arguing that "the challenges to sovereignty were successfully resisted and the central institutions failed to obtain the qualities of supranationalism."[2] His academic analysis echoed the cover of the *Economist* on March 20, 1982, showing a tombstone with the words, "EEC born March 25th, 1957, moribund March 25th, 1982, *capax imperii nisi imperasset*" (it seemed capable of power until it tried to wield it).[3] Even after agreement on the Single European Act, as Albert Bressand points out, the significance of the Act was underestimated both by skeptics and by federalists. Margaret Thatcher referred to it as a "modest decision," and Altiero Spinelli predicted that it "will almost certainly have proven its ineffectiveness within two years."[4] The *Economist* commented that "Europe has laboured long to produce a mouse."[5]

The unexpected success of European institutional change in the mid-1980s makes a more general theoretical point, which could be reinforced by the collapse of the Soviet empire in Eastern Europe in 1989. Because informed observers failed to anticipate such a centralization of Community policymaking any more than they later forecast the reunification of Germany and democratization in Eastern Europe, our efforts to explain Europe's institutional dynamism should be viewed with skepticism. What was unpredicted by analysts working with established theories cannot, in general, be adequately explained post hoc through the use of such theories.[6]

This volume seeks to describe and interpret the adoption and implementation of the Single European Act and the accompanying institutional changes that have taken place in the European Community during the 1980s. Our focus is institutional: We are interested in how political processes and practices have changed. Special attention is therefore paid to the principal Community institutions, in chapters by Peter Ludlow on the Commission, Wolfgang Wessels on the Council, Shirley Williams on the European Parliament and the problem of democratic accountability, and G. Federico Mancini on the European Court of Justice. The present chapter seeks both to locate European institutional changes in a wider global setting and to explore the relevance of some theories of European political change that were devised in the 1950s and 1960s. Andrew Moravcsik's interpretation of the origins of the Single European Act provides a detailed account of key events, along with his own evaluation of the relative merits of various theoretical perspectives often employed to account for the SEA.

We begin this chapter by briefly reviewing institutional changes in the European Community during the 1980s and their impact on other European countries, in the light of developments in the international political economy. In the second section we consider three general propositions about the nature of EC institutions, characterizing the EC as a network whose operations are well described as "supranational" in a specific sense but that have always rested on a set of intergovernmental bargains. In the third section we evaluate three competing hypotheses about EC institutional change, which focus on "spillover," pressures from a competitive world political economy, and convergence of preferences among various European polities. In our concluding section we offer some speculations about the European future—recognizing that in a period of rapid change, speculations can be dangerous if taken too seriously.

EUROPEAN INSTITUTIONAL CHANGE:
A BRIEF REVIEW

Western Europe's remarkable institutional transformation, from a collection of fractious nation-states to a partially amalgamated community, took place in the shadow of the Cold War (1947–1989).[7] Throughout the Cold War, Europe was a central focus of political struggle between the superpowers and a locus of economic transformation, as it had been before 1939. The first attempts at unity were inspired by a desire to prevent a repetition of World War II; these and subsequent measures were encouraged by the United States as part of its own Cold War strategy. Even during the 1970s and 1980s, Germany remained divided and restrained by formal limitations on its sovereignty, and Western Europe as a whole was a military protectorate of the United States. As long as the Cold War lasted, security threats from the Soviet Union were a source of cooperation within the West, reinforcing the NATO alliance as well as promoting U.S. support for the Community.

The Background to the Single European Act

The Single European Act was adopted and implemented while the Cold War persisted, and as its initial steps were being taken in 1984 and 1985, few observers foresaw a rapid thaw in U.S.-Soviet relations. The end of the Cold War must therefore not be regarded as playing any causal role in the mid-1980s' revival of European integration. From the standpoint of Europe at this time, the Cold War was a more or less frightening background condition, not a precipitating agent of change.

In the 1970s and through most of the 1980s, the more dynamic external pressures facing Europe were political-economic, emanating from the transformation of the world political economy and the competitive pressures that this transformation induced, rather than deriving from the Cold War. Since the formation of the Common Market in 1958, international trade and finance have grown immensely and have changed correspondingly. Capital movements rather than trade balances have become the dominant force on exchange rates. Since 1971 the price of oil has fluctuated sharply, depending on political and military events in the Middle East as well as economic conditions. During the 1970s and 1980s, technology-based oligopolistic competition among increasing internationalized firms, dependent on large-scale operations for profitability, intensified.

During these last two decades, East Asian economies have been transformed so rapidly that both Europe and the United States have had to adjust, especially to Japanese exports, technological competition, and financial expansion. Since the early 1970s it has become more difficult for Europe and the United States to determine the course of the world political economy without the participation of others—Japan on industrial issues, the oil-producing countries on energy issues in the 1970s. Furthermore, the economic turbulence of the 1970s created incentives for the United States to be less supportive of European policy than it had been previously and tempted European governments to make arrangements with oil-producing states that were at odds with their traditional deference to U.S. leadership. As the European Community has developed independent and sometimes quite assertive economic policies toward Japan and the United States, trade frictions have grown.

Until the very end of the 1980s, the socialist economies were largely cut off from this economic dynamism and the technological transformations that propelled it: Eastern Europe and the Soviet Union became economic backwaters and ecological disasters, using obsolete technology to produce increasingly obsolete products. But among the capitalist countries, international economic regimes became more elaborate, as the result of a series of tariff-lowering trade rounds, attempts to limit nontariff barriers, and efforts to coordinate policy in areas such as finance and energy.

As Western capitalism has engaged in its restless process of creative destruction during the last forty years, the fortunes of the European Community have waxed and waned. Prompted by a desire to prevent another war in Europe, as well as by visions of economic advantage, the postwar generation of leaders in France, Germany, Italy, and the Benelux countries created a remarkable set of institutions, culminating in the signing of the Treaty of Rome in 1957, which established the European Economic Community and Euratom (European Atomic Energy Community) to accompany the European Coal and Steel Community, which came into operation in 1952. After an initial period of success in lowering trade barriers and establishing common policies for agriculture and a number of other sectors, the Community's institutional transformation slowed down enormously in the mid-1960s, as a result of Charles de Gaulle's opposition to supranationality. Indeed, on most important issues the Community operated with a veto between 1966 and 1985. The European Council, an institutionalized summit meeting of heads of state or government, which supplemented but did not replace the Council of Ministers, was established in 1974. And the Community did expand, adding Britain, Denmark, and Ireland in 1973; Greece in 1981; and Portugal and Spain in 1986. But for its first decade of existence, the European Council was "at best a holding operation designed to prevent total collapse and at worst a dismal capitulation."[8] Expansion itself created problems for the Community's institutional machinery— most notably, the struggle over Britain's contribution to the budget, only resolved at the Fontainebleau council meeting in 1984. The intersecting struggles meant that throughout the period from 1966 to 1985, Europe was often viewed as politically and economically stagnant: In the early 1980s, "Eurosclerosis" was the fashionable term.

Almost as soon as they were made, however, forecasts of Eurosclerosis were falsified by the dramatic institutional transformation of Europe, exemplified by the negotiation and final ratification (in early 1987) of the Single European Act. Since 1987, furthermore, the movement toward completion of the internal market mandated by the Single European Act has been remarkably smooth. The vast majority of the 279 directives proposed in the Commission White Paper of 1985 had been adopted or were in the process of adoption by the Council by 1990. The new doctrine of mutual recognition—that each member country must accept products made under each other's product laws, subject to Europe-wide standards—has facilitated the enactment of directives to stop national product regulations and safety rules from blocking the free flow of goods.[9]

The scope of the Single European Act is not exhausted by its provisions for completion of the internal market. The Act represents a bargain on other issues as well, including limited foreign policy cooperation. Decisionmaking procedures have also changed. Under the Single Act, the Council decides issues relating to the adoption of measures required for the establishment and functioning of the internal market (Article 100a), as well as certain other issues, by qualified majority voting. Thus the scope of the Luxembourg compromise of 1966, an informal agreement that required unanimity on all questions a member deemed important to "national interest," has been sharply restricted. In December 1986 the Council amended its procedures on voting to require the President to call for a vote on such issues, at the request of a member of the Council or the Commission, whenever a majority of the members of the Council favor a measure. In 1988 the Commission reported that "the now fully accepted possibility of adopting a decision by a qualified majority forces the delegations to display flexibility throughout the debate, thus making decisionmaking easier."[10]

Despite the significance of these changes, it is important not to exaggerate the discontinuity in voting procedures created by the Single Act. In Chapter 2 Andrew Moravcsik shows that the scope of majority voting in the Single Act was limited to areas in which the British government favored reform. And in Chapter 3 Peter Ludlow points out that the new, expanded agenda of the Community in the mid-1980s led to increased reliance on majority voting even before the adoption of the Single Act. After all, the crucial decision at the Milan summit in June 1985 to call an Intergovernmental Conference—the key decision leading to the Single Act—was itself adopted by a qualified majority.

By the time the present work is published, further constitutional changes are likely to be in process; as mentioned above, a new Intergovernmental Conference convened in December 1990. Yet even without taking any such changes into account, the extent to which governments have sacrificed their legal freedom of action—sovereignty in the operational sense—is remarkable.

In other words, the EC has recently been continuing, even accelerating, its practice of "pooling sovereignty" through incremental change: sharing the capability to make decisions among governments, through a process of qualified majority rule. For issues on which sovereignty is pooled, authority to make decisions is removed from individual states. Many of these decisions have the force of Community law and are interpreted by the European Court of Justice. Yet authority is not transferred to a supranational body because the crucial decisionmaking role is taken by an interstate body (the EC Council of Ministers, as discussed in the chapter by Wolfgang Wessels), and because these decisions are implemented by national governments or—if these governments fail to carry out this task—through national courts, enforcing Community law.[11]

The central puzzle addressed in this chapter, and in various ways in all the chapters in this book, is how to account for the pooling of sovereignty and the unexpected set of institutional changes that have accompanied this process. Political scientists interested in theory development thrive on such puzzles—contradictions between what we should expect based on the conventional wisdom, or what passes for theory, and what we actually observe. During the past two decades, such contradictions have appeared between the realist state-centric view of world politics and the spread of transnational relations; and between the view that hegemony is essential to cooperation and the reality of extensive cooperation after the waning of U.S. dominance. The sudden and unexpected success of the Single European Act similarly confronts us with an analytical challenge.

Analyzing the Community in a Time of Flux

In the "dark ages" of the 1970s, positive institutional changes in Europe, such as the direct election of the European Parliament, were obscured to many observers by the Community's ineffectual response to the 1973 oil crisis, decisionmaking gridlock in the Council, and fears of Eurosclerosis. Nevertheless, during this period the European Community continued to display a magnetic attraction for countries on its periphery. The most striking indication of this attraction was the doubling of its membership after 1970. By the early 1980s, it was clear that members of the European Free Trade Area (EFTA) were anxious for closer association with the Community. Negotiations between the EC and the members of EFTA[12] led in 1984 to an EEC-EFTA Free Trade Area and continued at the end of the decade with more ambitious plans for a "European economic space." In 1989 Austria, a member of EFTA, applied to join the Community; Sweden has declared its intention to do so; and the East European democracies are already proclaiming EC membership as their long-term goal. A Community of twenty-four rather than twelve members is a distinct possibility by the end of the century.

These dramatic changes in Central Europe call into question even recent strategies, as they were formulated when the division of Germany appeared permanent. In early 1989 it seemed clear that the European

Community had begun a process of "deepening," extending its functions and strengthening its institutions, prior to any extension of membership. The accession of eastern Germany to the Federal Republic, however, has already added sixteen million people to the Community, without official Community action. As other governments adjust to the reality of German reunification, and as the Germans themselves react to the economic difficulties created by this historic turn of events, attitudes on EC issues change. During summer and fall 1990, for instance, German, Spanish, and Dutch finance ministers took the lead in criticizing the Delors Plan for a European union of central banks, counseling greater institutional caution; but in late October, eleven Community members (all except Britain) formally committed themselves to a January 1, 1994, starting date for the second stage of EMU. Rather than seeking to slow down institutional integration, furthermore, Chancellor Helmut Kohl of Germany began urging increased powers for the European Parliament.[13]

In such a situation of flux, forecasting is a hazardous enterprise, especially in a book to be published more than six months after the prediction is made. Nevertheless, whatever the details agreed to at the conferences on EMU and constitutional changes, there seems little doubt that European institutions will continue to become stronger and more encompassing, partly as a way of attaching Germany firmly to its partners. And there seems little doubt that Western Europe as a whole, and the institutions of the European Community in particular, will play the leading role in providing finance, investment, markets, and political guidance for those Eastern European countries whose politics enable them to become linked closely to Western capitalism.

As this expansion and strengthening of the Community continues, it will become increasingly important for scholars to understand its origins and dynamics. In view of our failure to predict developments using older theories, perhaps a new interpretation of joint European decisionmaking should be invented, discarding loaded terms such as "supranationality" and "spillover," and drawing instead on contemporary theories of strategic choice in collective situations, or recent attempts to understand institutional innovation.[14]

Before casting aside older theories, particularly neofunctionalist theories of change, however, we should reexamine them to see what insights they may yet contain—insights that may well have been buried by decades of stereotyping engaged in by critics of neofunctionalism. It seems unfortunate to us that many of the accounts of European Community politics have discarded neofunctional theory without putting anything theoretical in its place: Recourse is made to mere description of processes and events. Attempts to avoid theory, however, not only miss interesting questions but rely implicitly on a framework for analysis that remains unexamined precisely because it is implicit. Hence, the next two sections of this chapter take neofunctional theory seriously, to determine whether its insights may help us to understand the Europe of the 1980s and perhaps even to glean some clues to future developments.

THREE PROPOSITIONS
ABOUT EUROPEAN INSTITUTIONS

We begin with three propositions about the nature of the institutions of the European Community, which will form the basis for our subsequent exploration of institutional change. These propositions are largely static, although the third edges into description of processes of change. They can be summarized as follows:

1. The EC is best characterized as neither an international regime nor an emerging state but as a network involving the pooling of sovereignty.
2. The political process of the EC is well described by the term "supranationality" as used by Ernst Haas in the 1960s (although not as often used subsequently).
3. However, the EC has always rested on a set of *intergovernmental bargains*, and the Single European Act is no exception to this generalization.

The European Community as a Network

Like international regimes, such as the trade regime under the auspices of the General Agreement on Tariffs and Trade (GATT), the European Community establishes common expectations, provides information, and facilitates arm's-length intergovernmental negotiations. It is designed to protect its members against the consequences of uncertainty, as the formation of the European Monetary System (EMS) during a period of dollar volatility and weakness indicates. Yet the flexible and dynamic Community is much more centralized and institutionalized than an international regime and receives a much higher level of commitment from its members. It has gone well beyond any known "international organization."

The originality of the Community is also evident in foreign affairs. Traditionally, confederations, federations, and unitary states confer to their central institutions what Locke had called the "federative power"— the power to act for the state in international affairs, or, to use the correct legal term, external sovereignty. This is not the case in the EC, whose central institutions have full jurisdiction over only external trade, no more than a power of coordination over the rest of foreign policy, and no power yet over defense. In international meetings other than those of the GATT, the Community is not yet a distinctive actor. At best it is represented along with its members (as at the Group of Seven, or G7, meetings); usually the member states are the actors in world monetary, diplomatic, and military affairs. The "principle of subsidiarity," which prescribes that, in the creation of the single market, the Community take over only those functions the states cannot adequately perform, has not really been applied in foreign affairs and defense, for if it had been, the role of the EC as an actor would be far more important than it is—indeed it would perhaps even be the exclusive actor in matters of security.

As students of world politics and political economy, we are struck by the distinctiveness of the Community among contemporary international organizations. Most evident, perhaps, is the Commission, a coherent executive body composed of over 10,000 professionals that is able to take initiatives and whose President plays a role at summit meetings of heads of government of industrialized countries. When Jacques Delors became its head in early 1985, he decided that the best realm for a *relance* (or "relaunch") of the Community would be the internal market rather than either monetary union or diplomacy and defense, areas in which there was no good prospect of inter-state bargains and convergence of interests. And when the Council met in Milan in June 1985, it found on its table the Commission's famous White Paper on the creation of a single market. It is hard to imagine the European Community without the initiatives undertaken by the Commission. In Chapter 3, Ludlow analyzes the Commission's role in detail, stressing the "bureaucratic intermingling" of Commission, Council, and national administrations. Figure 3.4 provides a graphic portrayal of this distinctive European political process.

Another distinction of the European Community is its legal status: No other international organization enjoys such reliably effective supremacy of its law over the laws of member governments, with a recognized Court of Justice to adjudicate disputes. The Community legal process has a dynamic of its own. Despite a number of cases of nonimplementation of Community law, by the standards of international organizations implementation has been extraordinary. A recent study concludes that national administrations implement Community law about as effectively as they apply national law, and in its own analysis of such issues, the Commission has concluded that most national courts "are collaborating effectively in the implementation of Community law."[15] Indeed, of all Community institutions, the Court has gone farthest in limiting national autonomy, by asserting the principles of superiority of

Community law and of the obligation of member states to implement binding national acts consistent with Community directives.[16]

In addition to its executive capacity and legal powers, the Community has financial resources at its disposal. Furthermore, unlike any other organization in the world political economy, it makes trade policies for twelve states, constituting the largest market in the world. The contrast with the new North American Free Trade Area is instructive: The latter constitutes an agreement between two sovereign countries, with arrangements for dispute settlement between the United States and Canada but without common policymaking institutions with authority to negotiate with the rest of the world on behalf of both countries. From an institutional standpoint, the transformation of Europe during the last two or three decades has been dissimilar to the evolution of institutions elsewhere in the area of the Organization for Economic Cooperation and Development (OECD).

Boundaries are difficult to draw in a world of complex interdependence: Because relationships cross boundaries and coalitional patterns vary from issue to issue, it is never possible to classify all actors neatly into mutually exclusive categories. Europe is no exception. But institutional boundaries are clearer than those of trade or loyalty. The twelve EC states make decisions jointly, whereas EFTA members, no matter how important they are to the European economy, do not participate in that decisionmaking process. Europe has an institutional core, which is the European Community.

The kind of entity that is emerging does not, however, much resemble the sort of entity that the most enthusiastic functionalists and federalists had in mind. For they envisaged a transfer of powers to institutions whose authority would not derive from the governments of the member states, and a transfer of political loyalty to the center. According to the most optimistic scenarios, a "United States of Europe" would have come into being—a state with the key attributes of internal and external sovereignty: "supremacy over all other authorities within that territory and population" and "independence of outside authorities."[17]

Portrayals of the state are often bedeviled by the image of an idealtypical "state" whose authority is unquestioned and whose institutions work smoothly. No such state has ever existed; viewed close up, all modern states appear riddled with inefficiencies and contradictions. Nevertheless, the European Community by no means approximates a realistic image of a modern state, much less an idealized one. If in comparison with the authority of contemporary international organizations the Community looks strong, in comparison with highly institutionalized modern states it appears quite weak indeed. This weakness is reflected in that individual economic agents do not have direct access to the European Court of Justice for redress of grievances. But it is also political: As discussed elsewhere in this book and later in this chapter, the Community depends inordinately on one state—Germany. The European Community political system rests on national political systems, especially that of the Federal Republic.

The European Community looks anomalous from the standpoint of traditional state-centric theory because it is essentially organized as a network that involves the pooling and sharing of sovereignty rather than the transfer of sovereignty to a higher level. Unlike international organizations, the European Community as a whole has gained some share of states' sovereignty: The member states no longer have supremacy over all other authorities within their traditional territory, nor are they independent of outside authorities. Its institutions have some of the authority that we associate with institutions of sovereign governments: On certain issues individual states can no longer veto proposals before the Council; members of the Commission are independent figures rather than instructed agents. Especially with a leader of vision and method, such as Delors, the Commission is an indispensable fount of proposals and prodding; under the complex provisions of the Single European Act, furthermore, the Council can amend Commission recommendations only with great difficulty.

Yet national governments continue to play a dominant role in the decisionmaking process. Ludlow's analysis of the Commission (Chapter 3) and Wessels's discussion of the Council of Ministers (Chapter 4) reinforce the assessment of Heinrich Siedentopf and Jacques Ziller, who point out that "Community institutions and national government bodies involved do not act autonomously, but in common."[18] Policy is fragmented by sector, although within sectors a great deal of informal coordination, among national bureaucrats and interest groups, takes place. There are innumerable committees of national experts and bureaucrats preparing the Commission's proposals and the Council's decisions.[19] The execution of the Council's directives by the Commission is closely supervised by committees of national bureaucrats, some of which can overrule the Commission's moves. The Community has a highly complex policymaking process in which formal and informal institutions at different levels in the formal structure, if in the formal structure at all, are linked by a variety of networks.

The European Community operates neither as a political "market"—characterized by arm's-length transactions among independent entities—nor as a "hierarchy," in which the dominant mode of regulation is authoritative rule. Rather, the EC exemplifies what sociologists refer to as a "network form of organization," in which individual units are defined not by themselves but in relation to other units.[20] Actors in a

network have a preference for interaction with one another rather than
with outsiders, in part because intense interactions create incentives for
self-interested cooperation and for the maintenance of reputations for
reliability. In the Community, authority remains dispersed, but joint
benefits can be gained by the exchange of reliable information—which
long-term partners have more incentives to provide than do rivals.[21]
Wessels shows how the complex system of committees, working groups,
and expert groups creates networks of European bureaucrats and of
national administrators who play a dual role as representatives of their
states and as European agents. Transnational networks associated with
each council of ministers link Europe-wide interest groups, national and
Commission administrations, and committees of the European Parliament.
As Wessels says, the EC is not run by a few European specialists but
is serious business "for the ministers and high civil servants alike."

The notion of a network is more a metaphor than a theory. It helps
to emphasize the horizontal ties among actors and the complexity of
their relationships, but it does not elaborate clear hypotheses about
behavior. In 1975 Ernst Haas sought to take related notions a step
farther by characterizing the European Community as a "semi-lattice"
form of organization, somewhat between a hierarchy and a simple matrix:
"There is a clear center of authority for some activities and decisions,
but not for all. Lines of authority duplicate and overlap; tasks are
performed in fragments by many subsystems; sometimes authority flows
sideways and upwards, at other times the flow is downward."

Haas went on to predict that in a semi-lattice form of organization,
actors would first react to increased complexity and interdependence by
incremental, piecemeal approaches—seeking to "decompose" issues. In
the longer run, he speculated, these actors might realize that they were
sacrificing potential benefits with such a response and might devise new
policies.[22] As Haas recognized, the networks of the European Community
constitute neither a hierarchy nor a gemeinschaft, despite the community
rhetoric. With respect to the latter, it is enough to recall the quarrels
during the early 1980s over Britain's payments to the Community budget.
Britain argued on the basis of equity, whereas its Continental opponents
lamented what they saw as reinstitution of the principle of *juste retour*,
characterized by Foreign Minister Claude Cheysson of France as "not
a community idea."[23] Reciprocity in Europe is often quite specific—
demanding tit-for-tat exchanges of equivalent value. Yet as in the Community's North-South bargain, actors in the EC sometimes practice
"diffuse reciprocity," transferring resources to others in the expectation
that doing so will increase the legitimacy of the Community and its
long-term stability, as well as providing the donors with political influence
in the interim.[24]

The inappropriateness of statist, strictly intergovernmental, or even confederal models of how European politics operates stems from the inconsistency of these images with the network metaphor or the semi-lattice model, which serve as the best approximation to the evolving reality. "Supranationality," despite the unfortunate connotations of federalism encrusted onto the term, is compatible with these notions. The Community political system can best be visualized as an elaborate set of networks, closely linked in some ways, particularly decomposed in others, whose results depend on the political style in ascendance at the moment. When conditions are propitious and leadership strategies appropriate, as they have been since 1985, the political style of supranationality enables connections to be made among points in the network, and for an expanded conception of tasks. When conditions are less benign or strategies inappropriate, the results are policy stagnation and separation of policy spheres.

Supranationality in the European Community

Perhaps surprisingly, the most appropriate label for the political process of the European Community is Haas's notion of "supranationality." The conception of supranationality, rarely referred to in the recent literature on Europe except with disdain, has suffered grievous misinterpretation and stereotyping over the years. For Haas, supranationality did not mean that Community institutions exercise authority over national governments: "General de Gaulle equates supranationality with a federalism which he detests; Jean Monnet identifies it with a federalism of which he is a leading partisan. Both gentlemen mistake the essence of the phenomenon." Haas also denied a necessary association between supranationality and a "Community viewpoint." That is, supranationality is not at the end of a continuum, whose other end is occupied by strict intergovernmentalism. Instead, supranationality refers to a process or style of decisionmaking, "a cumulative pattern of accommodation in which the participants refrain from unconditionally vetoing proposals and instead seek to attain agreement by means of compromises upgrading common interests."[25] Haas saw this process as implying, structurally, "the existence of governmental authorities closer to the archetype of federation than any past international organization, but not yet identical with it."[26]

Haas viewed supranationality as a style of political behavior through which political interests would be realized, not as a depoliticized form of technical decisionmaking. What Haas called the "three core assumptions" on which theories of regional integration were based can be seen more accurately as the institutional results of the supranational decisionmaking style: "1) that a definable institutional pattern must mark the outcome of the process of integration, 2) that conflicts of interests involving trade-offs between ties with regional partners and ties with nonmembers should be resolved in favor of regional partners, and 3) that decisions be made on the basis of disjointed incrementalism."[27] Haas emphasized that "learning is based on the perceptions of self-interest displayed by the actors," and that lessons will only be generalized "if the actors, on the basis of their interest-inspired perceptions, desire to adapt integrative lessons learned in one context to a new situation."[28] And he emphasized connections between politics and economics: "The supranational style stresses the indirect penetration of the political by way of the economic because the 'purely' economic decisions always acquire political significance in the minds of the participants. In short, the kind of economic and social questions here dealt with are those at the very core of the modern welfare state."[29]

The Single European Act reinvigorated Community institutions, particularly by providing for qualified majority voting on issues related to the internal market. It can be argued that what this accomplished, in institutional terms, was the dramatic revival of a largely supranational decisionmaking style that was lost after 1966, frequently lamented in the years thereafter, and only partially restored with the reforms after the Paris Summit of 1974.[30] Yet this style is supranationality without supranational institutions: The Council is a body of state representatives; the Commission is not a supranational entity in the sense of being an authoritative decisionmaker above the nation-state, nor has loyalty been transferred from the nation-state to the Commission. "Progressive regional centralization of decisionmaking," as Haas calls it, has taken place. But we do not observe political integration in the more demanding sense of Haas's formulation in *The Uniting of Europe*: "The process whereby political actors in several distinct national settings are persuaded to shift their loyalties, expectations and political activities toward a new center, whose institutions possess or demand jurisdiction over the pre-existing national states."[31]

The current ascendancy of a qualified supranational style of decisionmaking is shown by the way in which, thanks to the Single Act, the Council now functions. There are no permanent coalitions in it, no country can either dominate or paralyze it, and the major players have repeatedly modified their initial positions in order to reach compromises. But the success of this style does not assure its continuation: The intergovernmental decisions on which the current situation rests (analyzed in the next section) could collapse, or entropy could set in as present goals are accomplished without new ones being agreed upon. Least of all does our use of the language of supranationality imply that Europe possesses sovereignty in any simple, unitary way. Quite to the contrary, as emphasized in the previous section, the European Community is an exercise in the pooling and sharing of sovereignty.

Intergovernmental Bargains and the European Community

Although the *process* of European Community policymaking is supranational, all this negotiation and coalition-building takes place within the context of agreements between governments. Without the original Franco-German accord, neither the European Coal and Steel Community nor the Common Market would have ever existed. Likewise, as Moravcsik argues in Chapter 2, any attempt to understand the Single European Act must begin with a recognition that *governments* took the final crucial steps leading to its negotiation and ratification.[32] Franco-German relations, based on a series of mutually beneficial bargains, have always been at the core of the politics of the European Community. The revival of a supranational style of decisionmaking and the strengthening of European institutions in the Single Act resulted most immediately from decisions by governments to press, in their own interests, for a removal of internal economic barriers and for institutional changes that would permit such a policy to be carried out.

Our argument is that successful spillover requires prior programmatic agreement among governments, expressed in an intergovernmental bargain. Such a bargain is clearly important in accounting for the Single European Act. Without the turnaround of French economic policy in 1983 and the decision by the British government to accept Treaty amendment in order to institutionalize deregulation, no consensus could have been reached on a program to dismantle barriers within Europe. The British government was very clear that it was entering into a bargain and not acting on the basis of an ideology of unity or solidarity with Europe. When Margaret Thatcher was asked in May 1989 why she had agreed to ratify the Single European Act, she replied simply that "we wished to have many of the directives under majority voting because things which we wanted were being stopped by others using a single vote. For instance, we have not yet got insurance freely in Germany as we wished."[33]

To say this is not to declare that a state-centric perspective will provide a satisfactory explanation of the Single European Act, only that such an explanation must begin with governmental actions, for these actions are what we observe as leading directly to the Act. The analyst must eventually go beyond these interstate bargains to the domestic political processes of the member states, on the one hand, and to the constraints of international institutions, on the other. Yet these interstate bargains remain the necessary conditions for European integration and must be recognized as such.

THREE COMPETING HYPOTHESES
ABOUT EC INSTITUTIONAL CHANGE

Even a reader who accepts our argument so far might entertain three quite different hypotheses about the sources of European institutional change in the 1980s. One hypothesis locates the sources of change within Europe, in the political institutions and processes of the Community. Haas made such an argument when he discussed what he called "spillover" from one sector to another.

A second view, the "political economy hypothesis," argues quite straightforwardly that institutional change in the European Community should be seen principally as a form of adaptation to pressures from the world political economy. This hypothesis is, broadly speaking, functional: The form of the European Community follows the functions it must perform to keep its firms, and economies, competitive in a rapidly changing world economy.

The third hypothesis is less often discussed but is consistent with our view that large-scale social change is typically the result of conjunctions of events that are not tightly related to one another. This "preference-convergence hypothesis" holds that a necessary condition for new EC-wide policies, or more centralized decisionmaking procedures, is convergence of governments' preferences about economic policy, for reasons that do not result principally from prior EC policies or from the pressures of the world political economy.

"Spillover"

Writing in the late 1950s, Haas characterized the process of spillover not as a manifestation of enthusiasm for the ideology of Europe but as a more prosaic result of "swapping concessions from a variety of sectors":

> Lack of agreement among governments can give rise to increased delegated powers on the part of these [supranational] institutions. Dissatisfaction with the results of partial economic steps may lead labor and industry to demand new central action. Supranational institutions and national groups may create situations which can be dealt with only through central action, unless the nations are willing to suffer deprivations in welfare. . . . No statesman, even if he deeply dislikes the process, can permanently isolate his nation from a commitment to unity which is only partially implemented, unless he is willing to pay the price in diminished welfare.[34]

Haas was sophisticated about the politics of spillover—in contrast to the distortions of his views common in the contemporary literature. "The spillover process," as he said, "is far from automatic." It depends on the continued division of Germany and "the tacit recognition of that status in the minds of West German leaders." Furthermore, spillover does not presume continued enthusiasm on the part of elites; indeed, its significance is most evident in the continuation of regional integration even as élan declines.[35]

"Spillover" is, as we have said, an ambiguous term. It can be used simply descriptively, to refer to the enlargement of "an authoritative and legitimate international task."[36] But its theoretical interest derives from a causal conceptualization. Joseph S. Nye, for instance, defines spillover as referring to a situation in which "imbalances created by the functional interdependence or inherent linkages of tasks can press political actors to redefine their common tasks."[37] This latter definition can be used either to characterize changing incentives facing states or to a more complex pattern of transnational activity in which national actors "appear as *differentiated* actors, a plurality of negotiating units (classes, status groups, subregions, *clienteles*, bureaucratic agencies, ideological clusters, etc.)."[38]

Neofunctionalists disagreed whether the changing incentives posited by the causal conception of spillover provided an explanation for task expansion. Nye argued that "the functional linkage of tasks has been a less powerful mechanism than was originally believed to be the case" and sought to construct a "revised neofunctionalist process model" in which deliberate linkages, actions of external actors, elite socialization, and other factors played comparable roles. Leon N. Lindberg and Stuart A. Scheingold even sought to refute Haas's conception that spillover led to the Common Market: "The successful transformation that gave birth to the Common Market was not a result of functional spillover."[39]

As argued above, we believe that spillover does not adequately account for major decisions such as those of the Milan summit in 1985 and, subsequently, those that led to the Single Act. If spillover and pressure from the European institutions had been sufficient to create such a step-level change, it would have occurred much earlier. After all, the members had repeatedly committed themselves to full economic union, but such a union had not been consummated. It is plausible to conjecture that spillover leads to task expansion in the wake of a major intergovernmental bargain, but it would be more difficult to argue that such bargains are themselves explained by endogenous changes in incentives, as a result of past policy change. The 1992 program was much more strongly affected by events in the world political economy outside of Europe— especially by concern about international competitiveness—than it was driven by the internal logic of spillover.

Spillover is an important concept, but it can only be usefully employed within a carefully delimited sphere. Before it is used effectively in

20   Robert O. Keohane and Stanley Hoffmann

research, different meanings will need to be distinguished, as above, and the *conditions* under which spillover can be expected to operate must be kept in mind.[40] The "theory of spillover" has therefore not been discredited: In the wake of an intergovernmental bargain based on subjective similarity and a common policy orientation, actors can have incentives to promote task expansion into new sectors in order to protect gains already achieved. But it remains to be seen, from empirical research, how much this theory will explain of the institutional changes now being observed in the European Community.

Bargains that cover only certain sectors, omitting to provide for sectors linked to these, can stimulate a spillover process either on an interstate basis (as incentives facing states change) or on a transnational one. This core idea of the neofunctionalists is consistent with much of what we know about how changes in the international political economy affect incentives for states. It leaves open for investigation, however, the question of how fast and how far spillover from an initial bargain will extend.

Any explanation of the institutional changes in the Single European Act must take into account that for a decade before the mid-1980s, the Community was preoccupied by its expansion to include twelve governments rather than the original six or the nine of the 1970s. A number of quiet institutional accomplishments occurred during those years: The creation of the European Council in 1974, the decision to have the European Parliament elected directly by the people, the establishment of the European Monetary System, and the enlargement negotiations that added six new members to the original six, all prepared the way for the dramatic events between 1985 and 1990.[41] During these years much concern was expressed about the negative consequences enlargement was expected to have on decisionmaking. For the better part of a decade, the Commission declared that "with twelve members, the institutions and decisionmaking procedures will be under considerable strain and the Community will be exposed to possible stalemate and dilution unless its practical *modus operandi* is improved."[42] As William Wallace put the issue in 1978:

> The fundamental question is . . . can one at the same time enlarge the Community and strengthen it? M. Calvo-Sotelo insisted that we could and would; many interventions in the Working Group discussions implied that we couldn't and wouldn't. My own conclusion is that we can—but that we are unlikely to, unless the current members accept the full responsibilities of enlargement and act towards each other and towards the Communities in approaching enlargement in a more positive spirit.[43]

Despite prevailing doubts, enlargement did contribute to strengthening Community institutions, not because of idealism or governments' senses of obligations but because governments sought to use Europe to promote deregulation and because decisionmaking was becoming virtually impossible under the practice of unanimity. By the mid-1980s, even the British government believed that it could not attain the predicted large benefits from deregulation without some way to ensure that its partners would open up their markets, and the most credible guarantee that this would occur was Treaty amendment, institutionalizing the deregulatory process and instituting qualified majority rule over it. With twelve members, the unit-veto system of the European Council would, in the absence of complex package deals, lead to stalemate on increasing numbers of issues. For a major advance in policy integration to take place, these package deals would have had to be so complex that the costs of negotiating them would have become prohibitive.

The contrast with the French position between 1965 and 1966 is quite instructive. The Common Agricultural Policy (CAP) had been agreed upon, as had the customs union. Both could and did continue without implementation of the EC Treaty provisions for qualified majority voting. De Gaulle could therefore block qualified majority voting, as well as increases in the power of the Commission, without jeopardizing France's economic policy goals. Britain, in 1985, could not do this: Changes in the voting procedures, and indeed Treaty amendments, were the price to be paid for the 1992 program to complete the internal market, because to achieve this objective, recalcitrant governments had to be outvoted.

Ultimate British willingness to accept majority voting reflected its acceptance of the argument that enlargement made effective use of unanimity impossible. In June 1985 the Minister of State at the Foreign and Commonwealth Office, Malcolm Rifkind, declared: "We believe that enlargement of the Community to 12 will make the existing procedures more unlikely to be capable of reaching early agreement on matters of importance." Similarly, in the French Senate debates on ratification of the Single Act, the French Minister of Foreign Affairs, Jean-Bernard Raimond, stated that "the Europe of twelve could not be administered as was the Community of six and must adapt its decisionmaking mechanisms to this new enlargement."[44]

Part of the story of the Single European Act, therefore, is that governments decided to strike a bargain on deregulation, which seemed to them to require, were it to be effective, reform of the decisionmaking system. Indeed, the Single European Act can even be seen as partly a way of completing arrangements for the enlargement of the Community to twelve members.[45] A new form of spillover, not from one economic sector to another but from one institutional dimension to another, took place. Under conditions of unanimous decisionmaking, expansion of the

Community led to anticipation of institutional stalemate, and (because the key actors sought policy changes) created incentives for formal institutional change.

Thus in a dialectical manner, the enlargement from the six to twelve, first appearing as an antithesis to effective decisionmaking, became a decisive element in decisionmaking reform. Spillover took place not as a functional expansion of tasks but rather in the form of the creation, as a result of enlargement, of incentives for institutional change. Of course, as Haas recognized, spillover was not automatic. Policy change and institutional change also required a convergence of interests between states.

The Political Economy Hypothesis

As we emphasized at the outset of this chapter, decisions on European integration during the 1980s were made in the context of a political economy of the 1980s that was greatly changed from that of the previous decade. U.S. policy had facilitated European integration in the 1950s and early 1960s, but the economic turbulence of the 1970s had created incentives for competitive extra-European affiliations (especially with oil-producing states). In the 1980s, oligopolistic competition intensified, but for European industry, it appeared increasingly necessary to merge or collaborate to attain sufficient economies of scale and the technological capability to cope with U.S. and Japanese competitors. The "conversion" of the French government in 1983 and the enthusiasm of Britain for deregulation opened the way for elites from big business and the Commission, concerned about the "waning competitiveness" of the EC vis-à-vis the United States and Japan and the perception that "international business seemed to turn its back on the EC." The "national champion" strategy of the 1970s, which had increased the perceived diversity of national situations and competition among European states, was now seen as a failure; European firms could only compete on an international scale if their home market became united rather than fragmented.[46] Thus events in the world political economy were important influences on the governmental decisions associated with the Community's revival.

Yet the political economy hypothesis, however important as part of the puzzle, is not sufficient to explain the sudden strengthening of European institutions during the 1980s. After all, Europe faced serious economic challenges in the late 1960s—when Jean-Jacques Servan-Schreiber coined the phrase, "the American challenge"—and in the 1970s, when a combination of U.S. political and economic policies and events in the Middle East produced turbulence in the markets for money and for oil. Had Europe unified itself more strongly in the 1970s, one could have "explained" those actions in functionalist terms as a reaction to instability, and indeed the formation of the European Monetary System in 1978 is often attributed to European concern about errant U.S. policy. Furthermore, from a rational-adaptive perspective the Europeans should have anticipated the effects of technological change on economies of scale and prospects for corporate competitiveness, and altered their institutions in the 1970s in preparation for the competitive struggles of the 1980s. Instead, decisive moves toward the Single European Act were delayed until the perception of crisis was widespread. The political economy hypothesis indeed would have predicted the strengthening of European institutions, but that revival could have occurred at any time after 1973. To understand the timing of the Single European Act, one also has to look at events within the domestic politics of European countries.

The Preference-Convergence Hypothesis

We have argued that although both the spillover and the political economy hypotheses contain some elements of truth, neither alone explains institutional change in Europe. Nor, in our view, are they sufficient for explanation together. A third hypothesis, which focuses on the convergence of preferences of major European governments, is necessary. In formulating this hypothesis, we should keep in mind Haas's own warning that incrementalist strategies, which are necessary for spillover, depend on shared objectives, based on a common understanding of causality as well as ultimate goals. In the 1950s and early 1960s, Europe thrived on what Haas called "a pragmatic synthesis of capitalism and socialism in the form of democratic planning." With such shared objectives, tactics and means can vary as interests and alignments change; furthermore, the specific objectives of the participants can be quite diverse as long as they are complementary with respect to proposed Europe-wide policies. Haas explained the ratification of the European Coal and Steel Community Treaty in the early 1950s as "the convergence, not of six separate national interests, but of a sufficiently large number of separate national party positions to push the Treaty over the top. . . . The very ambiguity of the Treaty, of course, made this pattern of convergence possible. Something seemed to be 'in it' for everybody and a large enough body of otherwise quarreling politicians was persuaded to launch the first experiment in deliberate integration."[48]

There is much in this description that could be applied to the Single European Act. Like the Treaty of Rome, its ratification resulted less from a coherent burst of idealism than from a convergence of national interests around a new pattern of economic policymaking: not the Keynesian synthesis of the 1950s and 1960s but the neoliberal, deregulatory program of the 1980s. Reliance on "mutual recognition" rather than harmonization reflected the decision to focus Community attention on removal of barriers rather than on means of economic intervention.[49] This particular bargain illustrates the general point that the members of a regional organization must regard themselves as having a great deal in common, distinguishing themselves from outsiders. It is, as one of us wrote during the earlier debates, "not that the units be in 'objectively' similar situations but that there be 'subjective' similarity—a conviction on the part of the policymakers that the similarity exists."[50] It was only after the shift in French economic policy in 1983 and the general turn toward deregulatory preferences that such subjective similarity reappeared in Europe.

Focusing on an intergovernmental bargain leaves out one actor: the Commission. When Delors became its head in early 1985, he decided that the best realm in which to relaunch the Community would be the internal market rather than either monetary union or diplomacy and defense, areas in which there was no good prospect of interstate bargains and convergence of interests. When the Council met in Milan in June 1985, it found on its table the famous White Paper prepared by the Commission about the creation of a single market. The Milan summit endorsed that program and also decided on the institutional reform that led to the Single Act. Still, it can be argued that Delors's major contribution was to focus states' attention on the one issue—the single market—that was acceptable to the three major actors, Britain, West Germany, and France.

If policy convergence among major governments was so important, we are left with the task of trying to explain why the interests of the major actors became convergent after having failed to be "subjectively similar" for so long, despite many earlier attempts at creating a single market. In the case of Britain, the decisive factor was external: a change in Britain's relation to the EC, whose Council finally made large concessions to Thatcher's demands aimed at reducing Britain's budgetary contribution. This made it possible for her to move on to the task she deemed important, deregulation, and to overcome her own objections to the abandonment of the rule of unanimity, as a qualified majority rule was necessary to the adoption of the single-market program.

The decisive concession to Thatcher had been made possible by a change in French policy. In order to account for the new definition of France's interest, we have to examine both international and domestic factors. The fiasco of the Socialist policy of 1981–1983 did not require a turn to the EC. Many Socialist leaders and businesspeople, as well as the Communists, advocated autarky and the removal of the franc from the EMS. But such a choice would have (1) put François Mitterrand at the mercy of his Communist allies and of the Left of his party, (2) cut France off from West Germany and the United States, to which Mitterrand, at that time, wanted France to cling, and (3) most probably undercut even further France's competitiveness.

Thus we end with a tentative conclusion congruent with regime theory: The existence of a "regime"—in this case, the EC—though it did not provoke the new definition of British and French interests, affected these states' calculations of incentives and made it possible for them to see a policy of relaunching Europe as advantageous. And while this relaunch is not a simple case of spillover, the four major actions taken during the period 1973–1984 and other moves, such as creating new programs of cooperation in technology and in higher education, made such a relaunch more attractive by making it appear more capable of succeeding. Nevertheless, in contrast to that period, when any institutional change required protracted and painful negotiation, there is little doubt that European decisionmaking has since 1985 been more expeditious and effective; we attribute a decisive role in that change not only to incentives for the world political economy and spillover but also to intergovernmental bargains made possible by convergence of preferences of major European states.

SPECULATIONS ABOUT THE FUTURE

At the end, we return to our starting point. EC institutional change was not determined either by spillover or by changes in the international political economy—significant as these both were. The SEA depended on a *conjunction* of events, which included:

1. Expansion of membership
2. Solution of the UK budgetary crisis
3. Intensification of pressures from the world political economy
4. Failure of old regulatory policies, involving a move toward market economies
5. The decision of the French Socialists to move toward the right

If developments in the EC during the 1980s were conjunctural— dependent on a combination of events, partly external to the EC, partly domestic—surely this is even more likely to be true for the 1990s. There is internal momentum in the EC. But to forecast the future one would need to know:

1. The effects of German reunification on the now-enlarged Federal Republic
2. The extent and intensity of German nationalism
3. The reactions of Germany's EC partners to the new, united Germany and to its policies
4. The likelihood of instability in Eastern Europe and the USSR
5. The effects of Eastern European developments and needs on the North-South bargain within the Community
6. Whether U.S. policy will be supportive
7. The ultimate effects on the members of the Community (and on their evaluation of their interests) of the Gulf war of 1991 and the U.S. recession of 1990–1991

Spillover will not be unimportant. The realization of the single market will create demands for further measures. Adopted by the Council in February 1988, the "Delors package"—an agreement to increase the resources of the Community and the funds for the poorer countries— is an example of meeting such demands. The current controversy over monetary union provides another case in point. If the full benefit is to be derived from the single market, stable exchange rates are essential within the Community. Yet the very success of the European Monetary System in creating exchange-rate stability and helping governments and central banks fight inflation has generated concern in Italy and France that their monetary policies are being controlled by the German Bundesbank. The only effective remedy for this political problem from their point of view is to create a European monetary union with a genuinely European central bank at its center, thus reinforcing Community powers through a classic spillover process.

Yet it is equally important to be aware of the limitations on spillover. Nothing in the functional logic of spillover requires a European central bank or a single currency. Ultimately, unless there is a radical change of policy in London, its partners will have to choose between a compromise or a break with Britain. Compromise would probably mean a European currency (such as the "hard Ecu," or European currency unit, which would never be devalued vis-à-vis any Community currency) and no European central bank. To create a system with a central bank would require not only overruling British objections but stifling the reservations of other influential parties, including the Bundesbank itself. It is not certain that the French and the Italians—much less the Spaniards— would ultimately prefer the second outcome to the first. If the French end up choosing the second, it will be more for political reasons— locking the Federal Republic into a "deepened" Community, even at the cost of accepting Bundesbank hegemony—than for economic ones. The

German government may also prefer a common currency, such as the hard-Ecu scheme envisages, to a continental EMU in which the de facto hegemony and de jure autonomy of the Bundesbank could be reduced through institutionalized decisionmaking procedures.

On social issues, the same combination of pressure for spillover, and resistance to it, is evident. The free circulation of persons will create strong pressures for a Community policy on immigration, but the issue is so explosive and divisive in many of the member states that such a common policy will be very difficult to devise. The labor unions are pressing for a common "social dimension"; the French government has argued for a common policy of restrictions on foreign (i.e., U.S.) programs on television, and for a single withholding tax on income from capital. However, as in the realm of monetary affairs, there is more evidence of the "expansive logic sector of integration" than of ready acceptance of new central powers. The single market is proceeding through such principles as "mutual recognition" and home-country control rather than through harmonization and common rules. Over television, only a compromise around a nonbinding directive could be reached. In the fields of taxation and social policy, the Commission's proposals have met such opposition that a relatively loose scheme of regulation, under which each member will be left free to set its own course within broad limits, is likely to emerge. Thus the principles of mutual recognition and subsidiarity may result in a clever "European" camouflaging of different national practices and in eliminating the conflict between national regulation and Community rules by giving a European label to the former. The chief beneficiaries of such a policy would be owners of mobile factors of production—capital and highly skilled professional people—and the economies of countries with cheap fixed factors of production (land and cheap, unskilled labor in particular).[51] As long as democratic politics prevailed in such a Europe at the national level, it would be vulnerable to social democratic or populist rebellion.

The strong new demand for European political cooperation (EPC) is not created principally by the establishment of the single market, although "spillover" is not absent. Behind EPC one finds both the changing position of Western Europe in world politics after the Cold War and the impossibility, in the long run, of keeping negotiations on economic issues entrusted to the Community's institutions separate from the definition of a common foreign policy. In coming years, international politics will increasingly be played on the chessboard of economic interdependence, where Community authority is predominant: association agreements, applications for membership, deals with EFTA countries, bargains in GATT and the OECD, and the like. But these issues will be closely linked to traditional diplomatic concerns, as both relations with Eastern Europe and the occasional impingement of economic issues on alliance politics (in both the U.S.-European and U.S.-Japanese relationship) make clear. Furthermore, economic and military issues are becoming increasingly entangled with one another, as the war in the Persian Gulf has shown.

Yet for political cooperation as well as monetary and social policies, there are manifest limits on spillover. So far, there is little evidence of any spillover into defense policy. For the Federal Republic, NATO and the CSCE are the pillars of its security policy, as they guarantee not only U.S. protection should a new threat arise but also Soviet cooperation. And even in a period of expanding political cooperation, this common function under the Single Act (unlike foreign economic policy under the Treaty of Rome) leads to pooled powers rather than to power for a central authority distinct from the states. Spillover depends on prior intergovernmental bargains. When those bargains are fresh and viable, pressures appear for intensified cooperation in sectors where the bargains were made and for extended cooperation in related sectors. But these pressures by no means automatically lead to new common policies.

Thus we must distinguish between the preservation of the Community and its further development, in scope and institutional autonomy alike. The former appears reasonably secure, not because there is a single purpose but because the Community, as it has evolved, both serves the multiple purposes of its members and can accommodate changes of purpose and policy within certain limits (the EMS is more of a constraint than almost any other Community policy). Thus the EC serves the French strategy of reaching through "Europe" national goals that can no longer be achieved at a purely national level; the Spanish strategy of economic modernization and political return to Europe; the British ideology of deregulation and realization of economies of scale; and the German desire for a zone of monetary stability, a broad market for German goods, and an anchor in the West. The lesson of the 1970s is probably vivid enough to prevent destruction of the Community even in case of a recession. An economic slump might put a temporary halt to the dismantling of barriers, to the opening of public procurement, to the tightening of monetary and fiscal cooperation required by the Madrid Council. It might lead members to use the various safeguards and provisions for temporary restrictions (Articles 36 and 100). But, as in the 1970s, the Community would survive, not only because of its capacity to accommodate different views but because of the habits of cooperation created by its many networks of private and public bargaining, which characterize the European mode of governance.

Still, further development of the Community in what might be called, in short, the Delors direction, is more problematic. It would require a new set of intergovernmental bargains, perhaps generated by prior spillover pressures but by no means preordained by them. In spring 1990, the Council's decision to accelerate work on monetary union and to prepare a conference on institutional reform showed that after the tensions that cracked the Franco-German axis in late 1989 because of Chancellor Kohl's tempo and methods for German unification, a new bargain was being considered. The October 1990 decision to move to the second stage of EMU clarified that this bargain is likely to involve greater economic policy integration. However, the Community's inability, at the same meeting, to agree on agricultural issues raised questions about the implications of internal coherence for global cooperation and, in particular, whether agreement within Europe would be purchased at the price of global trade liberalization.

As of October 1990, the institutional features of this new bargain— for example, the role to be played by the European Parliament—are still vague. Stage 2 of EMU will involve "a new monetary institution comprising member states' central banks and a central organ, exercising full responsibility for monetary policy"; in the final phase, exchange rates are to be irrevocably fixed and the Ecu established.[52] In addition to these institutions of monetary integration, whether involving a European central bank or a "Eurofed" on the U.S. model, the new bargain could lead to an institutional reform that would deal with the "democratic deficit," as Shirley Williams discusses in Chapter 5. In such a system the Council and the Commission would be the two components of the executive, and the European Parliament would become a real legislature (perhaps with a second chamber composed of delegations of national parliaments, although Delors dismisses the idea as a gimmick). An institutionally strengthened Community could also expand its functions into the field of defense, after drastic arms reductions in Europe negotiated by the two rival alliance systems and a substantial withdrawal of U.S. forces.

A recession could, however, bring to the fore claims for redistribution, the clamor of young people provided with mass education without adequate outlets, the cries of chauvinists blaming foreigners for unemployment and insecurity, coupled with increased pressures from those foreigners for liberalization of barriers toward the outside world. Even if the world recession were not severe, progress could be prevented by a set of domestic backlashes against the economic hardships the single market might impose on certain sectors, professions, or regions (the high pro–Le Pen vote in Alsace, the votes for a slate of "hunters and fishermen" in France in the European election in June 1989, and the republican vote in Germany are different manifestations of a nationalist undercurrent). If the disadvantaged turn to Brussels for relief and find that Brussels simply doesn't have either the financial means to provide it or the political clout to force significant redistribution, such revolts may become more serious.

New international tensions, whether arising from the Persian Gulf, Eastern Europe, or elsewhere, could prolong the grip of the United States on European security matters; revive the temptation of national *Grosspolitik* that always lurks in the hearts of political leaders; or widen the traditional differences among the international predispositions and stances of the key actors: Britain, France, and Germany. It is significant that neither France nor Germany is so far willing to curtail the full jurisdiction of the Council and the rule of unanimity in matters of foreign policy and defense, although Delors hopes to expand the Commission's role in these realms.

Ultimately, despite the revival of supranationality and the emergence of a Community-wide political system in which state sovereignty is both pooled and shrunk, what matters most are the bargains among the major players. The two indispensable ones remain France and Germany, whose alliance continues to provide the political motor of the enterprise. Suspicion of "Europe," even of supranationality, has dramatically declined in France, especially in the present generation of elites (cf. the evolution of the Gaullist party and also of the Socialists). But this is not irreversible. Indeed, parliamentarians from various parties have begun to object to the bureaucratic regulations coming from Brussels and to the French courts' willingness to accept the supremacy of Community law over French law.

On the right as well as on the left, one finds a growing fear that the resurgence of the economic and financial power of a united Federal Republic, its new eminence in East-West relations, and the economic and above all national opportunities provided to it by the decomposition of communism in Eastern Europe, may make Germany an unreliable partner. Some fear that a united and powerful Germany will be much less committed to the Community. By 1992, Germany could be in a situation comparable to that of de Gaulle in 1965, satisfied with arrangements completed (including monetary union, if it is on German terms), but unwilling to extend them further. Its government, absorbed by the costly "rehabilitation" of former East Germany and by calls for aid in Eastern Europe, might become less willing to pay large sums to the CAP and to regional funds, its industrialists and bankers less willing to cooperate and merge with others, its diplomats less eager to seek a European legitimation, once the single market—a major opportunity for the German economy—is achieved. The French have been especially worried about a combination of a drift of the Federal Republic to the East and a new German nationalism in the West. The speedy unification of Germany has intensified these fears.[53] The French are already disturbed by the unilateral moves Bonn took during the unification process (clearly an issue Bonn has deemed not to be within the Community's jurisdiction) and to aid Eastern Europe (in addition to Community moves).

Should such a policy change occur in Germany, the willingness of Germany to make concessions to its regional partners and to pay for economic development in the southern European states of the EC would decline. In sum, the French worry both about an "emancipated" Germany and about a Germany whose conception of the Community would be very different from France's: "purely mercantile" (and thus serving above all German financial and industrial interests), and not interested in developing the diplomatic and defense functions of the EC. In the French foreign minister's words, "security is the business of all of us, defense is the business of each of us."[54]

Will France and other Continental members be willing to pay a price in order to make a further development of the Community—limiting German autonomy—more attractive to Germany? What new benefits would make the balance of gains and costs irresistibly positive for the much enlarged Federal Republic? If these benefits amount to expanded German economic and monetary hegemony and a dominant role for Bonn (or Berlin) in EPC, will France, in turn, find the balance negative for itself? Already, some Gaullists and some Socialists warn that France's policy of encasing Germany in a more powerful European Community may well result in a Community controlled by Germany. De Gaulle had denounced supranationality as a trap because an external "federator," the United States, would be the puppeteer. Now there is fear of a far more redoubtable, internal hegemon: the new Germany.

At a concrete level of analysis, the issue raised here is the centrality of Germany to the Community—which, as many chapters in this volume demonstrate, is already impressive and becoming more so all the time. The future of the Community depends above all on the stability of German politics and the steadiness and moderation of German policy. At a structural level, the issue is the degree to which the Community can adapt to increased German power. The EC was established without a hegemon, for there was a "balance of imbalances" among its bigger members: France and Britain had nuclear weapons, West Germany had industrial *"force de frappe,"* and those three countries and Italy had populations of comparable size. In the new European politics, though nuclear might has lost much of its salience, Germany continues to grow in industrial strength but (unlike the United States in NATO) does not provide military security to its partners in exchange for deference to its leadership. Furthermore, Germany's national identity is at stake.

The stresses that result from these political changes may be relieved by the institutional strength of the EC and the considerable commitments of its members—both much greater than those commanded by ordinary international regimes. The key question, then, can be put as follows: Can the Community's existence and policies help dampen a rising hegemon's national aspirations so that they remain acceptable to the less powerful states, without at the same time appearing too burdensome to the hegemon? This is, obviously, a very different issue from those considered in recent arguments about U.S. hegemony and cooperation "after hegemony."[55]

In the longer run, there is some question as to the ability of the Community to create among its members ties so wide and so deep that a Germany reunified on Western terms would accept them without upsetting the equilibrium within the Community and in Europe overall. There is a race between this objective, which is Delors's, and British design for a far looser Community, a kind of free-trade area that would facilitate accession of Eastern European nations to an enlarged EC and that has an understandable attractiveness to East European countries. Germany resisted Thatcher's appeal, partly because she coupled it, self-destructively, with distrust of German unity. Indeed, she made her appeal so stridently at the Rome summit in October 1990 that a revolt within the Conservative party removed her from her prime ministerial position. Now that unity has been achieved, however, Germany may seek a compromise among French fears, British traditions, and German interests, leading to a Community tighter and more centralized than Thatcher had sought, yet quite far from Delors's quasi-federal ideal.

Also at issue is the ability of the Community to extend its sphere (perhaps through the Western European Union) to the military domain, and thus to provide an alternative to NATO. In a few years, neither the U.S. Congress nor the German public may accept a continued military presence no longer justified by a "Soviet threat." A West European security arrangement allied to the United States would be a better solution than having Germany become, in effect, the dominant member of NATO, and perpetuating the split in matters of reference between France and its European partners. On European security, the French so far only talk about a Community approach and prefer autonomy to NATO; the Germans and the British prefer NATO. On "out-of-area" issues such as the Persian Gulf, the British prefer their "special relationship" with the United States; the French, as usual, autonomy; and the Germans, as little participation as possible.[56] The West European Union, in the Gulf war, has served far more as a forum in which these divergences can be disguised and the minimal common points underlined than as a coordinating body in which policies are combined.

At present, one can only note that the evolution of world politics and the strength of ties already established among businesspeople and officials still favor the reinforcement of links among the partners of the Community. Even vis-à-vis Eastern Europe and the Soviet Union, the Federal Republic is stronger as a member of the Community than as a separate actor; a common Western European policy (as in the monetary realm) may well be a way both for Germany to obtain broader legitimacy for its *Ostpolitik* and for Germany's partners to try to exert some control over it. Furthermore, German leaders know that a fully autonomous united Germany would be frightening to many Europeans and therefore that Germany can actually exercise power more effectively, without engendering fear, as a member of the Community than alone.[57] Germany's interest is to seek influence through economic and monetary power—a capability in huge demand all over Europe—rather than through military power—a capability that antagonizes more than it reassures. The Community, if equipped with institutions that do not put Germany into a straitjacket, is a good vehicle for such influence.

France's insistence on nuclear independence will weigh less heavily in a world of expanded arms control and decreasingly militarized relations among major powers; and in the economic realm there is already very little room left for effective French independence. As a guideline for global policy, the "special relationship" with the United States is a sentimental mirage that has stopped fascinating most Britons. In such an environment, ties created by European networks could deepen as habits of pooling sovereignty develop. Spillover could lead to incremental expansion of joint decisionmaking, and European organizations would, like all organizations, seek to extend their authority. Thus, barring a major slump in the world economy, catastrophic events in the Soviet Union whose international fallout cannot be predicted, or a sudden turn of the German Republic away from the course it had followed as long as it was divided, there are reasons to be at least moderately optimistic about the Community's future.

NOTES

An earlier version of this chapter was published in William Wallace, ed., *The Dynamics of European Integration* (London: Frances Pinter, 1990), pp. 276–300. Used with permission.

The authors are particularly indebted to Victoria Gerus for research assistance. We thank James A. Caporaso, Ernst Haas, Peter Hall, Helen Milner, Andrew Moravcsik, Kalypso Nicolaïdis, Helen Wallace, and William Wallace for extensive written comments on an earlier draft of this manuscript. Jeff Frieden, Joseph S. Nye, and participants in the Florence Workshop on the Dynamics of European

Integration, September 10–12, 1989, and the Harvard Seminar on European Political Institutions also offered valuable suggestions and criticisms. We are grateful to William Wallace for commissioning the earlier version of this paper and for organizing the Florence conference at which it was given.

1. "Survey" of the European Community, *The Economist*, July 7, 1990, pp. 15; 6.

2. Paul Taylor, *The Limits of European Integration* (New York: Columbia University Press, 1983), p. 56. Writing in the mid-1970s, William Wallace perceptively pointed out the continuing strength of the Commission and the extent to which Community institutions facilitated coordination of national policymaking; and he anticipated the possibility of the Communities' having by the mid-1980s "widened and strengthened their ability to formulate and implement policies in concert or in common." However, he argued that if this occurred, "it is unlikely to have been the result of any overall strategy." William Wallace, "Walking Backwards Towards Unity," in Helen Wallace, William Wallace, and Carole Webb, eds. *Policy-Making in the European Communities* (London and New York: Wiley, 1977), p. 322.

3. Taylor, *Limits of European Integration*, p. 231.

4. Albert Bressand, "Beyond Interdependence: 1992 as a Global Challenge," paper presented at the Conference on the Dynamics of European Integration, Florence, September 10–12, 1989, p. 8.

5. *The Economist*, December 7, 1985, cited in *Project PROMETHEE, Perspectives No. 9* (March 1989), p. 5.

6. The present authors doubt whether any theory that can perfectly predict strategic behavior of states will ever be devised. Unconstrained strategic behavior is inherently unpredictable insofar as optimal action changes depending on each party's perception of the expectations of others. Theory, if widely known and accepted, creates expectations, which provide incentives for actors to devise strategies exploiting those who have such (now conventional) expectations— thus invalidating the theory. This conundrum applies to theories about much market behavior, insofar as it depends on interactor strategies, and also to politics. However, to the extent that rules and practices structure incentives and constrain behavior, *patterns* of action may become understandable, although surprises will, in the nature of politics, continue to occur.

7. For a path-breaking discussion of security communities, see Karl W. Deutsch et al., *Political Community and the North Atlantic Area* (Princeton: Princeton University Press, 1957).

8. Peter Ludlow, *Beyond 1992: Europe and Its Western Partners* (Brussels: Center for European Policy Studies, 1989), p. 18.

9. "Survey on Europe's Internal Market," *The Economist*, July 8, 1989, p. 12.

10. EC, *22nd General Report on the Activities of the European Communities* (Brussels, 1988), pp. 31–32. See also Helen Wallace, "Making Multilateralism Work" (mimeograph, August 1988), p. 17; EC, *20th General Report* (Brussels, 1986), pp. 28–36. The dramatic effect of the Single European Act on voting practices was not universally anticipated: For instance, former French Foreign Minister Maurice Couve de Murville, speaking in the French Senate's ratification

debate, claimed that with respect to the Luxembourg compromise, "the new treaty will not change anything." French Senate *Debates*, December 10, 1986, p. 5969.

11. In his essay, Wolfgang Wessels questions whether "pooling of sovereignty" sufficiently takes account of the evolution of Community law. We regard this issue as principally semantic. What "pooling of sovereignty" means to us is the transfer of states' legal authority over internal and external affairs to the Community as a whole, although not to supranational organs as such.

12. In the 1980s EFTA, which had originally been sponsored in the 1960s by Britain as an alternative to the EC, included Austria, Finland, Iceland, Norway, Sweden, and Switzerland.

13. *Financial Times*, October 29, 1990, p. 1. For indications of the uncertainty surrounding attitudes toward economic and monetary union, see *Financial Times*, July 2, 1990, p. 3; *Financial Times*, September 11, 1990, p. 16.

14. One source of insight would come from the "new economic history," exploring institutional change with theories of transaction costs, as in Douglass C. North, *Structure and Change in Economic History* (New York: W. W. Norton, 1981). Another worthwhile line of analysis would be to investigate the impact of increased trade on domestic political institutions, as done by Peter Gourevitch, *Politics in Hard Times: Comparative Responses to International Economic Crises* (Ithaca: Cornell University Press, 1986), and by Ronald Rogowski, *Commerce and Coalitions* (Princeton: Princeton University Press, 1989). Equally promising are institutionally detailed rational-choice models, exploring the impact of agenda control, veto power, and decisionmaking sequence on legislative outcomes, as in Kenneth A. Shepsle and Barry R. Weingast, "The Institutional Foundations of Committee Power," *American Political Science Review* 81, 1 (March 1987), pp. 85–104. We are indebted to Leon Lindberg for suggesting some of these possible lines of analysis.

15. For a good discussion, see the chapter by Renaud Dehousse and Joseph H. H. Weiler in William Wallace, ed., *Dynamics of European Integration* (London: Frances Pinter, 1990). To our text, it must quickly be added that the 1992 legislation will test the Community's implementation and compliance procedures. Signs of stress are already evident: Between the end of 1985 and the end of 1987, the number of cases of Court of Justice judgments not yet complied with, listed by the Commission, had risen from thirty-three to fifty-three. Compare the Third Annual Report to the European Parliament on Commission Monitoring of the Application of Community Law (1985), *Official Journal of the European Communities*, 1986 (86/C 220), with the Fifth Annual Report to the European Parliament on Commission Monitoring of the Application of Community Law (1987), *Official Journal of the European Communities*, 1988 (88/C 310), p. 43. For a good review of implementation, see Heinrich Siedentopf and Jacques Ziller, eds., *Making European Policies Work: The Implementation of Community Legislation in the Member States, vol. 1, Comparative Synthesis* (Beverley Hills, Calif.: Sage, for the European Institute of Public Administration, 1988), p. 58.

16. In this volume see Chapter 6 by G. Federico Mancini. Nevertheless, it remains the case that governments may fail to comply with Community law,

either deliberately, as a result of difficulties in the legislative process (as in Italy), or because of problems in enforcement. See Hjalte Rasmussen, "Les Etats membres et l'inexécution des obligations communautaires," in *Pouvoirs* 48 (1989), pp. 39–56.

17. Hedley Bull, *The Anarchical Society* (New York: Columbia University Press, 1977), p. 8.

18. Siedentopf and Ziller, vol. 1, p. 30. On the dominance of national governments in the process, see ibid., p. 71.

19. See Dusan Sidjanski, "Communauté européenne 1992: gouvernement de comité?" in *Pouvoirs*, issue on Europe 1993, 48 (1989), pp. 71–80.

20. Walter W. Powell, "Neither Market nor Hierarchy: Network Forms of Organization," draft (July 1988) prepared for Barry M. Shaw and Larry L. Cummings, eds., *Research in Organizational Behavior*, vol. 12 (Greenwich, Conn.: JAI Press).

21. Networks may eventually extend beyond the limits set by farsighted self-interest: As Powell comments in "Neither Market nor Hierarchy," "entangling strings of reputation, friendship, interdependence and altruism [may] become integral parts of the relationship." Shared identities can become important; a sense of solidarity may develop among elites even though a sense of community, as it is used by Karl Deutsch, may never come into being. See Deutsch et al., *Political Community.*

22. Ernst B. Haas, "Is There a Hole in the Whole? Knowledge, Technology, Interdependence and the Construction of International Regimes," *International Organization* 29, 3 (Summer 1975), pp. 827–876. The quotation appears in note 36 on p. 856.

23. Taylor, *Limits of European Integration*, p. 240. Cheysson's comment was made on January 28, 1982. Helen Wallace has kindly corrected our interpretation of this point.

24. See Robert O. Keohane, "Reciprocity in International Relations," *International Organization* 40, 1 (Winter 1986), pp. 1–27.

25. Ernst B. Haas, "Technocracy, Pluralism and the New Europe," in Stephen R. Graubard, ed., *A New Europe?* (Boston: Houghton Mifflin, 1964), pp. 64, 66.

26. Ernst B. Haas, *The Uniting of Europe: Political, Economic and Social Forces, 1950–1957* (London: Stevens and Sons, and Stanford: Stanford University Press, 1958), p. 59.

27. Ernst B. Haas, "Turbulent Fields and the Theory of Regional Integration," *International Organization* 30, 2 (Spring 1976), p. 173.

28. Ernst B. Haas, *Beyond the Nation-State: Functionalism and International Organization* (Stanford: Stanford University Press, 1964), p. 48.

29. Haas, "Technocracy," p. 65.

30. Europe's paper trail is littered with complaints about the Luxembourg compromise and proposals for a return to what the Commission in 1969 called "normal functioning of the institutions as laid down in the Treaties" (*Bulletin of the European Communities*, 1 [January 1970], p. 18). See also the Tindemans Report, *Bulletin of the EC, Supplement* (January 1976); the conclusions of the "Three Wise Men" who reported to the Council on institutional arrangements

in 1979 (*Bulletin of the EC* [November 1979], pp. 25–28); and of course the report of the ad hoc Committee on Institutional Affairs (Dooge Report), *Bulletin of the EC* (March 1985), pp. 102–111.

31. Haas, *Uniting of Europe*, p. 16.

32. Intergovernmental "bargains" are also emphasized by Wayne Sandholtz and John Zysman, "1992: Recasting the European Bargain," *World Politics* 42, 1 (October 1989), pp. 1–30.

33. Editorial, *Financial Times*, May 19, 1989.

34. Haas, *Uniting of Europe*, pp. 243, 283–317.

35. Taylor, *Limits of European Integration*, p. 299.

36. Haas, *Beyond the Nation-State*, p. 407. This is similar to his usage in *Uniting of Europe*, in which he talks about "spill-over" (in quotation marks) to describe the movement of policy integration into "new economic and political sectors" (p. 292). Haas uses the term similarly, to describe *task expansion*, in "The Study of Regional Integration: Reflections on the Joy and Anguish of Pretheorizing," in Leon N. Lindberg and Stuart A. Scheingold, eds., *Regional Integration: Theory and Research* (Cambridge: Harvard University Press, 1971), pp. 3–44.

37. Joseph S. Nye, Jr., "Comparing Common Markets: A Revised Neofunctional Model," in Lindberg and Scheingold, *Regional Integration*, p. 200. This is a restatement in propositional terms of a formulation by Haas, which indicates imperatives (or incentives): "Policies made in carrying out an initial task and grant of power can be made real only if the task itself is expanded" (*Beyond the Nation-State*, p. 111). Philippe Schmitter defines the "spillover hypothesis" ("the basic functionalist proposition") as follows: "Tensions from the global environment and/or contradictions generated by past performance give rise to unexpected performance in the pursuit of agreed-upon common objectives. These frustrations and/or dissatisfactions are likely to result in the search for alternative means for reaching the same goals, i.e., to induce actions to revise their respective strategies vis-à-vis the scope and level of regional decisionmaking." "A Revised Theory of Regional Integration," in Lindberg and Scheingold, *Regional Integration*, p. 243.

38. Schmitter, "Revised Theory," p. 260; italics in the original.

39. Joseph S. Nye, Jr., *Peace in Parts: Integration and Conflict in Regional Organization* (Boston: Little, Brown, 1971), pp. 65, 76; Leon N. Lindberg and Stuart A. Scheingold, *Europe's Would-Be Polity: Patterns of Change in the European Community* (Englewood Cliffs, N.J.: Prentice-Hall, 1970), p. 242.

40. The predictions of a theory can fail to be borne out by events for one of two distinct reasons: (1) because the propositions of the theory were false, so that even if the preconditions specified in the theory apply, anticipated results do not occur; or (2) because the conditions for the operation of the theory are simply not met. In the latter case, the theory is not falsified but just appears irrelevant to the situation.

41. We are grateful to Philippe de Schoucheete for pointing this out to us in comments prepared for the September 1989 conference in Florence on the Dynamics of European Integration.

42. "Report of the Commission on Enlargement of the European Community: General Considerations," *Bulletin of the EC, Supplement* (January 1978), p. 15.

43. William Wallace, "Conclusions, Working Groups A and C," in W. Wallace and I. Herreman, eds., *A Community of Twelve? The Impact of Further Enlargement on the European Communities* (Bruges: College of Europe, 1978), p. 412. The usual view in the late 1970s was that the enlargement of the community would make it more like a free-trade area. However, when President Valéry Giscard d'Estaing was asked by *Le Monde* in July 1978 if a Community of twelve could function normally, he replied that "enlargement provides a golden opportunity to look into ways of improving" Community institutions, and he proposed a committee of "three wise men," subsequently appointed, to examine desirable institutional reforms. See Emanuelle Gazzo, "Enlargement of the Community: Attitudes of Member States," in J. W. Schneider, ed., *From Nine to Twelve: Europe's Destiny?* (Alphen aan den Rijn, Netherlands: Sijthoff & Noordhoff, 1980), p. 13.

44. *United Kingdom House of Commons Parliamentary Debates*, vol. 81, c. 246 (June 26, 1985), p. 465; French Senate *Debates*, December 10, 1986, p. 5956 (author's translation).

45. For this point we are indebted to Helen Wallace.

46. Sandholtz and Zysman emphasize the role of international competition, particularly from Japan, in prompting action on Europe's internal market. See also Jacques Pelkmans and Alan Winters, *Europe's Domestic Market* (London: Royal Institute of International Affairs, Chatham House Paper no. 43, 1988); and Paolo Ceccini, *The European Challenge, 1992: The Benefits of a Single Market* (Aldershot, U.K.: Wildwood House, 1988).

47. Jean-Jacques Servan-Schreiber, *The American Challenge*, trans. Ronald Steel (New York: Atheneum, 1968).

48. Haas, "Technocracy," p. 68; Haas, "Turbulent Fields," p. 183; Haas, *Uniting of Europe*, pp. 154–155.

49. In his 1983 volume, *The Limits to European Integration*, Taylor distinguished "negative integration"—the removal of barriers—from "positive integration," which he defined as the establishment of common ways of intervening in economies. He characterized the former, in Europe, as generally successful and the latter as unsuccessful. The revival of European integration after 1985 can be seen as a validation of this insight: The strategy chosen by European elites was successful, in this interpretation, because it relied on negative rather than positive intervention. The Commission White Paper of June 1985, "Completing the Internal Market," classifies all proposed measures under three categories: "the removal of physical barriers, the removal of technical barriers, and the removal of physical barriers."

50. Stanley Hoffmann, "Obstinate or Obsolete? France, European Integration and the Fate of the Nation-State," in Stanley Hoffmann et al., eds., *Decline or Renewal? France Since the 1930s* (New York: Viking Press, 1974), p. 395, adapted from Hoffmann, "Obstinate or Obsolete? The Fate of the Nation-State and the Case of Western Europe," *Daedalus* (Summer 1966), pp. 862–915. Hoffmann added: "Integration means a common choice of a common future, but that

requires certain attitudes about the past and the present." It is worth noting that imperfect scholarly memories have stereotyped the debate of the late 1960s between neofunctionalists and statists. As we have seen, Haas never believed that spillover was automatic. Nor did the critics see a resurgence of integration as impossible. Hoffmann argued in 1966 that "one can conceive of a set of circumstances in which a speedy forward march could succeed" ("Obstinate or Obsolete?" p. 393). The question is not so much "Will European integration succeed?" as "Under what conditions can integration progress?" Haas recognized this in 1976 in "Turbulent Fields," which characterized integration theory as "obsolescent but not obsolete": "Theories of regional integration," he declared, "retain a good deal of relevance wherever and whenever the setting they were designed to describe and explain continues to exist" ("Turbulent Fields," p. 177). It is our contention in this chapter that the conditions for the relevance of neofunctionalist theory in Europe are stronger now than they have been since the 1960s.

51. To someone from the United States, the relevant phrase would be the "Delawarization of Europe," Delaware being the state in which many U.S. corporations are legally domiciled because its laws are most favorable to their operation.

52. Final Statement of the European Council, October 28, 1990, *Financial Times*, October 29, 1990, p. 4.

53. In some respects, the very speed of unification will reduce disruption to the Community, as exemplified by the recent history of the Schengen agreement. This treaty, lifting all border controls on people passing between France, Germany, and Benelux, was due to be signed in December 1989 but was temporarily frozen as a result of the German unification process. Concerns were expressed over the right of free circulation that would be granted to citizens of the German Democratic Republic throughout the EC, and even about the possible access of the East German secret police to the Schengen Information System computer. In June 1990, with full unification in sight and the Stasi in process of dissolution, the treaty was concluded.

54. *Le Monde*, October 12, 1990, p. 10.

55. Robert O. Keohane, *After Hegemony: Cooperation and Discord in the World Political Economy* (Princeton: Princeton University Press, 1984).

56. On these points, see Stanley Hoffmann, "La France dans le nouvel ordre européen," *Politique étrangère* (March 1990), pp. 503–512, and "Away from the Past," *Foreign Policy* 81 (Winter 1990–1991), pp. 20–38.

57. This point was made by Shirley Williams during a recent discussion with us.

2

Negotiating the Single European Act

Andrew Moravcsik

The European Community (EC) is experiencing its most important period of reform since the completion of the Common Market in 1968. This new impulse toward European integration—the "relaunching" of Europe, the French call it—was unexpected. The late 1970s and early 1980s were periods of "Europessimism" and "Eurosclerosis," when politicians and academics alike lost faith in European institutions. The current period is one of optimism and institutional momentum. The source of this transformation was the Single European Act (SEA), a document approved by European heads of government in 1986.[1]

The SEA links liberalization of the European market with procedural reform. The first half of this reform package, incorporating 279 proposals contained in the 1985 EC Commission White Paper, aims to create "an area without internal frontiers in which the free movement of goods, persons, services, and capital is ensured."[2] To realize this goal, European leaders committed themselves to addressing issues never successfully tackled in a multinational forum, such as the comprehensive liberalization of trade in services and the removal of domestic regulations that act as nontariff barriers. Previous attempts to set detailed and uniform European standards for domestic regulations ("harmonization") had proven time-consuming and fruitless. With this in mind, the White Paper called for a "new approach" based on "mutual recognition"—a less invasive form of liberalization whereby only minimal standards would be harmonized.

Reprinted from Andrew Moravcsik, "Negotiating the Single European Act: National Interests and Conventional Statecraft in the European Community," *International Organization* 45, 1 (1991): 651–688. Used with permission.

The second half of the SEA reform package consists of procedural reforms designed to streamline decision making in the governing body of the EC, the Council of Ministers. Since January 1966, qualified majority voting had been limited in practice by the "Luxembourg compromise," in which France unilaterally asserted the right to veto a proposal in the Council of Ministers by declaring that a "vital" or "very important" interest was at stake.[3] The SEA expands the use of qualified majority voting in the Council of Ministers, although only on matters pertaining to the internal market.[4]

What accounts for the timing and the content of the reform package that relaunched Europe? Why did this reform succeed when so many previous efforts had failed? As a first step toward answering these questions, this article presents a history of the negotiations that led to the approval of the SEA by the European Council in February 1986, formulates and evaluates two stylized explanations for their unexpected success, and relates the findings to theories of international cooperation.

The findings challenge the prominent view that institutional reform resulted from an elite alliance between EC officials and pan-European business interest groups. The negotiating history is more consistent with the alternative explanation that EC reform rested on interstate bargains between Britain, France, and Germany. An essential precondition for reform was the convergence of the economic policy prescriptions of ruling party coalitions in these countries following the election of the British Conservative party in 1979 and the reversal of French Socialist party policy in 1983. Also essential was the negotiating leverage that France and Germany gained by exploiting the threat to create a "two-track" Europe and excluding Britain from it. This "intergovernmental institutionalist" explanation is more consistent with what Robert Keohane calls the "modified structural realist" view of regime change, a view that stresses traditional conceptions of national interest and power,[5] than it is with supranational variants of neofunctionalist integration theory. For the source of state interests, however, scholars must turn away from structural theories and toward domestic politics, where the existence of several competing explanations invites further research.

EXPLANATIONS FOR THE SUCCESS
OF THE SEA

Journalistic reportage, academic analysis, and interviews with European officials reveal a bewilderingly wide range of explanations, some contradictory, for the timing, content, and process of adopting the White Paper and the SEA. One French official I interviewed in Brussels quipped, "When the little boy turns out well, everyone claims paternity!" The various accounts cluster around two stylized explanations, the first stressing the independent activism of international or transnational actors and the second emphasizing bargaining between leaders of the most powerful states of Europe.

Supranational Institutionalism *& EC Reform*

Three supranational factors consistently recur in accounts of EC reform: pressure from EC institutions, particularly the Parliament and Court; lobbying by transnational business interest groups; and the political entrepreneurship of the Commission, led by President Jacques Delors and Internal Market Commissioner Lord Arthur Cockfield.[6] Together these supranational factors offer an account of reform guided by actors and institutions acting "above" the nation-state.

European Institutions

Between 1980 and 1985, pressure for reform grew within the EC institutions. In the European Parliament, resolutions and reports supported the programs of two groups, one "maximalist" and the other "minimalist" in approach. The first group, which included many Italians and quite a number of Germans, advocated European federalism and a broad expansion in the scope of EC activities, backed by procedural reforms focusing particularly on increasing the power of the Parliament.[7] Following the Europarliamentary penchant for animal names, these activists called themselves the "Crocodile Group," after the Strasbourg restaurant where they first met. Led by the venerable Altiero Spinelli, a founding father of the EC, their efforts culminated in the European Parliament resolution of February 1984 proposing a "Draft Treaty Establishing the European Union"—a new, more ambitious document to replace the Treaty of Rome.

The second group, founded in 1981 and consisting of Parliament members who were skeptical of federalism and parliamentary reform, focused on working with national leaders to liberalize the internal market. These activists called themselves the "Kangaroo Group," based on the Australian marsupial's ability to "hop over borders." Their efforts were funded by sympathetic business interests (primarily British and Dutch), and they counted Basil de Ferranti, a leading British industrialist and Tory parliamentarian, among their leaders.[8] The Kangaroos encouraged parliamentary studies on economic topics and in 1983 launched a public campaign in favor of a detailed EC timetable for abolishing administrative, technical, and fiscal barriers, a reference to which was included in the draft treaty.

Transnational Business Interest Groups

According to Wisse Dekker, chief executive officer of Philips, European integration in the 1950s was initiated by politicians, while in its current "industrial" phase it is initiated by business leaders.[9] The evidence presented to date by partisans of this view stresses the actions of pan-European business interest groups. The Commission has long sought to encourage the development of a sort of pan-European corporatist network by granting these groups privileged access to the policy process, though this effort has met with little success.[10]

In the mid-1980s, business interest groups, at times working together with EC officials, hoped to bolster the competitiveness of European firms by calling for a more liberal EC market. Viscount Etienne Davignon, the internal market commissioner from 1976 through 1984, brought together a group of large European information technology firms in 1981 to form the Thorn-Davignon Commission, which developed proposals for technology programs and European technical norms and reportedly also discussed market liberalization. In 1983, Pehr Gyllenhammer, the chief executive officer of Volvo, and Wisse Dekker helped found the Roundtable of European Industrialists, made up of the heads of a number of Europe's largest multinational corporations, some of whom were selected on Davignon's suggestion.[11] Once the SEA was adopted, the Roundtable formed a "watchdog" committee to press for its implementation. In February 1984, the Union des Confédérations de l'Industrie et des Employeurs d'Europe (UNICE), the leading EC industrial interest group, called for majority voting, and it has been active since then in promoting market liberalization.[12]

In a series of speeches delivered in the autumn of 1984 and early 1985, Dekker proposed what became the best-known business plan for market liberalization, the "Europa 1990" plan.[13] Its focus on internal market liberalization, its division of the task into categories (reform of fiscal, commercial, technical, and government procurement policies), its ideology of economies of scale, its recognition of the link between commercial liberalization and tax harmonization, its identification of the ultimate goal with a certain date, and many of its other details were echoed in Delors' proposal to the European Parliament a few months later and in the White Paper of June 1985. Transnational business pressure, some have argued, was "indispensable" to the passage of the SEA.[14]

International Political Leaders

The Commission has traditionally been viewed as the agenda-setting arm of the EC. When Delors was nominated for the presidency of the

Commission, he immediately sought a major initiative to rejuvenate the EC. When he assumed the office in January 1985, he visited government, business, and labor leaders in each of the European capitals to discuss possible reforms. According to his account, he considered reform in three areas—the EC decision-making institutions, European monetary policy, and political and defense collaboration—before deciding to "return to the origins" of the EC, the construction of a single internal market.[15] Like Jean Monnet two decades before, Delors identified the goal with a date. He aimed to render the achievement of the program irreversible by 1988 and to complete it by 1992, coeval with the duration of two four-year terms of commissioners. It is commonly argued that Delors used the institutional power of the presidency as a platform from which to forge the link between the procedural improvements proposed by Parliament and the internal market liberalization advocated by Brussels-based business groups. According to this view, he encouraged Cockfield to elaborate the internal market agenda in the White Paper and then exaggerated the sense of economic decline to secure its approval by European heads of government.[16]

Supranational Institutionalism and Neofunctionalism

An elite alliance between transnationally organized big business groups and EC officials, led by Delors, constitutes the core of the supranational institutionalist explanation for the 1992 initiative. The explanation is theoretically coherent insofar as each of its elements emphasizes the autonomy and influence enjoyed by international institutions and transnational groups acting "above the state." Two leading scholars have recently argued that the key role played by supranational actors decisively distinguishes the politics of the SEA from those of the Treaty of Rome three decades earlier: "Leadership for 1992 came from outside the national settings. . . . It came from the Commission."[17]

This explanation is consistent with a certain variant of neofunctionalist theory. In *The Uniting of Europe*, Ernst Haas distinguishes between processes of integration that take place at what he called the "supranational" and "national" levels. Three key elements of the supranational process are the ability of a central institution (the EC) "to assert itself in such a way as to cause strong positive or negative expectations," the tendency of "business and labor . . . to unite beyond their former national confines in an effort to make common policy," and the "demonstration by a resourceful supranational executive that ends already agreed to cannot be attained without further united steps."[18] An examination of the role of supranational actors in initiating the SEA tests this particular variant of neofunctionalism, though not, of course, the entire approach.

TABLE [2.1]   Comparison of Two Approaches to Explaining the Success of the 1992 Initiative

	Supranational Institutionalism	Intergovernmental Institutionalism
Key actors initiating the negotiations and compromises	Transnational interest groups and supranational officials	Heads of government and top officials of the largest member states, with specific policy goals determined by their domestic political system and by the preferences of policy makers, technocrats, political parties, and interest groups
Nature of the bargaining	Logrolling and linkages that upgrade the common interest of member states	Lowest-common-denominator (veto group) decisions among the largest member states, with smaller states receiving side-payments and larger states subject to threats of exclusion
Nature of the agreement	Fluid issue-areas and spillover	Rigid issue-areas that are subject to change only by further interstate agreement under the unanimity rule

Intergovernmental Institutionalism

An alternative approach to explaining the success of the 1992 initiative focuses on interstate bargains between heads of government in the three largest member states of the EC. This approach, which can be called "intergovernmental institutionalism,"[19] stresses the central importance of power and interests, with the latter not simply dictated by position in the international system (see Table [2.1]). Intergovernmental institutionalism is based on three principles: intergovernmentalism, lowest-common-denominator bargaining, and strict limits on future transfers of sovereignty.

Intergovernmentalism

From its inception, the EC has been based on interstate bargains between its leading member states. Heads of government, backed by a small group of ministers and advisers, initiate and negotiate major initiatives in the Council of Ministers or the European Council. Each government views the EC through the lens of its own policy preferences; EC politics is the continuation of domestic policies by other means.[20] Even when societal interests are transnational, the principal form of their political expression remains national.

Lowest-Common-Denominator Bargaining

Without a "European hegemon" capable of providing universal incentives or threats to promote regime formation and without the widespread use of linkages and logrolling, the bargains struck in the EC reflect the relative power positions of the member states. Small states can be bought off with side-payments, but larger states exercise a de facto veto over fundamental changes in the scope or rules of the core element of the EC, which remains economic liberalization. Thus, bargaining tends to converge toward the minimum common denominator of large state interests. The bargains initially consisted of bilateral agreements between France and Germany; now they consist of trilateral agreements including Britain.[21]

The only tool that can impel a state to accept an outcome on a major issue that it does not prefer to the status quo is the threat of exclusion. Once an international institution has been created, exclusion can be expensive both because the nonmember forfeits input into further decision making and because it forgoes whatever benefits result. If two major states can isolate the third and credibly threaten it with exclusion and if such exclusion undermines the substantive interests of the excluded state, the coercive threat may bring about an agreement at a level of integration above the lowest common denominator.

Protection of Sovereignty

The decision to join a regime involves some sacrifice of national sovereignty in exchange for certain advantages. Policymakers safeguard their countries against the future erosion of sovereignty by demanding the unanimous consent of regime members to sovereignty-related reforms. They also avoid granting open-ended authority to central institutions that might infringe on their sovereignty, preferring instead to work through intergovernmental institutions such as the Council of Ministers,

rather than through supranational bodies such as the Commission and
Parliament.

Intergovernmental Institutionalism
and Modified Structural Realism

Convergent national interests, interstate bargains, and constraints on
further reform constitute the intergovernmental institutionalist explanation for the SEA. This explanation is theoretically coherent insofar as
it stresses the autonomy and influence of national leaders vis-à-vis
international institutions as well as the importance of power resources
in determining the outcomes of intergovernmental bargains.

Intergovernmental institutionalism affirms the realist foundations of
what Keohane calls the "modified structural realist" explanation of
regime formation and maintenance.[22] States are the principal actors in
the international system. Interstate bargains reflect national interests and
relative power. International regimes shape interstate politics by providing
a common framework that reduces the uncertainty and transaction costs
of interstate interactions. In the postwar system, Keohane argues, regimes
have preserved established patterns of cooperation after the relative
decline of the United States. Similarly, the EC regime, though neither
created nor maintained by a hegemon, fixes interstate bargains until the
major European powers choose to negotiate changes.

The emphasis of intergovernmental institutionalism differs decisively
from that of modified structural realism, however, in that it locates the
sources of regime reform not only in the changing power distribution
but also in the changing interests of states. States are not "black boxes";
they are entities entrusted to governments, which themselves are responsible to domestic constituencies. State interests change over time,
often in ways which are decisive for the integration process but which
cannot be traced to shifts in the relative power of states.

NATIONAL INTERESTS AND 1992

The intergovernmental approach suggests that an analysis of the 1992
initiative must begin by examining the underlying preferences of Germany,
France, and Britain. As indicated above, Delors identified four issue-
areas that might have served as the vehicle for major EC reform: monetary
coordination, political and defense cooperation, institutional reform, and
internal market liberalization. A glance at the national preferences for
monetary coordination and for political and defense cooperation suggests
that there was little possibility of a formal agreement, since in both
cases, France was opposed by Britain and Germany (see Table [2.2]).

TABLE [2.2]   Preferences of the Three Largest EC Member States, 1980–86

	Germany	France	Britain
Monetary coordination	Opposed, at least until capital flows are liberalized	In favor; advocates moving toward a European central bank	Opposed; is not a participant in the EMS
Political and defense cooperation	Opposed; advocates codifying current cooperation	In favor of creating the position of Secretariat-General; opposed to extending defense cooperation	Opposed; advocates codifying current cooperation
Procedural reform in EC decision-making institutions	In favor of revising the treaty to strengthen Parliament's role; opposed to the Luxembourg compromise; in favor of more majority voting	In favor of revising the treaty or drafting a new treaty to allow for "variable geometry" programs; after 1984, opposed to strengthening Parliament's role, opposed to the Luxembourg compromise, and in favor of more majority voting	Opposed to revising the treaty; in favor of the Luxembourg compromise but advocates informal efforts to facilitate more majority voting
Internal market	In favor in principle	Opposed at first; after 1983, increasingly in favor	In favor in principle, but only if budgetary issues are resolved prior to liberalization

Procedural reform in the EC decision-making institutions and liberalization of the internal market offered more promise and later became the two components of the 1992 initiative.

Germany: Consistent Support

Among the three largest member states of the EC, Germany has enjoyed since the late 1950s the least partisan opposition to further European integration. As Europe's leading exporter, dependent on the EC for nearly half its exports, Germany profits directly from economic integration. German Foreign Minister Hans-Dietrich Genscher, leader of the Free Democrats, has also been a strong supporter of European political cooperation, which he views as a vital complement to *Ostpolitik*.[23] Moreover, a greater role for the European Parliament is widely viewed as a desirable step toward political union.[24] On the other hand, in the mid-1980s, Germany was suspicious of proposals for a European defense organization, was ambivalent about altering the agricultural policy so it would pay more or receive less, and was opposed to further monetary integration, at least until capital flows were liberalized.[25]

France: The Road to Damascus

Although traditionally pro-European, the French Socialist party all but ignored the EC during the first few years of the Mitterrand presidency.[26] France did call for more qualified majority voting and, to the surprise of many, supported a majority vote to override the threatened British veto of the cereal price package in May 1982. But substantive disagreements undermined Franco-German cooperation for EC reform. The most important French initiatives of this period, one in October 1981 on *un espace social européen* [a European social space] and another in the autumn of 1983 on *un espace industriel européen* [a European industrial space] did not amount to much. The first initiative, which was an antiunemployment program of fiscal stimulation billed as the initial step toward a "socialist Europe," found few friends in either Bonn or London and was never discussed at the Council. The second offered support for technology policies already in the process of adoption by the EC.

France's role as a European outsider during this period reflected its unorthodox domestic economic policies, which ran counter to the more conservative policies of Germany and Britain. Until 1983, French economic policy was conceived by the more radical wing of the Socialist party, led by politicians such as Jean-Pierre Chevènement and Pierre Bérégovoy. Nationalization, direct intervention to increase employment, and increases in social welfare spending undermined international business and financial confidence in the French economy. By March 1983, the French government had already negotiated two devaluations of the franc within the European Monetary System (EMS) and was rapidly heading for a third. The governments of other European states, particularly Germany, made it clear that a continuation of expansive policies was incompatible with continued membership in the EMS.

Many Socialists urged Mitterrand to move toward autarky—import protection, capital controls, and repudiation of the EMS—to protect expansionist domestic policies. Others in the moderate wing of the Socialist party, represented by politicians Michel Rocard and Jacques Delors and backed nearly unanimously by the French economic technocracy, advocated continued EMS membership, external free trade, and an austerity policy consisting of wage restraint and cuts in public expenditures. Some moderates also realized that the economic fundamentals underlying traditional French support for the Common Agricultural Policy (CAP) were shifting. Although domestic politics dictated that the government not move too quickly against agricultural interests, France was no longer a large net beneficiary from the EC budget, and its prospects after the entry of Spain and Portugal were even bleaker.[27]

Mitterrand's decision to remain in the EMS, announced on 21 March 1983, marked a turning point not only in French domestic politics but also in French policy toward the EC. While the EMS decision may have been influenced in part by an independent desire to remain "European," other factors included the failure of the autarkic policies, which would ultimately have compelled the French government to impose as much austerity as the policy they chose, and the decline of the Communist party, which allowed Mitterrand to align himself with moderate Socialists.[28] French economic decision making was thus vested in the hands of Rocard, Delors, and other politicians convinced of the virtues of conservative economic policies and firm in their belief that France must work within Europe to achieve its economic goals.

With the advent in January 1984 of the French presidency in the Council of Ministers and with elections to the European Parliament just two months away, Mitterrand—true to the European idealism he had espoused since the 1940s but undoubtedly also conscious of the political advantage to be gained by making a virtue out of necessity—announced a major diplomatic initiative for a relaunching of Europe. From that point on, Mitterrand played a decisive role in settling European disputes. French leadership and concessions helped resolve British agricultural and budget complaints. French negotiators began to support internal market liberalization and collaborative research and development. Mitterrand began to adopt the rhetoric of European federalism. He spoke of reconsidering the Luxembourg compromise and supporting procedural reform, as long as it was limited to the Council and the Commission and did not imply a radical democratization of EC politics.[29] Although committed to using the EC to combat economic decline, the French government remained uncertain whether monetary policy, internal market liberalization, or cooperative research and development should be the heart of the new initiative. Thus, Mitterrand, without being entirely sure where the initiative was leading, became the primary spokesman for relaunching Europe. One senior French diplomat observed dryly, "Monsieur Mitterrand's term as president of the European Council has become his road to Damascus."[30]

Britain: The Road to Milan

With France converted to the European cause, Britain remained the major obstacle to an initiative linking internal market liberalization and procedural reform. Britain's entry into the EC in 1973 had expanded the Community without strengthening it. Insofar as Thatcher was pro-European, it was largely because she saw the EC almost exclusively as an organization for promoting economic liberalism in the industrial and service sectors. By British standards, however, this represented a considerable commitment, since the opposition Labour party opposed market liberalization and European integration. Having abolished exchange controls in 1979, having begun liberalization of telecommunications services in 1981, having publicly promised to lower European air fares, and, last but not least, being fully aware that the city of London contained highly competitive banking and insurance sectors, Thatcher began to call for pan-European deregulation of services.[31] The British government also favored strengthening European political cooperation, although without creating an independent bureaucracy.

In the early 1980s, the most important British objection to EC policy stemmed from the heavy British deficit under the CAP. With its small, efficient agricultural sector concentrated in areas not generously subsidized by the CAP (for example, in sheep husbandry), Britain gained little from the agricultural programs that comprise 70 percent of the EC budget. At the same time, Britain was by far the largest per capita *net* contributor to the budget. Thatcher campaigned to get "her money back" from the EC, and her frugality bolstered British opposition to the budgetary policy. When she was elected to office, she insisted that two-thirds of the British deficit over the past few years be rebated and that permanent adjustments be made to limit agricultural spending and to prevent future budgetary disequilibria.

More was at stake in the British objections than temporary budgetary imbalances. In 1973, Britain had been forced to accept the agricultural and budgetary policies as part of the *acquis communautaire,* the corpus of existing EC institutions. For those who had worked for decades in the Community and who saw the CAP as part of the initial Franco-German bargain at the heart of the EC, the British demand called into question the very foundation of European cooperation. French Foreign Minister Claude Cheysson declared in 1982 that "the United Kingdom [seeks] *juste retour,* which is not a Community idea. We and the British are not speaking of the same community."[32]

The Thatcher government, even more than previous British governments, was wary of attempts to strengthen the Commission and Parliament and to expand EC competence into areas not directly connected with trade, such as indirect taxation and social legislation. Thatcher also firmly opposed formal changes in Council procedures, in part because of a suspicion of written constitutions, a suspicion shared by most British conservatives. Although opposed to any treaty changes that undermined the sovereign prerogatives recognized by the Luxembourg compromise, she recognized the need for some movement away from unanimous decision making and thus favored informal means of encouraging majority voting.

SETTING AN AGENDA FOR EUROPE:
A POLICY HISTORY OF THE 1992 INITIATIVE

From the Height of "Europessimism" to the French Presidency

The early 1980s marked the apogee of Europessimism. Disputes over agricultural policy, the accession of Spain and Portugal, and budgetary reform festered. Ideas of splitting the EC into subgroups proliferated: *Europe à deux vitesses,* a two-tier Community, *abgestufte Integration.* The divergent economic policies of France and Germany undermined their traditional axis of collaboration within the EC. With the exception of the launching of the European Strategic Programme for Research and Development in Information Technology (ESPRIT) in 1983, appeals for a renewed commitment to Europe came to naught. The most significant of these appeals, the Genscher-Columbo initiative and the Stuttgart Declaration, are sometimes interpreted as precursors of the SEA.[33] In fact, however, they demonstrate the utter absence of a European consensus for reform before 1984.

The Genscher-Columbo initiative of 1981 was a Council declaration calling for greater movement toward European unity. It was proposed by the German foreign minister, who was later joined by his Italian counterpart, and backed by the Commission. The two foreign ministers justified the initiative with reference to economic recession and institutional malaise in the EC, but disagreements between member states prevented the development of specific proposals, outside of political cooperation. To address the completion of the internal market, which had been discussed in the Council since its inception in 1974, a report was commissioned.

Despite its vagueness and ambiguous legal status, the Genscher-Columbo initiative was immediately criticized by France, whose interest in Europe was still limited to sporadic proposals for steps toward a socialist Europe, and by Britain, for whom resolution of the budget wrangle remained the *sine qua non* for negotiations over anything else. André Chandernagor, French Minister for European Affairs, observed sarcastically before the Assemblée Nationale that some Europeans were trying to build Europe from the roof down.[34]

The Council did set up an ad hoc working group to look into the initiative, but when it reported back to the Stuttgart summit of June 1983, its recommendations did little more than codify the status quo. The Council issued the "Solemn Declaration on European Union," which was based on the ad hoc group's report and reaffirmed in general terms the member states' desire to reinforce and develop both economic and security cooperation. It called for the completion of the internal market alongside numerous other proposals of widely varying promise, including coordinated reflation, social programs, reinforcement of the monetary system, and a European industrial policy. The document again reflected the lack of consensus on procedural reform, suggesting only that member states voluntarily abstain rather than invoke the veto. Nonetheless, it elicited immediate *procès-verbaux* reaffirming the Luxembourg compromise from Britain, Denmark, France, Greece, and Ireland. Shortly thereafter, French Prime Minister Pierre Mauroy launched a public attack on the Stuttgart Declaration, reasserting the veto right.[35] In the end, the only solid achievement of the meeting was acceptance of Genscher's proposal to link together four outstanding issues in the Community—an increase in EC funds, agricultural reform, internal market liberalization, and the entry of Spain and Portugal—in the hope that they would be resolved as a package at the Athens summit later that year.

The Turning Point: The French Presidency

All this changed unexpectedly with France's accession to the revolving presidency of the EC in January 1984, less than a year after the moderate wing of the Socialist party assumed power in France. Mitterrand's extraordinary personal involvement in the six-month presidency prompted one French observer to call him a "one-man orchestra."[36] He began the year with a personal tour of all the European capitals to seek a consensus for relaunching the EC. Throughout 1984, he and French Foreign Minister Roland Dumas practiced "shuttle diplomacy" between Paris, Bonn, and London. Mitterrand's speeches, most notably in May before the European Parliament, underscored the economic nature of the current crisis and elaborated a vision of the future EC as an instrument to combat the economic decline of Europe. "Europe," he warned, "is beginning to look like an abandoned building site."[37] He proposed political cooperation, technological programs, and reform of the CAP. Two constant refrains were decision making and internal market reform.

The outlines of an interstate bargain were becoming clear. Germany and Britain were agreed on the need for liberalization, with weak support from France, while Germany and France were agreed on the need for procedural reform, with weak support from Britain.[38] But Mitterrand's plan to resolve these issues by calling a conference to "preserve Europe" was blocked by the long-standing disputes over CAP reform, Britain's demand for compensation, the accession of Spain and Portugal, and the need for greater EC financial resources. Within a year, these issues had been resolved, in each case largely owing to an unexpected French willingness to compromise.[39]

The first steps were taken in early 1984, when the French government put its farmers on notice that France would no longer unquestioningly support their interests in Brussels. "The revitalization of agricultural policy," declared Michel Rocard, then Minister of Agriculture, "can no longer serve as the instrument of European unification."[40] Under Rocard's direction, a compromise was reached in March 1984, marking the first of several initiatives to bring agricultural spending under control.

Agricultural disputes were also at the heart of the enlargement issue. French farmers, fearing the import of cheap vegetables and wine from Spain and Portugal, had long encouraged the French government to stall on this issue. In the EC, the related conflicts manifested themselves through threats and counterthreats about the budget. EC finances were overextended, so much so that the Council had decided in October 1983 to delay payments under the CAP for lack of funds. Germany had insisted at Stuttgart that Spain and Portugal enter by the end of 1984 and had threatened to block increases in EC funding until the enlargement issue was settled. Thatcher had also promised to block any funding increases until the budget issue was resolved. With the EC fiscal situation growing more perilous, Mitterrand, whose government had reversed its opposition to budgetary increases after the pro-European turn in 1983, announced that he would complete the negotiations by September 1984.[41]

Mitterrand wasted no time. In Brussels in March 1984, French negotiators offered a series of concessions, agreeing for the first time that the British net contribution should be cut permanently and should reflect Britain's lower per capita income. But France also kept up the pressure by joining Italy in blocking the British rebate for 1983, which totalled £457 million. Thatcher considered retaliating by withholding the British budget contribution for 1984, but she reportedly was dissuaded by Cabinet opposition and by the fear of losing a challenge before the British or European courts.[42]

The heads of government agreed to a system for limiting agricultural spending that would keep any growth in Britain's contribution roughly in line with its percentage of the EC gross domestic product. But the budget rebate for 1984 and following years remained unsettled, with the others offering ECU 1 billion and Thatcher demanding ECU 1.5 billion. After days of face-to-face haggling, the heads of government seemed to have reached a deal at ECU 1.2 billion. British officials were drafting a communiqué announcing the success when agreement was blocked by Kohl's sudden refusal to pay Germany's share of any sum larger than ECU 1 billion. His unexpected stubbornness grounded the negotiations, leaving an angry Thatcher the scapegoat.

After the Brussels meeting, Mitterrand called for a conference to discuss relaunching the EC among those member states which would "stand up and be counted."[43] In his May 1984 speech to the Parliament, he picked up the thread again, speaking frankly about the possible need for a Europe *à geométrie variable*. Dumas announced that if a budget agreement was not reached, his government would call a meeting without the British to discuss various proposals for reform, and he boldly raised the possibility of a two-track Europe during Thatcher's visit to the Elysée. For his part, Kohl announced shortly thereafter that the "decisive conditions had been created" to move toward completion of the European market and majority voting in the Council. He called for movement toward greater European unity within a year, whether or not all countries agreed.

Britain became increasingly isolated as Mitterrand and Kohl repeated the threat of a two-tier Europe that would leave Britain without a say in the details of the new agreements. The lesson of the 1950s, when Britain had refused to join the EC, was that exclusion could be costly in the long run. Decades later, the British were still trying to reverse priorities set in their absence.

Mitterrand exploited the threat of exclusion with great finesse, a stratagem facilitated by the fact that the threat was more credible than it may seem in retrospect. France had long promoted two-track initiatives, especially in the area of high technology. During this period, moreover, a two-track EC had found a number of prominent exponents among European academics and commentators.[44] It is thus no surprise that the threat was understood as such across the Channel. The British press picked up the theme, and a Tory think tank issued a report calling for a more conciliatory negotiating position to head off the exclusion of Britain from future European initiatives.[45]

The Breakthrough: The Fontainebleau Summit Meeting

In the weeks leading to the Fontainebleau summit of June 1984, Thatcher seemed sobered by her experience at Brussels. She exhibited a new positive spirit, quietly circulating a paper entitled "Europe: The Future," which outlined her government's vision for relaunching Europe. At the head of the list of priorities was liberalization of the internal market, particularly in services. British Foreign Minister Geoffrey Howe called for the removal of "all—and I mean all, economic barriers," suggesting 1990 as a deadline.[46] These proposals were quietly supported by France. "Europe: The Future" also addressed the decision-making issue, calling for qualified majority voting to be respected in cases in which the treaty provided for it: nations should be able to veto "where a very important national interest is at stake" but "should be required . . . to set out their reasons fully" before the other Council members.[47]

Mitterrand seemed to choreograph the Fontainebleau summit in a manner designed to remind Thatcher once again of the possibility of a two-track Europe. Heads of government cooled their heels for two hours when the opening meeting was delayed to allow Mitterrand to present an extemporaneous exposition of his "dreams of Europe" before the television cameras.[48] Whatever the cause, Thatcher was more conciliatory at Fontainebleau than she had been at Brussels. The decisive issue, which took more than thirty-six hours to resolve, was again the size of the British rebate. A compromise was finally reached at a figure roughly equivalent to what the British had been offered (and had rejected) in Brussels, with the French assuming a sizable portion of the burden. Moreover, the Council agreed to generalize the principle of *juste retour* to payments into the budget: no member state should be required to sustain a "budgetary burden which is excessive in relation to its relative prosperity."[49]

Fontainebleau marked the moment when momentum toward a package deal containing internal market liberalization and decision-making reform became unmistakable. The heads of government called for a package of internal liberalization, coordinated stimulation, and collaborative research and development designed to give the EC "an economic impulse comparable to that given by the Common Market in the 1960s."[50] They further agreed that customs controls would eventually be abolished. At their summit meeting in Saarbrücken shortly after Fontainebleau, Mitterrand and Kohl demonstrated the seriousness of their commitment to internal market reform (while renewing the threat of a two-tier Europe) by entering into negotiations over the abolition of all controls on normal goods traffic, the harmonization of domestic veterinary and sanitary legislation, the free movement of people, the adoption of common streamlined administrative procedures, and the eventual accession to the Benelux customs union. This would create a "super EEC" among the five states.[51]

Mitterrand also sought agreement on expanding majority voting at Fontainebleau but was forced to settle for the creation of two committees. The first, the Ad Hoc Committee on a People's Europe (later called the Adonnino Committee), received a mandate to investigate aspects of the EC that were directly visible to the common citizen: customs formalities for individuals, equivalence of university diplomas, the creation of European symbols, and European volunteer programs. The second and far more significant committee, the Ad Hoc Committee for Institutional Affairs (later called the Dooge Committee, after its Irish chairman), had a mandate to consider institutional, political, and economic reform.

The symbolic significance of the Dooge Committee was enormous. According to the Fontainebleau communiqué, it was to be set up on the lines of the Spaak Committee, the group formed in 1955 by the Council of the European Coal and Steel Community (ECSC) to develop proposals for the *relance européenne* of that decade. Those proposals led in 1957 to the signing of the Treaty of Rome and the founding of the EC.[52] Mitterrand immediately signaled grand ambitions for the Dooge Committee by appointing Maurice Faure, a strong pan-European and a signatory to the Treaty of Rome, as his representative. Faure had Mitterrand's personal support, and he arrived at the second meeting with a draft report that had reportedly been approved by Mitterrand himself over the objections of the Quai d'Orsay.

It soon became clear that while the member states differed over political cooperation, monetary policy, defense, and procedural reform, all (with the possible exception of Greece) were in substantial agreement about the need for internal market liberalization, as had been reflected in the Fontainebleau communiqué. On detailed points, the report contained many proposals that were originally British, such as common EC standards, liberalization of transport and insurance services, and open public procurement.

Although the Committee devoted most of its time to procedural reform, which it viewed as its "real task," it was unable to agree on the decisive issues: qualified majority voting and veto rights. On these questions, the British delegation expected to find itself comfortably located in the center of the spectrum, alongside the French and perhaps the German delegations. But the French joined the Germans in calling for majority voting on internal market issues and for amendments to the treaty. Seven of the ten member states were willing to renounce the Luxembourg compromise and expand qualified majority voting through treaty changes, while Britain, Greece, and Denmark stuck to the British program, reasserting the right to veto when "very important national interests" were at stake and accepting only the voluntary, informal steps to encourage majority voting already acknowledged in the Stuttgart Declaration. The seven also called for an intergovernmental conference to negotiate a draft treaty of European union.[53]

As the Dooge Committee deliberated, it came time to name a new European Commission and, more important, a new president of the Commission. France and Germany, seeking to expedite the *relance européenne* by giving the position political status, pressed for a president from a large country. Domestic coalitional politics appear to have prevented Germany, whose informal turn it was, from nominating a suitable candidate. Davignon, a Belgian and the self-nominated front-runner, lacked national political experience, was considered by some to be an insufficiently inspiring leader, and was associated with interventionist economic policies. Delors, freed from the post of Minister of Finance just in time by a reshuffle in France, was nominated at the last minute by Mitterrand. His stature as a politician with senior ministerial experience, his years as a member of the EC Economic and Social Committee, and his reputation for sensible economic policymaking led Germany and Britain to signal immediate approval. Thatcher nonetheless took the precaution of naming Cockfield (a strong candidate with Cabinet-level experience, despite press commentary to the contrary) as a liberal counterweight.

Delors immediately embarked on his trip through the member states, exploring possibilities for reform. Upon returning, he quietly went to work, distributing portfolios to his fellow commissioners—usually the occasion for extended haggling—with unprecedented swiftness. He proposed his reform strategy to the new Commission in December 1984 and announced the goal of completing the internal market by 1992 in his maiden speech before the European Parliament on 14 January 1985.

At the Luxembourg summit of March 1985, France and Germany supported an initiative, largely based on the Dooge Report, to relaunch the EC by limiting the Luxembourg compromise, extending EC competence in foreign affairs, and completing the internal market. At Brussels a few weeks later, the Council endorsed the goal of a single market by 1992 and called upon the Commission to draw up a detailed program with a specific timetable. Lord Cockfield, now Internal Market Commissioner, interpreted his mandate broadly. Quickly assembling material that had long been languishing in the drawers of the Directorate-General III (responsible for internal market policy), he drafted the celebrated White Paper. In lieu of a firm definition of a "completed internal market," Cockfield set forth nearly three hundred specific proposals, including value-added tax (VAT) harmonization and mutual recognition, accompanied by a brief philosophical defense of free market liberalism.

In the run-up to the summit in Milan during the last days of June 1985, proposals began to multiply. In addition to the Dooge Report and the White Paper, Delors suggested an extension of the EC substantive responsibilities, including the doubling of research and development funding and reform of the monetary system. Delors' public speeches began linking internal liberalization to qualified majority voting, stressing that the first was unattainable without the second and that neither was possible without an intergovernmental conference to amend the Treaty of Rome. The British government, feeling marginalized but nonetheless hoping to channel momentum away from treaty amendments, launched a counteroffensive. The British initiative tied its previous proposal for internal market reform, a proposal announced prior to the Fontainebleau summit and now codified in the White Paper, to "gentleman's agreements" to abstain rather than invoke the veto. This procedural proposal now included two new elements: voluntary restraint in invoking the Luxembourg compromise at lower levels of the Council once the chiefs of state had set an objective and a separate treaty codifying principles of informal political cooperation.[54]

As the Milan summit opened, the heads of government unanimously approved the White Paper. They also immediately accepted the British proposal on informal improvements to decision making, but for most countries this was only a starting point. Genscher proposed a more ambitious agreement consisting of a "return to the decision-making procedure which existed before the so-called Luxembourg disagreement," majority voting on internal market issues, and informal agreement to abstain from invoking the veto.[55] But some, presumably including Thatcher, found renunciation of the Luxembourg compromise unacceptable. The text was rejected, even after being watered down with British amendments.

At this moment, Italian Foreign Minister Andreotti, skeptical of mere declarations of intention and anxious to avoid a failure under the Italian presidency, called for a majority vote on whether to convene an intergovernmental conference under Article 236. Germany and the Benelux countries immediately supported the Italian measure, and France and Ireland hesitatingly joined them, leaving only Britain, Denmark, and Greece opposed. On procedural grounds, Britain protested the invocation of a majority vote, but its protests were rejected and the conference was called.[56]

Thatcher returned from Milan in a fury but within a few days allowed herself to be persuaded that Britain should attend the conference. The reasons were varied. First, Britain had little to lose from qualified majority voting on the internal market program, which it favored in general and which jeopardized British interests, as Thatcher assessed them, in only a few areas. In areas outside the internal market, Thatcher appears to have assumed that reform proposals were simply rhetorical. The British were also sensitive to Delors' constant reminders that some procedural changes were needed to ensure implementation of the internal market plan. Second, the procedure for amending the treaty under Article 236 (as opposed to negotiating a new treaty) offered two advantages to the recalcitrant: it excluded the Parliament, and it required unanimity. There would be no two-track decisions. Third, Mitterrand continued to feed speculation about a two-tiered Europe, calling the decisions at Milan "a test of truth."[57] In the end, Britain attended the conference, where it played a skeptical but ultimately constructive role.

Victory for the Minimalists:
The Intergovernmental Conference

A draft of the SEA was written during the first month of the intergovernmental conference; the remaining details were worked out between the foreign ministers and heads of state at five meetings between 21 October and 1 December 1985; and the document was signed in February 1986.[58] Most of the central issues were resolved within the first two months.

The SEA negotiations can be interpreted as a process of limiting the scope and intensity of reform—a process necessary to gain the acceptance not only of Britain but also of other member states who, when it came to drafting a document, suddenly proved quite jealous of their sovereignty. The maximalist program of broad reform was progressively sacrificed in favor of the minimalist program limited to those procedural and substantive changes needed to liberalize the internal market. Minimalist limitations were negotiated in three stages. First, the negotiators continued the trend, evident since the appointment of the Dooge Committee, toward blocking significant reform in areas of cooperation not directly connected with the internal market. Second, they obstructed the extension of majority voting to a number of contentious internal market issues, such as fiscal and social regulation. And, third, they offset the implicit suppressions of the veto with generous exemptions and safeguard provisions regarding the harmonization of internal legislation.

In all cases other than internal market policy, the lack of a consensus among the major states reduced commitments to a minor or symbolic level. The fate of monetary reform is an important and typical example. Monetary coordination had long been a personal interest of Delors, and the Commission's proposals to the intergovernmental conference made progress toward a common monetary fund subject to the unanimous approval only of the group of member states that would choose to participate. The two-track proposal would have therefore granted EC legitimacy to any effort by a smaller group to proceed on its own. But shortly after the opening of the conference, this activism was curbed during an informal meeting of the ministers of economics and finance, who insisted that they be consulted before any further monetary proposals were made to the conference.

France, Italy, and some others felt that the Delors proposal was too weak, while Germany, Britain, and the Netherlands were opposed to the discussion of monetary policy at the conference.[59] Germany believed that freedom of capital markets and coordinated economic policy must precede the consideration of further monetary coordination. Thatcher felt that Britain, which does not participate in the existing exchange rate mechanism of the EMS, should not surrender any sovereignty at that time. When Germany and Britain lost patience and threatened to tie any monetary agreement to the complete liberalization of capital markets by the end of 1986, the others quickly agreed to a compromise that included no concrete steps beyond existing policies.

Reference to eventual monetary union was included in the preamble to the revised treaty, but so was language limiting the EMS to its present functions. Commission proposals permitting a two-track monetary system were rejected outright. Moreover, the SEA placed the EMS under the unanimity rule of Article 236, thereby granting Britain, a nonparticipant in the exchange rate mechanism, veto power over its future evolution. This has led some to argue that further progress toward monetary union "seems likely to be checked rather than encouraged." Even Delors could say only that the revised treaty makes "allowance for [its] evolution when this becomes necessary."[60]

One provision essential to the passage of the internal market program was the expansion of structural funds aimed at poorer regions of the EC. This provision, referred to as the "convergence policy," was not a vital element of economic liberalization, as the Commission at times claimed, but was instead a side-payment to Ireland and the Southern nations in exchange for their political support. The richer countries hesitated to pay more to the poorer countries but in the end agreed that structural and development funds would be "significantly increased in real terms within the limits of financial possibilities"—a phrase that laid the foundation for a sizable increase in transfers approved in 1988.[61] In contrast, proposals on political cooperation, technology policy, social and cultural policy, human rights, and energy policy did not go beyond a codification of current practice, while environmental policy, a new area, remains under unanimity rule.[62]

All states agreed on the need for significant exemptions and escape clauses with regard to internal market liberalization. Although the negotiators deliberately avoided discussing the Luxembourg compromise or the procedures for calling a majority vote (procedures later determined by the Council itself), the veto right was retained in a weaker form in Article 100(4) of the revised treaty, which permits nations outvoted in the Council or wishing to invoke a safeguard clause to retain their domestic regulations for reasons of *exigences importantes* under Article 36. To invoke this clause, however, governments must inform the Commission, which then determines whether a particular measure constitutes an arbitrary form of discrimination or a disguised restriction on commerce, rather than a legitimate derogation. The Commission or any government that believes a nation has abused the safeguard clause may seek relief before the European Court, using a special accelerated procedure. This clause shifts the locus of conflict over the veto from ratification by the Council to implementation by each nation. And the final arbiters have changed: the Court and, to a lesser extent, the Commission—not the member states, as under the Luxembourg compromise—now ultimately determine what constitutes proper justification for exempting a state from an EC decision.[63] It is important to note, however, that these procedures are strictly limited to matters pertaining to the internal market.

At the Luxembourg summit of December 1985, the heads of government resolved the remaining details. The ratification of the amendments was unproblematic, although it was delayed by Denmark, which had to fulfill its constitutional obligation to hold a referendum. In the wake of the Luxembourg summit, Kohl and Mitterrand stated (though perhaps only for posterity) that they would have been prepared to go further on the powers of the Parliament and on monetary policy, respectively, as well as on majority voting. Italian Prime Minister Craxi, who had voiced doubts that the SEA included enough of the maximalist agenda, promised support for the act only if the European Parliament approved it.

Thatcher, by contrast, hailed the results as "clear and decisive."[64] In many ways, the final agreement on substantive issues satisfied the British the most, as could be expected in cases of lowest-common-denominator bargaining. The outcome of the agricultural budget negotiations, for example, reflected the other member states' acknowledgment of the legitimacy of the British claim to reshape the *acquis communautaire* in fundamental ways, although it also reflected the changed perceptions of France with regard to agricultural spending. Time and time again during the negotiations, the British got their way on substantive and procedural issues—in part because the commitment of other countries turned out to be weaker than their rhetoric—until the final draft looked very much like the plan for eliminating all barriers to trade that Geoffrey Howe had called for in early 1984.

In the areas where the British government favored reform, such as liberalization of services trade, qualified majority voting triumphed. Elsewhere it failed. Although Britain did not succeed in blocking treaty revisions altogether, its negotiators did succeed in preventing an explicit revocation of the Luxembourg compromise. We cannot know for sure how far the French and Germans would actually have been prepared to go to carry out the threat of a two-tier Europe, but certainly they are now hampered from doing so, particularly in the monetary area, by the SEA.[65]

INTERPRETING THE NEGOTIATIONS

Assessing Supranational Institutionalism

The historical record does not confirm the importance of international and transnational factors. Let us consider each element in turn.

European Institutions

The supranational model stresses the role of EC institutions, particularly the Parliament. Yet after Fontainebleau, government representatives, abetted by the Commission, deliberately excluded representatives of the Parliament from decisive forums. One of the Dooge Committee's first actions was to reject the Parliament's "Draft Treaty Establishing European Union" and begin negotiations with a French government draft instead.[66] From that moment on, key decision makers ignored the maximalist agenda. National governments viewed the Parliament's proposals as too open-ended ("real reform . . . requires a treaty encompassing all Community policies and the institutions needed to implement them"), too democratic (the powers of the Parliament should be "extended to new spheres of activity"), and too automatic (the draft treaty would have gone into effect without unanimous Council approval).[67] The Parliament members' continuous protests against the emasculation of the draft treaty and their exclusion from the "real participation" in the discussions were ignored.[68] The fact that the member states parried parliamentary pressure with ease certainly casts doubt on the argument that the SEA was necessary to coopt rising demands for even more thoroughgoing institutional reform. In the end, the Parliament overwhelmingly passed a resolution protesting that the SEA "in no way represent[s] the real reform of the Community that our peoples need," but it had little alternative but to accept the fait accompli.[69]

Transnational Business Interest Groups

The internal market program, like the EC itself thirty years before, appears to have been launched independently of pressure from transnationally organized business interest groups.[70] The Kangaroo Group in Parliament, which had close contacts with business interests, remained relatively small until after the 1992 initiative was launched and established no formal links with the Council until 1986. The activities of the Roundtable of European Industrialists focused primarily on the concerns of its non-EC European membership. Before 1985, its chief involvement was in European infrastructure projects such as the Channel tunnel.[71] The Roundtable was based in Geneva and did not move to Brussels until 1988, when Dekker assumed its presidency.

Most transnational business lobbies got involved late. By the time Dekker delivered his oft-quoted speeches, nearly a year had passed since the beginning of the path-breaking French presidency and the discussions of the Dooge Committee were well under way. But a few business groups, such as UNICE, had been pushing vainly for liberalization for a long time. Given their persistence, what needs to be explained is why governments finally listened.

International Political Leaders

Cockfield's conceptual boldness and Delors' political dexterity are not in question. Cockfield and Delors acted on the margins to broaden the White Paper and the SEA, and they may have contributed to the remarkable speed of decision making at the intergovernmental conference. Nevertheless, the broader outlines of both documents were proposed, negotiated, and approved, often in advance of Commission initiatives, by the heads of government themselves. Indeed, the breakthrough in the relaunching of the EC had already occurred before Delors became president of the Commission. The causality of the supranational explanation is thus reversed: the selection of a prestigious politician for the presidency was merely a symptom of mounting trilateral pressure for reform. In this regard, ironically enough, Delors' actions as Finance Minister of France may have contributed more to the SEA than those as president of the Commission.

It is worth dwelling for a moment longer on the intergovernmental conference, for this is the point at which supranational institutionalist hypotheses about Commission influence might appear most plausible.

Four specific arguments can be advanced, but none suggests that supranational actors influenced the substance of the SEA. First, the remarkable speed of the conference might be attributed, at least in part,
to the role of Delors and the Commission in proposing and revising
the specific wording of treaty amendments. While logistical support from
the Commission may indeed have hastened a final agreement, there is
little evidence that it altered its substance. Second, the Commission
might be credited with having quietly slipped some new EC functions,
such as environmental and research and development programs, into
the revised treaty. But these were functions that the EC had been handling
under indirect authorization for a number of years, and there was little
opposition from member states to extending a concrete mandate to cover
them. Third, in late September and early October 1985, Delors dropped
strong advocacy of monetary and social reform and chose to stress
instead the links between internal market reform, majority voting, and
the increases in structural funds needed to gain support from Ireland
and the Southern countries.[72] Delors' conciliatory move, particularly the
proposal for structural funding, may have facilitated a political compromise, but his position on these issues was nonetheless closely circumscribed by the views of the major states. This is particularly true
in regard to monetary policy, where Delors' elimination of monetary
reform from the package, as we have seen, resulted from the direct
pressure of domestic officials. Fourth and finally, Cockfield's White Paper
might be seen as a key act of agenda setting. But the White Paper was
a response to a mandate from the member states expressed both in the
Council, which commissioned the paper, and in the interim report of
the Dooge Committee. In previous years, the Commission had proposed
many of the nearly three hundred items as part of various reform
proposals, but governments had simply rejected them.

   Delors' most important contributions to the process resulted not from
his role as an initiator of unforeseen policies but instead from his keen
awareness of the extreme constraints under which he was acting. A
reexamination of his memoirs reveals that his arguments (as distinct
from his tone) stress intergovernmental constraints rather than personal
influence.[73] Procedural reform without a substantive program, he rea-
soned, would get bogged down in ideological battles over sovereignty;
a plan for European monetary union would encounter the opposition
of the governors of the central banks, who, led by the Germans, had
just rejected an expansion of the EMS; and European defense cooperation
was neither within the current competence of the EC nor widely supported
among member states.[74] The sole remaining option was internal market
reform. In this regard, Delors' most statesmanlike judgments concerned

the proper moment to compromise—as he did in September and October 1985.[75]

Supranational Institutionalism and Neofunctionalism

None of the three supranational variables—European institutional momentum, transnational business interest group activity, and international political leadership—seems to account for the timing, content, and process of negotiating the SEA. Moreover, governments did not bargain by "upgrading" the common interest or by linking issues but, rather, by accepting the lowest common denominator, backed by the threat of exclusion. The resulting bargain places major obstacles in the path of attempts to extend the reform to new issues, such as monetary policy.

In this regard, one striking aspect of the negotiations for the SEA is their parallel to the negotiations for the ECSC and EC in the 1950s. Even regional integration theorists are inclined to accept that the founding of the ECSC was an extraordinary act of political statecraft, but they contend that once it occurred it sparked a qualitatively different and potentially self-sustaining process of spillover. The negotiating history of the SEA, however, suggests that three decades later the factors encouraging a greater commitment to European unity are essentially the same: the convergence of national interests, the pro-European idealism of heads of government, and the decisive role of the large member states.

The importance of interstate bargains in the SEA negotiations is consistent with the broader experience of the EC since the mid-1960s. European integration did not proceed steadily and incrementally; it proceeded in fits and starts. Moreover, since the Luxembourg compromise in 1966, the EC has moved toward intergovernmental ("state-to-state") decision making centered in the Council and summit meetings, rather than toward increasing authority for international bodies such as the Commission and Parliament.[76] One detailed study concluded that the systems change in the EC has in fact proved to be more political and less technical than Haas predicted.[77] While spillover and forward linkages may in some cases suffice to prompt the intensification of international decision making under a specific mandate within a given sector, they play a minimal role in the processes of opening new issues, reforming decision-making procedures, and ratifying the accession of new members. Movement in these areas requires active intervention by heads of state and a considerable amount of nontechnocratic interstate bargaining.

The SEA negotiations suggest, furthermore, that in the 1980s, just as in the 1950s, pan-European business groups were relatively ineffective at influencing policy.[78] Business, at least on the supranational level, was mobilized by the emerging interstate consensus for reform, rather than the reverse. This casts doubt on at least one mechanism underlying the long-term historical prediction underlying neofunctionalism—namely, that over time, growth in the autonomy and responsibility of supranational actors and organizations will facilitate further integration.

Assessing Intergovernmental Institutionalism

The historical record confirms the importance of the three elements of intergovernmental institutionalism. Again, these elements can be considered in turn.

Intergovernmentalism

Heads of government and their direct representatives carried out the negotiations. The result represents the convergence of domestic policy preferences in the largest member states. The dominance of the three largest states is revealed most clearly by the lack of cases (with the possible exception of the Danish stand on workers' rights) in which a smaller nation either initiated or vetoed a central initiative. The Southern nations and Ireland were appeased en masse with the promise of a side-payment in the form of increased structural funds; the Benelux countries had been prepared in any case to go further than the others. The election of a Conservative government in Britain and, more important, the shift in French economic policy preferences in 1983 were the key turning points on the road to 1992.

Lowest-Common-Denominator Bargaining

The only major exception to lowest-common-denominator bargaining concerned whether to amend the Treaty of Rome to promote majority voting on internal market matters. On this point, the British yielded to Franco-German pressure to convene an intergovernmental conference, at least in part because the Franco-German position was backed by the threat of exclusion. As Paul Taylor has observed, "British diplomacy . . . had to balance two objectives: that of satisfying specific interests, and that of staying in the game. A measure of compromise in the former [became] necessary to achieve the latter."[79] Nonetheless, given the lowest-common-denominator bargaining characteristic of systems change in the EC, it is not surprising that the British were most satisfied with the final outcome. Thatcher's success in negotiating a fundamental revision of the rules for calculating the net obligations to the EC budget can be viewed as the end of extended negotiations over the terms of British accession. While the agricultural *acquis communautaire* represented a

Franco-German deal, the new agreement reflected more closely the new trilateral balance of power within the EC. The British also succeeded in limiting institutional reform to internal market issues.[80]

Protection of Sovereignty

The steady narrowing of the institutional reform to a "minimalist" position in which majority voting is restricted to internal market policy, the power of the Parliament is limited, and the future spillover to areas such as monetary policy is blocked confirms the enduring preoccupation of all three major states with maintaining sovereignty and control over future changes in the scope of EC activities.

International Institutionalism and Domestic Politics

While the intergovernmental approach, based on the relative power of member states and the convergence of their national policy preferences, offers a satisfactory account of the SEA negotiations, it raises a second, equally important question: Why did underlying national policy preferences converge at this point in time? As indicated earlier, part of the answer can be found in the domestic politics of France, Germany, and Britain. Four paradigmatic explanations can also be identified: autonomous action by political leaders, pressure from state bureaucracies, support from centrist coalitions, and pressure to replace failed economic policies. Each offers a promising starting point for analyzing the domestic roots of European integration, but none is entirely satisfactory.

Statism: The Autonomy of Political Leaders

The convergence of policy preferences in the mid-1980s may have reflected the views, either pro-European or neoliberal, of the three major European leaders of the time—Mitterrand, Kohl, and Thatcher—and their close associates. The history of the SEA suggests that heads of government in the three largest member states possessed considerable autonomy from domestic bureaucracies, political parties, and interest groups, at least in the short run.

In 1984, Mitterrand's personal advocacy, against the opposition of the Quai d'Orsay and the left wing of his own party, gave a decisive impetus to reform efforts. Delors himself stressed the importance of Mitterrand's shuttle diplomacy, recalling that Mitterrand met six times each with Kohl and Thatcher during his 1984 Council presidency alone. The key decisions in France were made in meetings *à quatre* with Mitterrand, Dumas, Delors, and the French Minister of European Affairs.[81]

Like Adenauer and de Gaulle before them, Kohl and Mitterrand viewed economic integration as part of a geopolitical grand strategy. In this sense, French support for the EC could not be separated from French initiatives in areas such as armaments coproduction, coordinated conventional defense, and nuclear strategy. Similarly, Kohl followed Genscher in viewing German support for the EC as an indispensable precondition for German unification within a pan-European framework.[82]

Thatcher's role in the reform effort was as important as Mitterrand's role, though somewhat more ambivalent. Obstacles to reform stemmed from Thatcher's personal crusade to constrain European bureaucracy, particularly in the social and monetary areas, despite the more pro-European sentiments of her closest civil service advisers and a majority of her own party. On the other hand, her extreme neoliberalism lent the SEA much of its substance.

In the case of Mitterrand and Thatcher, current views toward European unification reflect positions held for decades. In the case of Cockfield, Rocard, Delors, and others, support may also reflect positive experiences working with and within EC institutions.

Bureaucratic Politics: The Role of Technocracy

The importance of bureaucracies is suggested by the long-term evolution of European policymaking. Since 1966, when the Luxembourg compromise was accepted, the EC has institutionalized an intergovernmental style of internal decision making, centered in the Council. Committees consisting of national bureaucrats, members of permanent delegations (COREPER), or ministers (the Council of Ministers) have met regularly in Brussels and interacted through an increasingly cooperative and specialized mode of decision making. By the early 1980s, a clear trend had emerged away from the traditional practice of consulting foreign ministries in each European state and toward specialization of functions in the Council. While the foreign ministries tended to be suspicious of transferring or pooling sovereignty through mechanisms such as majority voting, the bureaucratic specialists have often been strong supporters of European economic integration. Thus, increased specialization may have encouraged a steady increase in majority voting, with ten decisions based on qualified majority voting between 1966 and 1974, thirty-five between 1974 and 1979, and more than ninety between 1980 and 1984. In this sense, as Helen Wallace points out, the SEA represents "a return on investments made over many previous years" in developing a set of common norms for Council negotiating.[83]

According to the bureaucratic politics view, this evolution in EC negotiating style may also have had an effect at home. That is, as technocrats have internalized norms of cooperation, the national leaders have increasingly supported European integration. At a number of points in the negotiating history of the SEA, for example, domestic bureaucracies appear to have intervened to change the views of heads of government, most notably when British officials helped convince Thatcher to join the intergovernmental conference.

Like the statist explanation, the bureaucratic politics explanation has several weaknesses. First, both overlook the evidence that changes in domestic political support facilitated or frustrated the efforts of national leaders to implement policies favoring further European integration. Neither national leaders nor bureaucracies enjoy complete autonomy. Second, both of the explanations fail to offer a plausible account of the stop-and-go process of European integration over the past twenty years. Technocratic explanations overlook evidence of the splits between bureaucracies and the strong opposition among top officials to the dilution of national sovereignty through majority voting. But despite the weaknesses of these explanations, autonomous decision making by heads of state or bureaucrats should be retained as a null hypothesis in future research on the domestic roots of policy initiation in the EC.

Partisan Support: The Role of Centrist Coalitions

A more promising explanation for the convergence of national policies stresses the role of political parties. While heads of government have some autonomy in European affairs, they are constrained, in this view, by the party coalitions that support their rule. Since Europe is a low-priority issue for the voters of the three largest member states, it is implausible to posit a mechanism by which politicians launch policy initiatives to seek direct electoral advantage, except perhaps immediately before European elections. European integration remains an elite affair. Nonetheless, the evolution of conceptions of national interest over time and the key role of partisan splits over European policy, as demonstrated by the decisive French turnaround in 1983 and the importance of British Tory support for neoliberal policies, suggest that the autonomy of heads of government in pursuing a European policy may be constrained by elites within their domestic partisan base.

Over the years, centrist parties, particularly those of the center-right, have tended to support EC reforms, while the strongest opposition to further integration has been located on the extremes of the ideological spectrum. At the founding of the EC, Christian Democratic parties provided the core of partisan support for European integration. Over the years, Germany's center-weighted party system, which pivots on alliances with the pro-European Free Democrats, generated constant support for European integration. Since the completion of the Common Market in 1968 and Britain's accession in 1973, however, a reform package of internal market liberalization and majority voting was blocked by the presence of an anti-EC party in at least one ruling coalition. In the 1970s and early 1980s, the far left (the British Labour party, the West German Greens, the French Communist party, and the more radical French Socialists) remained suspicious of economic liberalization, while the far right (the Thatcherite wing of the British Conservative party, the Gaullists and the party of Jean-Marie Le Pen in France, and the German Republicans) opposed the dilution of national sovereignty. The SEA thus had to navigate a narrow passage between the Scylla of far left opposition to economic liberalization and the Charybdis of conservative opposition to institutional reform.

In the mid-1980s, the dominance of centrists in ruling coalitions created a rare opening for reform. The election of Thatcher and the shift to the moderate wing of the French Socialist party in early 1983 dramatically altered the political landscape. For the first time in over a decade, ruling coalitions in each of the three major states of Europe were ideologically committed to relatively liberal domestic economic policies and were also committed, in varying degrees and for diverse reasons, to liberalization of the European market. If the Labour party had held power in Britain or if either the Gaullists or the Communists had held power in France, reform would have encountered bitter opposition. The SEA still had to satisfy British complaints about agricultural policy and surmount Thatcherite opposition to institutional reform. The first obstacle was overcome by the carrot of budget reform and the second by the stick of threatened exclusion. The partisan support explanation thus accounts for the high level of international conflict over budget and institutional reform, as compared with the low level of conflict over the central substantive agenda of market liberalization. Yet this explanation nonetheless shares several weaknesses with the following explanation, as discussed below.

Economic Functionalism: The Role of Policy Failure

The convergence of policy preferences in the major European states may also have resulted from the failure of purely national strategies of economic policy, which created or legitimated pressure for coordinated liberalization at the European level.[84] According to the statements of European leaders, the plan for market liberalization by 1992 was in part a response to the declining industrial competitiveness of Europe. In the late 1970s and early 1980s, "Eurosclerosis"—the combination of persistent high unemployment, low growth rates relative to those of other countries in the Organization for Economic Cooperation and Development (OECD), and long-term decline in international competitiveness vis-à-vis the

United States and Japan in high-technology industries such as electronics and telecommunications—was widely interpreted as an indication of policy failure.

In the 1970s and early 1980s, the economic difficulties of Britain, France, and Germany could ostensibly be attributed to problems common to all OECD countries, such as disruption from the two oil shocks and the need for tight monetary policies to combat inflation. By 1982, however, French and German economic performance lagged significantly behind that of the United States and Japan.[85] This relative failure in economic performance undermined the last excuse for slow growth. After the British experience in the mid-1970s, the German experience with internationally coordinated reflation in 1977, and the French experience with "Keynesianism in one country," reflation was no longer credible. The business-labor bargains on which corporatism and incomes policy are based were disintegrating.[86]

Poor economic performance may have been translated into pressure for internal market liberalization through at least three distinct, though not mutually exclusive, mechanisms. The first mechanism is electoral. Although European integration itself is rarely an issue of electoral importance, leading politicians in advanced industrial democracies face a structural imperative to provide steady economic growth, on which electoral success often depends. Growth requires constant investment, which in turn is stimulated by business confidence. Internal market reform can thus be seen as a way to generate business confidence and stimulate investment by removing market barriers.[87]

The second mechanism is ideological. With other economic policies discredited, European governments turned to new ideas, particularly the American and Japanese models of development. The idea of creating an internal market the size of the United States was one of the few untried policies. It seemed particularly attractive when tied to firm-led high-technology cooperation programs patterned on the Japanese model, such as ESPRIT, the European Programme for High Technology Research and Development (EUREKA), and Research and Development in Advanced Communications (RACE). Moreover, the idea of economic renewal through economies of scale and industrial flexibility underlies the 1992 initiative and reflects the new supply-side and privatization orthodoxy that was sweeping Europe during this period.[88]

The third mechanism involves sectoral or firm-level business pressure at the domestic level.[89] In general, as trade and investment interdependence increase, these interests grow stronger. Specifically, the more competitive a given firm or sector and hence the greater the level of net exports or foreign investment, particularly within the EC, the greater is the likelihood that the firm or sector will support internal market liberalization.[90]

Moreover, as sectors become globalized and sensitive to competition from outside the EC, particularly from the United States and Japan, liberalization may appear necessary to create the economies of scale required to compete effectively.[91] The greater the potential for common gains vis-à-vis non-EC countries, the greater is the incentive to bear the costs of adjustments to liberalization within Europe.

This sort of sectoral logic might also be used to explain the initial bargain upon which the EC was founded. In the early years of the EC, Germany agreed to finance a disproportionate share of the budget, much of which went to France in the form of subsidies to its relatively efficient agricultural sector, in exchange for market liberalization for industrial goods, in which Germany enjoyed a comparative advantage. Today, British support would be expected from the financial and business service sectors, while German support would draw on industrial and capital-goods exporters.

The economic functionalist explanation and the partisan support explanation are both more plausible than the first two explanations set forth above.[92] Yet anomalies plague these accounts as well. Neither a functionalist nor a partisan sectoral approach seems to explain French support for internal market liberalization. France appears to lack a natural constituency analogous to German industry or British financial services. And if the 1992 initiative was a capitalist conspiracy, Mitterrand was a most unlikely instrument. The economic functionalist approach also faces difficulties in explaining the pressure in some member states for institutional change in areas other than internal market policy. Despite these anomalies, however, the activities of interest groups and political parties should serve as a springboard for further inquiry.

Domestic analysis is a precondition for systemic analysis, not a supplement to it. The existence of significant cross-national variance in state policy preferences and diplomatic strategies invites further research into the domestic roots of European integration. Yet most theories of international cooperation, including regime theory, have neglected the problem of domestic interest formation, often electing instead to specify interests by assumption.[93] None of this is meant to exclude theories of state interests based on international processes, such as economic and social interdependence. But at the very least, domestic politics offers a mechanism—a "transmission belt"—by which international impulses are translated into policy.[94] Testing domestic theories of integration invariably raises many questions traditionally treated by students of comparative politics: Which domestic actors take the lead in promoting and opposing economic liberalization? Are they state or societal actors? How do they perceive their interests? How do they influence one another? What is their relation to the world economy? Future research on these questions will necessarily connect the literatures on international cooperation and state-society relations in an interdependent world economy.[95]

CONCLUSION:
THE SEA IN PERSPECTIVE

Neofunctionalism remains the sole attempt to fashion a coherent and comprehensive theory of European integration. The standing of neofunctionalist theory among political scientists is a lagged function of the standing of the EC in the eyes of Europeans. When the EC stagnates, as in the 1970s, scholars speak of the obsolescence of regional integration theory; when it rebounds, as in 1985, they speak of the obsolescence of the nation-state. Regional integration theory, we read today, has been "unjustly consigned to the dustbin."[96]

This article challenges the notion, implicit in these statements, that progress in the EC necessarily supports all the claims of neofunctionalists.[97] It does so by testing and rejecting a particular variant of neofunctionalism, supranational institutionalism, which rests on the argument that international institutions and transnational interest groups play a vital and increasing role as integration progresses. The approach proposed here, intergovernmental institutionalism, accords an important role to supranational institutions in cementing existing interstate bargains as the foundation for renewed integration. But it also affirms that the primary source of integration lies in the interests of the states themselves and the relative power each brings to Brussels. Perhaps most important, the intergovernmental approach demonstrates that even this explanation is incomplete, thus clearing the ground for further research into the international implications of European domestic politics.

NOTES

For advice, encouragement, and comments on earlier drafts, I am indebted to Anne-Marie Burley, James Caporaso, David Dessler, Geoffrey Garrett, Peter Gourevitch, Ernst Haas, Peter Hall, Stanley Hoffmann, Peter Katzenstein, Robert Keohane, Stephen Krasner, Julius Moravcsik, Kalypso Nicolaïdis, Joseph Nye, Diane Orentlicher, Paul Pierson, Alec Stone, Helen Wallace, Fareed Zakaria, an anonymous referee, and the participants in colloquiums at Harvard University, Stanford University, the University of Chicago, and the University of California at San Diego. I am grateful to the European Community Visitors' Program and the Center for European Studies, Harvard University, for financial and logistical support. An earlier, more thoroughly documented version of this analysis appeared as Working Paper no. 21, Harvard University Center for European Studies, Cambridge, Massachusetts, October 1989.

1. The best negotiating history of the SEA, written by an intelligent insider who took comprehensive notes, is Jean De Ruyt's *L'acte unique européen: Commentaire* (The Single European Act: Commentary) (Bruxelles: Editions de l'Université de Bruxelles, 1987). For other useful histories and commentaries, see Pete Ludlow, *Beyond 1992: Europe and Its Western Partners* (Brussels: Center for European Policy Studies, 1989); Michael Calingaert, *The 1992 Challenge from Europe: Development of the European Community's Internal Market* (Washington, D.C.: National Planning Association, 1988); and Angelika Volle, *Grossbritannien und der europäische Einigungsprozess* (Great Britain and the process of European integration) (Bonn: Forschungsinstitut der Deutschen Gesellschaft für Auswärtige Politik, February 1989), pp. 46–76. For a collection of important German articles and documents between 1985 and 1989, see Jochen Thies and Wolfgang Wagner, eds., *Auf dem Wege zum Binnenmarkt: Europäische Integration and deutscher Föderalismus* (On the way to the internal market: European integration and German federalism) (Bonn: Verlag für Internationale Politik, 1989). For a path-breaking attempt to explain the SEA offered by two political scientists and incorporating nearly all existing hypotheses, see Wayne Sandholtz and John Zysman, "1992: Recasting the European Bargain," *World Politics* 42 (October 1989), pp. 95–128. For an excellent comparison of the SEA negotiations and previous negotiations, see Roy Pryce, ed., *The Dynamics of European Union* (London: Croom Helm, 1987). On the provisions of 1992 as a new form of multilateral economic negotiation, see Kalypso Nicolaïdis, "Mutual Recognition: The New Frontier of Multilateralism?" in *Network Politics*, Promethée Perspectives no. 10, Paris, June 1989, pp. 21–34.

2. Article 8A of the 1985 EC Commission White Paper, as amended by the SEA.

3. The Luxembourg compromise, which was announced to the world in a press communiqué, has no legal standing. Quite the opposite, it has been interpreted as an attempt to circumvent legal procedures outlined in Article 236 of the Treaty of Rome.

4. With the exception of a few minor initiatives (such as the inclusion of collaborative research and development programs under the SEA), other potential areas of European integration—including political cooperation, social legislation, monetary policy, further procedural reform, and fundamental constitutional issues such as the enlargement of EC membership—are subject to neither the new approach nor majority voting.

5. See Robert Keohane, *After Hegemony: Cooperation and Discord in the World Political Economy* (Princeton, N.J.: Princeton University Press, 1984), pp. 61–64; and Robert Keohane, ed., *Neo-Realism and Its Critics* (New York: Columbia University Press, 1986), pp. 192–95. In *After Hegemony*, p. 63, Keohane writes that "the concept of international regime is consistent with both the importance of differential power and with a sophisticated view of self-interest." It is not, however, consistent with the strong view of domestic politics as an independent determinant of interest defended here.

6. These factors are stressed by Calingaert in *The 1992 Challenge from Europe* and by Sandholtz and Zysman in "1992." See also Axel Krause, "What After

European Integration?" *European Affairs* 2 (Autumn 1988), pp. 46–55; and Peter Ludlow, "Beyond 1992," *European Affairs* 2 (Autumn 1988), pp. 19–21.

7. For strong claims about the importance of this group in inspiring reform, see Marina Gazzo, "Introduction," in Marina Gazzo, ed., *Towards European Union* (Brussels: Agence Europe, 1985), vol. 1, pp. 7–10. The advent of direct elections to the European Parliament in 1979, which endowed the body with democratic legitimacy, gave the activities of the group new impetus.

8. See Michel Albert and James Ball, *Toward European Economic Recovery in the 1980s: Report to the European Parliament* (New York: Praeger, 1984).

9. Wisse Dekker, "Europe's Economic Power: Potential and Perspectives," speech delivered to the Swiss Institute for International Studies, Geneva, 25 October 1988.

10. Philippe Schmitter and Wolfgang Streeck, "Organized Interests and the Europe of 1992," paper presented to the American Enterprise Institute, Washington, D.C., 6–8 March 1990.

11. Sandholtz and Zysman, "1992," p. 117.

12. For a discussion of the role of business, see Lawrence G. Franko, "Europe 1992: The Impact on Global Corporate Strategy and Multinational Corporate Strategy," mimeograph, University of Massachusetts, Boston, September 1989; Sandholtz and Zysman, "1992," pp. 108 and 116–20; *Financial Times*, 14 February 1984; Axel Krause, "Many Groups Lobby on Implementation of Market Plan," *Europe Magazine*, July–August 1988, pp. 24–25; Ludlow, *Beyond 1992*, pp. 27–30; Calingaert, *The 1992 Challenge from Europe*, p. 8; and Helen Wallace, "Making Multilateralism Work: Negotiations in the European Community," mimeograph, Chatham House, London, August 1988, p. 7.

13. For Dekker's proposals, see *Europe 1990: An Agenda for Action* (Eindhoven: N. V. Philips, 1984). The four aspects of the Dekker plan were administrative simplification of border formalities, harmonization of the value-added tax (VAT), standardization of technical norms, and liberalization of government procurement. Dekker outlined the new role of business in "Europe's Economic Power: Potential and Perspectives," a speech delivered to the Swiss Institute for International Studies, Geneva, 25 October 1988.

14. See Sandholtz and Zysman, "1992," p. 128.

15. Jacques Delors et al., *La France par l'Europe* (France through Europe) (Paris: Bernard Grasset, 1988), pp. 47 and 50–51. The tone is heroic, as the opening words of the chapter on Delors' initiative (p. 47) illustrate: "January 1985: the winter was harsh. In Brussels, as in Paris, people were shivering. On the top floor of the Berlaymont, in a vast office that didn't yet seem quite lived in, Jacques Delors gathered his closest associates around him."

16. Sandholtz and Zysman, "1992," p. 98.

17. Ibid., pp. 96–97; see also pp. 100, 108–9, and 128 for a discussion of the key role of supranational actors. Sandholtz and Zysman criticize neofunctionalism, but their description of the integration process is in fact compatible with neofunctionalism in all but a few particulars. For other supranational interpretations, see Ludlow, *Beyond 1992*, pp. 27–30; Calingaert, *The 1992 Challenge from Europe*; and Helen Wallace, "Europäische Integration" (European integration), in Thies and Wagner, *Aug dem Wege zum Binnenmarkt*, pp. 127–28.

18. Ernst B. Haas, *The Uniting of Europe: Political, Social and Economic Forces, 1950–1957* (London: Stevens & Sons, 1958), pp. xiii–xiv; see also pp. 389 and 483–84 and chaps. 8–12, in which Haas stressed the federating influence of an active supranational executive and of transnational groups. Haas and Schmitter subsequently stressed "creative personal action" using organization resources and skills, as seen, for example, when a central integrationist leader is able to promote trade-offs and package deals. See Ernst B. Haas and Philippe Schmitter, "Economics and Differential Patterns of Political Integration," *International Organization* 18 (Autumn 1964), pp. 736–37. This idea was picked up by later theorists. See Joseph S. Nye, Jr., *Peace in Parts: Integration and Conflict in Regional Organization* (Boston: Little, Brown, 1971), pp. 69 and 71–72.

19. I am grateful to Anne-Marie Burley for suggesting this rubric.

20. For summaries of the literature on intergovernmentalism, see Paul Taylor, *The Limits of European Integration* (Beckenham, U.K.: Croom Helm, 1983); and Helen Wallace, William Wallace, and Carole Webb, eds., *Policy-Making in the European Communities* (London: Wiley, 1977).

21. Helen Wallace, "Bilateral, Trilateral and Multilateral Negotiations in the European Community," in Roger Morgan and Caroline Bray, eds., *Partners and Rivals in Western Europe: Britain, France and Germany* (Aldershot, U.K.: Gower, 1986), pp. 156–74.

22. See Keohane, *After Hegemony*, pp. 61–64; and Keohane, *Neo-Realism and Its Critics*, pp. 192–95.

23. For a summary of Genscher's comments at the opening session of the intergovernmental conference, see Gazzo, *Towards European Union*, vol. 2, pp. 28–29.

24. For a summary of Germany's draft proposal on new powers for the Parliament, see Gazzo, *Towards European Union*, vol. 1, pp. 39–40.

25. For a discussion of German views about the agricultural policy, see Gisela Hendriks, "Germany and the CAP: National Interests and the European Community," *International Affairs* 65 (Winter 1988–89), pp. 75–87. The German stand against more intensive monetary cooperation softened in 1988–89, once the initial condition of increased capital mobility was being met.

26. This account of French foreign policy during the first Mitterrand presidency draws heavily on Gabriel Robin's *La diplomatie de Mitterrand ou le triomphe des apparences, 1981–1985* (Mitterrand's diplomacy or the triumph of appearances, 1981–1985) (Paris: Editions de la Bièvre, 1985).

27. Mitterrand and his ministers may have been looking for a way to limit agricultural spending without appearing to be responsible for doing so. This would account for the attempts to cast Thatcher as a scapegoat and for the fact that although the French government became more accommodating of agricultural reform and the French ministers spoke out occasionally about overgenerous support, France remained one of the staunchest supporters of generous agricultural subsidies as late as the Brussels summit of February 1988. See Paul Taylor, "The New Dynamics of EC Integration in the 1980s," in Juliet Lodge, ed., *The European Community and the Challenge of the Future* (London: Pinter, 1989), p. 6.

28. The reasoning behind Mitterrand's decision is disputed. The decisive economic argument appears to have been made by the French treasury via

Laurent Fabius, who told Mitterrand that leaving the EMS would undermine confidence in the economy and ultimately compel the French government to impose as much austerity as would continued membership. The decisive political condition appears to have been the decline of the French Communist party, which allowed Mitterrand to align himself with the moderate wing of the Socialist party. See David Cameron, *The Colors of a Rose: On the Ambiguous Record of French Socialism* (Cambridge, Mass.: Harvard University Center for European Studies, 1987); Peter Hall, *Governing the Economy: The Politics of State Intervention in Britain and France* (New York: Oxford University Press, 1986), pp. 193 and 201 ff.; Organization for Economic Cooperation and Development (OECD), *Why Economic Policies Change Course* (Paris: OECD, 1988), pp. 56–64; and Philippe Bauchard, *La guerre des deux roses: Du rêve à la realité, 1981–1985* (The war of two roses: From dream to reality, 1981–1985) (Paris: Bernard Grasset, 1986).

29. Mitterrand, speech delivered to the European Parliament, Brussels, 24 May 1984; reprinted in Gazzo, *Towards European Union,* vol. 1, pp. 82–85.

30. Robin, *La diplomatie de Mitterrand,* p. 145; see also p. 219. For another, equally ironic but more positive assessment, see Philippe Moreau-Defarges, "'J'ai fait un rêve . . .' Le président François Mitterrand, artisan de l'union européenne" ("I had a dream . . ." President François Mitterrand, craftsman of European union) *Politique Etrangère* 50 (Fall 1985), pp. 359–75.

31. The Conservative government began pushing deregulation of services during the British presidency of the Council in 1981. See Simon Bulmer and William Paterson, *The Federal Republic of Germany and the European Community* (London: Allen & Unwin, 1987), p. 48.

32. Cheysson, cited in *Financial Times,* 26 January 1982. Howe echoed Cheysson's point of view: "The negotiation launched at Stuttgart and continued at Athens in December 1983 is not just about the budget and the CAP. It is about the whole future shape and direction of Europe." Geoffrey Howe, "The Future of the European Community: Britain's Approach to the Negotiations," *International Affairs* 60 (Spring 1984), p. 190.

33. See David Cameron, "Sovereign States in a Single Market: Integration and Intergovernmentalism in the European Community," paper presented at the Brookings Institution, Washington, D.C., 29–30 March 1990.

34. Chandernagor, cited in Robin, *La diplomatie de Mitterrand,* p. 219. See also Gianni Bonvicini, "The Genscher-Columbo Plan and the 'Solemn Declaration on European Union', 1981–1983," in Pryce, *The Dynamics of European Union,* pp. 174–87; and Joseph Weiler, "The Genscher-Columbo Draft European Act: The Politics of Indecision," *Revue d'Intégration Européenne* 6 (Spring 1983), pp. 129–54.

35. See Robin, *La diplomatie de Mitterrand,* p. 219; and De Ruyt, *L'acte unique européen,* pp. 35 and 315–24.

36. Moreau-Defarges, " 'J'ai fait un rêve . . .' " p. 368.

37. "Speech of François Mitterrand Before the Netherlands Government, 7 February 1984," released by the Ambassade de France à Londres (CTL/DISCOM/ 29/84).

38. See Heinz Stadlmann. "Die europäische Gemeinschaft nach der französischen Ratspräsidentschaft" (The European Community after the French presidency of the Council), *Europa-Archiv* 39 (October 1984), pp. 447–54. The Franco-German agreement on procedure was only partial, since France did not support German efforts to strengthen the Parliament. France preferred to replace Article 235 of the treaty with one that would have sanctioned the creation of a "differentiated Europe," with different sets of members involved in different programs. The French have traditionally supported diplomatic flexibility to facilitate projects which, like EUREKA, involve only some EC countries and also involve non-EC countries. See De Ruyt, *L'acte unique européen*, p. 99.

39. See Stadlmann, "Die europäische Gemeinschaft"; De Ruyt, *L'acte unique européen*, pp. 47–49; *The Guardian*, 25 January 1984; and press conference with Mitterrand, 2 April 1984. For a contemporary critique of Mitterrand's policy changes, see Robin, *La diplomatie de Mitterrand*, pp. 69–81, 133–45 and 211–29.

40. Interview with Michel Rocard, *Intervention*, February–April 1984, p. 102.

41. See Robin, *La diplomatie de Mitterrand*, p. 215.

42. See Ludlow, *Beyond 1992*, pp. x–xi; and Howe, "The Future of the European Community," pp. 188–89. Britain did delay payment of an emergency levy requested by the EC.

43. This account of the threat of excluding Britain draws heavily on Taylor's insights in "The New Dynamics of EC Integration in the 1980s." For earlier versions of the same thesis, see Richard Corbett, "The 1985 Intergovernmental Conference and the Single European Act," in Pryce, *The Dynamics of European Union*, pp. 268–69; and Françoise de la Serre, *La Grande-Bretagne et le Communauté Européenne* (Great Britain and the European Community) (Paris: Presses Universitaires de France, 1987), pp. 193–94 and 207–9.

44. For a summary of the debate about a two-track EC, see Helen Wallace and Adam Ridley, *Europe: The Challenge of Diversity* (London: Routledge & Kegan Paul, 1985), especially chap. 5; and Eberhard Grabitz, ed., *Abgestufte Integration: Eine Alternative zum herkömmlichen Integrationskonzept?* (Multi-tiered integration: An alternative to the existing concept of integration?) (Kehl am Rhein: Engel Verlag, 1984).

45. See the *Guardian*, 30 May 1984; and Centre for Policy Studies, *Making It Work: The Future of the European Community* (London: Centre for Policy Studies, 1984). See also *Le Monde*, 18 March 1984 and 5 May 1984; and Kohl, speech delivered to the Bundestag, Bonn, 28 June 1984, and excerpted in Gazzo, *Towards European Union*, vol. 1, p. 98.

46. Howe, quoted in *Financial Times*, 22 March 1984.

47. See "Europe: The Future—United Kingdom Memorandum, June 1984"; reprinted in Gazzo, *Towards European Union*, vol. 1, pp. 86–95.

48. In "The New Dynamics of EC Integration in the 1980s," p. 7, Taylor argues that the mood of conciliation was due to the fact that during the British and French failure in March at Brussels, they had "looked into the abyss, and were shocked into an awareness of the need to hold themselves back." According to Taylor, by taking time to confess his personal ideals, Mitterrand was letting Thatcher "see the future."

49. See De Ruyt, *L'acte unique européen*, p. 261. The Commission later adopted a standard to measure the burden.

50. See Gazzo, *Towards European Union*, vol. 1, pp. 96–97.

51. The Benelux countries assented in late October 1984, and a memorandum setting out objectives was approved on 12 December 1984. See Geoffrey Howe, "Grossbritannien und die Bundesrepublik Deutschland als europäische Partner" (Great Britain and the Federal Republic of Germany as European partners), *Europa-Archiv* 39 (November 1984), p. 637. France reportedly insisted that Italy be excluded, for fear that Italian participation would slow the negotiations. The negotiations were concluded in early 1990.

52. See "Conclusions of the European Council at Its Meeting in Fontainebleau, 26 June 1984"; reprinted in Gazzo, *Towards European Union*, vol. 1, pp. 96–97. For a discussion of the Spaak Committee, see Hans Jürgen Küsters, "The Treaties of Rome, 1955–1957," in Pryce, *The Dynamics of European Union*, pp. 84 ff.

53. See *Financial Times*, 30 November 1984, 3 December 1984, 22 March 1985, and 10 May 1985; and *Le Monde*, 30 March 1985. France, too, accepted that the first priority of the EC must be the creation of an *espace économique intérieur homogène*. For a discussion of the objections of the Quai d'Orsay, presumably to the renunciation of the Luxembourg compromise, see Corbett, "1985 Intergovernmental Conference," p. 269.

54. See De Ruyt, *L'acte unique européen*, pp. 57–59. The proposals of Britain, as well as those of the Benelux countries, France, Germany, and Italy, are reprinted in Gazzo, *Towards European Union*, supplement. For commentary, see *The Times* (London), 21 June 1985.

55. See Gazzo, *Towards European Union*, supplement, pp. 27–32.

56. See De Ruyt, *L'acte unique européen*, pp. 60–61. In a memorandum written by the Italians prior to the Milan summit, the option of invoking Article 236 (which allows amendment by unanimous consent of the Council) was presented as a possible compromise between a new treaty and the more ad hoc British approach. Nonetheless, the vote taken at the summit does not seem to have been planned in advance by the governments that voted affirmatively. See Gazzo, *Towards European Union*, supplement, pp. 3–8.

57. Taylor, "The New Dynamics of EC Integration in the 1980s," p. 10.

58. De Ruyt, *L'acte unique européen*, pp. 67–91.

59. This account of the conference negotiations follows Corbett's "1985 Intergovernmental Conference," pp. 247–48. See also Ludlow, *Beyond 1992*, p. vi; and Gazzo, *Towards European Union*, vol. 1, p. 38. Delors' speech and his press conference of 27 November 1985, which offer his characterization of the role of Germany and Britain, are reprinted in Gazzo, *Towards European Union*, vol. 2, p. 86.

60. Delors, cited in Gazzo, *Towards European Union*, vol. 1, p. 8; see also pp. 25–26.

61. See Corbett, "1985 Intergovernmental Conference," p. 249.

62. Ibid., pp. 249–50 and 259.

63. De Ruyt, *L'acte unique européen*, pp. 172 ff.

64. See Taylor, "The New Dynamics of EC Integration in the 1980s."

65. For speculation on Franco-German intentions, see De Ruyt, *L'acte unique européen*, p. 272; and Corbett, "1985 Intergovernmental Conference," p. 268. The view that the outcome reflected a triumph for British negotiators has been most cogently argued by Taylor in "The New Dynamics of EC Integration in the 1980s."

66. De Ruyt, *L'acte unique européen*, p. 56.

67. See the European Parliament's opinion of 9 July 1985 regarding the proposal for an intergovernmental conference; reprinted in Gazzo, *Towards European Union*, vol. 2, pp. 13–14.

68. For an account of the debate, see Gazzo, *Toward European Union*, vol. 2, pp. 17–20, 27, 30, and 41.

69. Parliament resolution; cited in Gazzo, *Towards European Union*, vol. 2, p. 104. See also the programmatic statement of Spinelli and two associates made in the inaugural issue of the "Crocodile" newsletter and reprinted in Gazzo, *Towards European Union*, vol. 1, pp. 11–17; and De Ruyt, *L'acte unique européen*, p. 85.

70. For a discussion of the lack of active elite business support for the early European initiatives, see Haas, *The Uniting of Europe*, chap. 5. Transnationally active business interests may have had an effect at the domestic level, as outlined in the next section of this article.

71. Krause, "Many Groups Lobby on Implementation of Market Plan," p. 24.

72. *Financial Times*, 9 October 1989. I am indebted to Peter Ludlow for suggestions that helped sharpen this hypothesis.

73. See Delors et al., *La France par l'Europe*, pp. 49–50.

74. Interview with Jacques Delors, Cambridge, Massachusetts, 22 September 1989. See also Calingaert, *The 1992 Challenge from Europe*, p. 9.

75. The initial draft amendments submitted by the Commission to the intergovernmental conference went far beyond the final settlement (except on the powers of the Parliament), a fact which hardly lends credence to Delors' claim that he foresaw all in January 1985. But this may underestimate Delors' skill in setting the agenda, where aggressiveness did pay dividends.

76. See Juliet Lodge, "EC Policymaking: Institutional Considerations," in Lodge, *The European Community and the Challenge of the Future*, p. 28; and Taylor, *The Limits of European Integration*, chaps. 3 and 10.

77. Leon Lindberg and Stuart Scheingold, *Europe's Would-Be Polity: Patterns of Change in the European Community* (Englewood Cliffs, N.J.: Prentice-Hall, 1970).

78. For a discussion of the role of business groups in the 1950s, see Haas, *The Uniting of Europe*, p. 353.

79. Taylor, "The New Dynamics of EC Integration in the 1980s," p. 3.

80. See Wallace, "Bilateral, Trilateral and Multilateral Negotiations in the European Community," pp. 158–59. I am indebted to Helen Wallace for discussions on the British negotiating position.

81. Interview with Delors, 22 September 1989.

82. See Anne-Marie Burley, "The Once and Future German Question," *Foreign Affairs* 68 (Winter 1989–90), pp. 65–83. Some have suggested that the 1992 initiative is a response to the threat of a U.S.-Soviet condominium. See, for example, Enrique Baron, *Europe 92: Le rapt du future* (Europe 92: The rape of the future) (Paris: Editions Bernard Coutas, 1989). Sandholtz and Zysman speculate, though with little evidence, that renewed European integration was a response to the decline of the United States, on which the Europeans were dependent for technology. See Sandholtz and Zysman, "1992," p. 96.

83. Wallace, "Making Multilateralism Work," p. 6.

84. Sandholtz and Zysman, "1992," p. 109.

85. I am indebted to Geoffrey Garrett, who encouraged me to develop this argument more precisely.

86. Manfred Wegner, "Preparing the 1990s: A Three-Pronged Strategy," in Wolfgang Wessels and Elfriede Regelsberger, eds., *The Federal Republic of Germany and the European Community* (Bonn: Europa Union Verlag, 1988), pp. 115–24.

87. See Charles Lindblom, *Politics and Markets* (New York: Basic Books, 1977); and Andrea Boltho, ed., *The European Economy: Growth and Crisis* (Oxford: Oxford University Press, 1982).

88. EC Commission, Directorate-General for Economic and Financial Affairs, *The Economics of 1992: An Assessment of the Potential Economic Effects of Completing the Internal Market of the European Community* (Luxembourg: EC, March 1988).

89. This hypothesis should be clearly distinguished from the supranational institutionalist hypothesis that pressure from *transnationally organized* business interest groups was an essential precondition for the SEA.

90. Helen Milner, *Resisting Protectionism: Global Industries and the Politics of International Trade* (Princeton, N.J.: Princeton University Press, 1988).

91. Keniche Ohmae, *Triad Power: The Coming Shape of Global Competition* (Singapore: McKinsey, 1985).

92. Sandholtz and Zysman attribute the SEA to a wide variety of factors, including economic policy failure and the decline of the European left (which seem the most promising elements of their explanation) as well as the transition from American to Japanese leadership in high-technology development, the changing global security environment, Commission activism, and pan-European interest group pressure. See Sandholtz and Zysman, "1992."

93. See Keohane, *After Hegemony*, p. 6. For a discussion of the relationship between domestic interests and the broader category of "liberal" theories of international relations, see Andrew Moravcsik, "Liberalism in International Life," chap. 8 in "The Roots of European Economic Cooperation," Ph.D. diss., Harvard University, forthcoming; and Robert Keohane, "International Liberalism Reconsidered," in John Dunn, ed., *The Economic Limits to Modern Politics* (Cambridge: Cambridge University Press, 1990). For a discussion of the problems involved in specifying interests by assumption, see Andrew Moravcsik, "Disciplining Trade Finance: The OECD Export Credit Arrangement," *International Organization* 43 (Summer 1989), pp. 441–45.

94. For this phrase, I am indebted to a seminar presentation by Robert Keohane. For a typology of theoretical approaches that combine international

and domestic factors, see Andrew Moravcsik, "International and Domestic Theories of International Relations: A Theoretical Introduction," in Peter Evans, Harold Jacobson, and Robert Putnam, eds., *International Bargaining and Domestic Politics: An Interactive Approach*, forthcoming.

95. For previous work focusing on state-society relations in the world economy, see Hall, *Governing the Economy;* Peter Gourevitch, *Politics in Hard Times: Comparative Responses to International Economic Crises* (Ithaca, N.Y.: Cornell University Press, 1986); Peter Katzenstein, *Small States in World Markets* (Ithaca, N.Y.: Cornell University Press, 1985); and Peter Katzenstein, ed., *Between Power and Plenty* (Madison: University of Wisconsin Press, 1977).

96. Robert Keohane and Stanley Hoffmann, "European Integration," unpublished manuscript, Harvard University, November 1989. See also Roy Pryce and Wolfgang Wessels, "The Search for an Ever Closer Union: A Framework for Analysis," in Pryce, *The Dynamics of European Union*, pp. 1–34.

97. Analysts who stress power and interests have traditionally been pessimistic. For a contrast of pessimistic and optimistic views in the 1960s and 1980s, respectively, see the following articles by Stanley Hoffmann: "Obstinate or Obsolete? The Fate of the Nation-State and the Case of Western Europe," *Daedalus* 95 (Summer 1966), pp. 892–908; and "Reflections on the Nation-State in Western Europe Today," *Journal of Common Market Studies* 21 (September–December 1982), pp. 33–35.

3

The European Commission

Peter Ludlow

The transformation of the European Community and more particularly of the status, morale, and impact of the European Commission in the past few years has been remarkable by any standards. The Commission has been at the heart of the far-reaching changes associated with the 1992 program, the development of plans for economic and monetary union, the formulation and implementation of a new generation of environmental policies, the design of a development strategy for the poorer regions of the European Community (which, in the areas concerned, is comparable in significance to the Marshall Plan for Western Europe after World War II), the construction of new collaborative research programs for the European private sector, and the development of major contributions to the debate about political union in advance of the second Intergovernmental Conference launched in December 1990. The Commission has also been much in evidence on the international scene as a privileged interlocutor of the U.S. administration following the latter's review of its European policy in 1989, as the coordinator and spearhead of Western assistance in the reconstruction of Central and Eastern Europe, as the European Council's designated instrument for the review of EC strategy toward the Soviet Union, and as a target and magnet for governments both near and far who want to create new and better relations with the new Europe.

This new dynamism is all the more remarkable in that it has been developed without any major redefinition of the constitutional role of the Commission or any fundamental restructuring of the organization itself. Formally, the functions of the Commission are still those set out in the Treaty of Rome more than thirty years ago. Organizationally, too, it is in many important respects very much the institution that it has always been. It has not, for example, grown in relation to the Community population. Its basic organizational units are much as they were in 1967, when the Coal and Steel Community, Euratom, and The European Economic Community merged, forming a single Council and Commission. Even its structural weaknesses, so clearly analyzed in 1979 in the Spierenberg Report,[1] are for the most part still there.

This curious combination of continuity and change constitutes the central theme of this chapter. Where has the new dynamism come from? How sustainable is it by an organization that is in several important respects so manifestly ill structured? What needs to be done over the coming months and years to ensure that the Commission can keep up with the whirlwind that it has generated and, when Europe eventually attains a new equilibrium, play the central role that is almost certain to be assigned to it?

The answer to the first of these questions—whence the dynamic?—is complex. The principal factors are undoubtedly in some senses external to the institution: changes in the agenda of the Community, themselves reflecting major revaluations of the priorities and capabilities of the member states; modifications in the internal structure, behavior patterns, and ambitions of the Commission's partner institutions, notably the Council and Parliament; and the parachuting into office from 1985 onward of a remarkable group of politicians and officials, headed by Jacques Delors. All these factors, as the second section of this essay suggests, are vitally important. They should not, however, be allowed to obscure the relevance of the original design. The architects of the 1950s and 1960s did well. The Commission alone could not create the new Community. It was never intended to do so. Given the right context and strong leadership, however, it could and did respond effectively to the opportunities that opened up before it.

In the first section of this chapter, I discuss the organization and functions of the Commission, as originally conceived and as developed over four decades, which enabled it to respond to recent opportunities. I give special attention to the functional orientation of the Treaties that provide the constitutional basis for the Community; the membership and organization of the Commission; its functions; and its tasks of political management, which involve it closely with the political leaderships and the bureaucracies of member states. In the following section I analyze the "dynamics of the new Community," examining the transformation of the agenda, relevant changes in the "partner institutions" of Council and Parliament, and the impact of Delors as President of the Commission since 1985.

The basic soundness of the original concept and the successes of recent years should not, however, serve as grounds for complacency.

On the contrary, continuity in a period of such significant change as the Commission has recently passed through is as much a problem as a cause for self-congratulation. There are signs, as the discussion in the first two sections of this chapter suggests, that the Commission has recently been driven to, and possibly even beyond, the limits of its capacity. Commission reform seems bound, therefore, to be an issue of growing importance over the coming years. The third section includes some ideas about priorities and possible solutions. Many of them concern efficiency; the most important are linked with the question of legitimacy. The point of departure must, however, be the organization and the functions of the Commission as originally conceived and developed over four decades.

ORGANIZATION AND FUNCTIONS
OF THE COMMISSION

The Commission and the System

The Commission is at "the heart of the Community system."[2] The Commission is, however, only part of the system. Before considering its specific functions, then, it is important to note some of the more significant features of the system as a whole. Two in particular require emphasis: the EC's quadripartite institutional structure[3] and the function-oriented character of the Treaties.

The long-term objective of Jean Monnet and Robert Schuman was, as the Schuman Plan stated, "a European federation."[4] The Community system that they devised is, though, radically different from the classical federal systems of the Western world. This is particularly apparent in the allocation of executive and legislative responsibilities and in the definition of federal and state roles. Far from separating the powers of the executive and legislative branches or distinguishing federal and state authorities, the Community system as defined in the Treaties and sanctioned by practice depends for its effectiveness on their intermingling.[5] The Commission has a crucial role in both legislative and executive processes: So, too, however, do the Council, acting collectively as part of the "supranational" system, and the member states, whose several interests are fed into the policy formation process before decisions are taken, and whose administrative apparatus is subsequently essential for policy implementation.

The practical implications of this complex interdependence as far as the Commission is concerned should become clear in the following pages. Suffice it to say at this point that an "adversarial" model of Commission-Council relations is seriously misleading. The Commission needs the Council and its member states and engages them in its business at every stage of the political process. For its part, the Council needs the Commission and, when the system is working properly, turns to it repeatedly both as a source of leadership and as the instrument specially designed to implement policies "in the general European interest." A system as complex as this is obviously open to abuse: The Council could become paralyzed by nationalism; the Commission may become unduly timid. Both possibilities have been amply illustrated in the history of the Community. The negative features should not, however, be exaggerated. The Community's quadripartite system is politically realistic: France is not California and the United Kingdom is not Pennsylvania. As the periods before 1966 and since 1985 have demonstrated, it can also be operational. The Community does not therefore have to choose, as is so often suggested, between intergovernmentalism and supranationalism. It functions best when it combines both.

The other distinctive feature of the Treaties establishing the Community is their functional orientation. The Community has, it is true, a general mission: In the Treaty of Rome it is "an ever closer union among the peoples of Europe" and in the Single European Act it is, more simply, a European union. This general object can furthermore have operational significance, particularly between Treaty revisions, as the Community machine moves into policy areas outside those specifically sanctioned by the Treaties. The hard core of Community activity is, however, defined and circumscribed by the Treaties' definition of what is or what is not Community business.

The adoption of a concrete, action-oriented plan as the catalyst of progress toward European union in the 1950s was realistic and, in the 1950s and 1960s, immensely fruitful. In the new world of the 1970s and 1980s, however, the mismatch between Community priorities as defined in the Treaties and the policies required by Europeans to master the new global situation was the source of persistent weakness. Hence the crucial importance of the new agenda that emerged informally in the course of the 1970s and 1980s and was sanctioned by the Single European Act. Legal bases are not the only preconditions nor even by themselves adequate guarantees of Community initiative: They are nevertheless critically important, not least for the Commission.

Membership and Organization

In the Treaties, the term "Commission" applies only to the seventeen men and women currently led by President Delors. In common parlance, however, the term is also used to refer to the significantly larger body in the administration over which the political Commission presides. This chapter is concerned with both, but where there is any risk of confusion, I have made separate references to the Commission as a political body and the administration.

Membership

The Commission currently consists of seventeen members. This number appears in the Treaties as they were revised after the last enlargement, but it can be changed without Treaty revision by the unanimous agreement of the Council. The Treaties do insist, however, that the Commission should include at least one national of each of the member states.[6] Any attempt to streamline the body by reducing its numbers to below twelve would therefore require Treaty revision. In addition to the one Commissioner per member state, the larger states (France, Germany, Italy, Spain, and the United Kingdom) are allowed an extra representative.

Members of the Commission are appointed "by common accord" of the member states in the European Council. In practice, each Commissioner except the President has an electoral college of one, namely, the Prime Minister of his or her member state. The Prime Ministers concerned exercise this patronage in different ways. On occasion, individual Prime Ministers have listened to the wishes of the incoming President, whose appointment or reappointment has traditionally been made some time before the rest of the Commission. However, even Roy Jenkins, who was the most successful in this regard, did not get all the Commissioners he wanted; and despite Delors's prestige after his first term, at least three Commissioners were replaced in 1988–1989 against Delors's wishes.

The appointment of the President has traditionally been handled rather differently. In the first place, it happens earlier, usually at the European Council meeting in June of the final year of the outgoing Commission. Second, the decision is usually more collective, though once again, there is no fixed procedure, making it difficult to generalize.[7]

The background of the Commissioners has varied over the years. There has, however, been a strong trend toward the appointment of politicians. Of the fourteen Commissioners who served between 1958 and 1967, only five had been senior government ministers, although Walter Hallstein had been a state secretary in the German Foreign Office and Georges Caron had been a junior minister and deputy. The remaining seven were civil servants, academics, or "experts."[8] The Jenkins Commission of thirteen, by contrast, included eight politicians and one, Cheysson, who made himself enough of one during his extended period in Brussels to be nominated Minister of Foreign Affairs by Mitterrand. Ironically, however, two of the remaining four, Etienne Davignon and

Finn-Olav Gundelach, proved to be much better at Community politics than any of their "political" colleagues.[9] With the second Delors Commission, the process has advanced still further. Of the seventeen Commissioners, only one, Jean Dondelinger, is not a politician by profession.

The Collegiate System

Once appointed, Commissioners constitute a college. The rule applies even to the President, who is formally no more than primus inter pares. He can be, and quite frequently is, outvoted, even if he is Jacques Delors. The practical and symbolic significance of the collegiate principle should not, therefore, be underestimated. Indeed, it is widely believed even now that a majority of member states would firmly resist a break with it. Their European vocation notwithstanding, Commissioners, and perhaps still more their Cabinets, are national champions who defend national positions in the Commission. At times, this aspect of their Brussels role has undoubtedly been abused. If, however, after two hundred years, there is nothing to stop a U.S. President showing a penchant for Texans, it is difficult to believe that there is anything inherently wrong with a system that guarantees comprehensive representation to member states. The collegiate system has other advantages. Backed up by an able Cabinet, a good Commissioner can speak with real authority on almost any business, to the general advantage of the policymaking process.

For much of the time, however, inequality is more obvious than equality. In the Commission, as in every other group, there are always stronger and weaker members. Furthermore, all Commissioners (except, in normal circumstances, the President) have special portfolios. As a result, each can usually expect to start with a certain advantage when presenting a proposal within his or her area of competence. Third, though technically the equal of all, the President is in fact in another league: The President has the largest Cabinet and alone has the right to attend the European Council, therefore taking a place beside the Community's heads of state and government. Since 1977 the President has also participated in the world economic summits and in bilateral relations has more often than not been treated as a head of government.

As a result of these various inequalities, the actual operation of successive Commissions has for much of the time diverged from a strict collegiate pattern. Nevertheless, this does not mean that any one alternative pattern has dominated. On the contrary, experience under Jenkins, Thorn, and Delors has differed considerably. Roy Jenkins (1977–1981) was an effective President on the international scene, particularly during the launch phase of the EMS, but his role in the Commission was far from consistently dominant. Indeed, he accepted what generally became known as government by and through a number of Commissioners known as "barons" because of their autonomy. In Gaston Thorn's presidency (1981–1985), the barons continued to rule. As I later suggest, it would be wrong to ignore the importance of the Thorn period for the subsequent relaunch of the Community under Delors, but the achievements of these years owed more to the political skills of Commissioner Davignon and some of his colleagues than to those of President Thorn.

I have already noted that all Commissioners, save the President, are allocated specific responsibilities within the Commission. There are, however, at least two other features of the portfolio system that merit discussion. The first concerns the process by which responsibilities are allocated, formally the job of the President working with the Commission. In practice, this duty has provided a severe and occasionally quite brutal test of the President's capacity to lead. By far the worst episode within the recent past was the distribution of tasks in the Thorn Commission. The troubles that Thorn experienced, however, have in one way or another plagued most if not all who preceded and succeeded him.

These difficulties include strong indirect and direct pressure from national governments. Any President is more or less obliged to assume that the senior representatives of France, Germany, and Britain must get big posts. This can cause problems if there are other important representatives around or, if as has often been the case with the Federal Republic, the larger countries' representatives do not have particular prestige.[10] Other governments make their wishes known more directly. In late 1988, for example, the Spanish Prime Minister indicated to Delors that he thought Abel Matutes, the second Spanish Commissioner, would be well suited for the External Affairs portfolio, which included Latin America. On this occasion, it was a hint. Other Prime Ministers are more forthright, and none more so than Thatcher. The peremptory telephone call from 10 Downing Street on behalf of Christopher Tugendhat at the beginning of 1981 still sends shudders down many spines.

Other pressures come from within the college. Every President has to cope with a number of colleagues who have already held office for at least four and sometimes eight years, and who sometimes have rather strong views on which job they would like to do. Finally, there has sometimes been a scramble toward the end of the appointment process to find a meaningful portfolio for one or another of the less well placed or well backed Commissioners, causing disappointment not only to the individual concerned but sometimes to the government of the Commissioner's home country.

The second feature of the portfolio system that requires attention is the mismatch between the responsibilities allocated to the Commissioners

TABLE 3.1   Principal Administrative Units in the Commission

Secretariat General
Legal Service
Spokesman's Service
Consumer Policy Service
Task Force "Human Resources, Education, Training, and Youth"
Translation Service
Joint Interpretation and Conference Service
Statistical Office

DG I	External Relations
DG II	Economic and Financial Affairs
DG III	Internal Market and Industrial Affairs
DG IV	Competition
DG V	Employment, Industrial Relationships, and Social Affairs
DG VI	Agriculture
DG VII	Transport
DG VIII	Development
DG IX	Personnel and Administration
DG X	Information, Communication, and Culture
DG XI	Environment, Nuclear Safety, and Civil Protection
DG XII	Science, Research, and Development Joint Research Center
DG XIII	Telecommunications, Information Industries, and Innovation
DG XIV	Fisheries
DG XV	Financial Institutions and Company Law
DG XVI	Regional Policies
DG XVII	Energy
DG XVIII	Credit and Investments
DG XIX	Budgets
DG XX	Financial Control
DG XXI	Customs Union and Indirect Taxation
DG XXII	Coordination of Structural Policies
DG XXIII	Enterprises' Policy, Distributive Trades, Tourism, and Social Economy

Euratom Supply Agency
Security Office

and the major units in the administration. Table 3.1 lists the principal administrative units as of 1990. As it indicates, there are twenty-three Directorate Generals (DGs) to match only seventeen Commissioners. Yet the obvious solution, the allocation of more than one Directorate General to certain Commissioners, is not consistently followed. Instead, several Director Generals report to more than one Commissioner, whereas one Commissioner, Matutes, does not have a Directorate General at all. There is nothing new about this untidiness. On the contrary, it has been a feature of every Commission. It is yet another theoretical expression of collegiality; in practice, it is a source of inefficiency.

The Cabinets ✓

The Cabinets attached to the various Commissioners also require discussion. The system has existed from the earliest days of the Commission, although in 1958 each Commissioner was allowed no more than two staff members. The principal functions of the Cabinets are

- to act as the personal staff of the Commissioners, organizing their personal program and serving as "special" political advisers
- to provide Commissioners with enough information about the activities of the Commission as a whole to enable them to fulfill their responsibilities as members of the college
- to ensure the coordination of Commission business at the political level (Every Monday the Chefs de Cabinet hold a meeting, chaired by the Secretary General, to coordinate the work of the Commission and more particularly to prepare for the Wednesday meeting of the Commissioners.)
- to maintain relations between Commissioners and Parliament
- to serve as the Commissioners' political representatives when they cannot be present at outside functions, and so on
- to serve as a link between Commissioners and their own member states

These are wide-ranging and important functions. It is not surprising, therefore, that certain Cabinets (and more particularly outstanding individuals within them) have made an important mark on Commission business. The adage that a Commissioner is only as good as his or her Chef de Cabinet goes too far, but it is true that a Commissioner who has made a poor choice of Cabinet staff, and more particularly of the Chef, will find it difficult to function well. This is especially true of the Commissioner's responsibilities in collegiate discussions. With a good Cabinet, an individual Commissioner can play a far more constructive and influential role in the general conduct of Commission business than departmental ministers under normal national systems.

On balance, the cabinet system has probably been beneficial. There is, however, a widespread feeling (already anticipated in the Spierenberg Report of 1979) that the Cabinets have become too large. According to the Commission's own figures, the total number of staff in the seventeen Cabinets at the end of 1989 exceeded 300. Even if allowance is made for secretaries and other support staff among this number, it is a very large body of people to be serving seventeen Commissioners. The Cabinets are, in fact, among the very few parts of the Commission in which there is a considerable amount of surplus fat to be eliminated.

The Administration

In complete contrast with the Cabinets, the first and most important feature of the Commission's administration is just how small it is. Excluding the research centers, which are administered by the Commission but which are quite separate from the main institution, the Commission's 1990 budget provides for 12,887 full-time permanent and temporary staff. This figure is significantly larger than the comparable figure from 1970, when the total number of staff was 5,234. Since then, however, the Community has gone through three enlargements. As a result, the ratio of full-time Commission staff per head of Community population has scarcely changed, despite a major widening of the Community's agenda.

As Richard Hay, present Director General responsible for personnel, noted:

> Comparisons with other organizations are difficult, because it is not easy to find any with comparable responsibilities or staff composition. In terms of total staff only, the Commission's policy and executive services are about the same size as the French Ministry of Culture or the Lord Chancellor's Department in the British Civil Service, and smaller than the total staff of the city of Amsterdam or the Comunidad Autonoma of Madrid.[11]

The Commission staff is organized into a number of horizontal and vertical units, as given in Table 3.1. There has been some growth in the number of vertical units over time, reflecting new responsibilities and priorities. There has also been some change in the staff weighting of certain Directorate Generals, again reflecting shifting priorities. These changes have been accomplished partly by the creation of new posts but also by the transfer of officials from one Directorate General to another. Since 1985, as the Community's business has exploded, this latter device has become particularly important, for the budgetary authorities have been notably stringent. In the first five years of the 1970s, Commission staff expanded by 50 percent. In the first five years of Delors's tenure as President, growth was somewhat less than 25 percent. Redeployment of existing personnel has therefore been inevitable. For example, DG I, the External Service of the Commission, which includes not only officials in Brussels but also a growing number of staff in embassies, delegations, and other offices abroad, has acquired a variegated collection of officials, sometimes at senior level, with backgrounds in agriculture, industry, statistics, and so on. Whatever the personal qualities of those concerned, it must be doubted whether this is, in a systemic sense, the best way to build up a professional foreign service.

The responsibilities of the Directorate Generals are evident from the titles listed in Table 3.1. Of the horizontal units, two require special discussion: the Legal Service and the Secretariat General.

The Legal Service is a central player in the Commission. Commissioners (and others) are not always aware when they arrive in Brussels that the European Community is, for better or for worse, a people of the book, as the head of the Legal Service has traditionally and sometimes painfully made clear. The Legal Service must approve any significant policy initiative, not to mention any draft proposal. It is also, of course, equally involved in the Commission's functions as guardian of the Treaties and as implementer of Community decisions.

The Secretary General is, by tradition and as a result of function, primus inter pares of senior officials in the Commission administration. The formal functions of the Secretary General (with a staff of 330) are various. At the simplest level, the Secretary General is secretary to the Commission and therefore the only non-Commissioner who sits at the Commission table when it meets. The Secretary General must also, however, coordinate the services and ensure the maximum coordination possible between the Commission as such and the administration, presiding over a meeting of Chefs de Cabinets each Monday and a weekly meeting of Director Generals each Thursday. The Secretary General is also responsible for Commission relations with the Council and Parliament and with intergovernmental institutions involving Community members, including, most importantly, European political cooperation: The Commission's Political Director, currently Gunter Burghardt, is part of the Secretary General's staff. Finally, the Secretary General oversees the policy planning unit, set up by Jenkins and expanded significantly under Delors.

The Commission has had only two Secretaries General since 1958: Emile Noël, a Frenchman, who occupied the post for thirty years, and David Williamson, an Englishman, who was appointed in 1987. At the height of his powers in the 1970s, Noël dominated the administration and was also a formidable figure at the political level. His style, however, was very personal, and coordination, where it occurred, was effected largely through his own actions and those of his trusted staff members planted throughout the administration. (A discussion of the Williamson system is best left until the next section, which deals in part with the Delors effect.)

The Functions of the Commission

The Commission is charged by the Treaties to act "in the general interest of the Communities." More specifically, it is given three functions:

- to initiate the policy process and more generally serve as the driving force behind European integration within the terms of reference laid down by the Treaties
- to act as guardian of the Treaties themselves, both in its own right and by recourse to the Court
- to implement Community policies in terms laid down by and with the Council

The Commission as Initiator

The Commission's mandate in this respect is not simply optional, it is binding. The Commission is obliged by the Treaties to take the initiative in ensuring that their provisions are transformed into practical policy. Its actual fulfillment of these tasks is probably best considered under five headings: strategic goal setting, policy formulation, the drafting of legislation, preparation of the budget, and political management.

Strategic Goal Setting. Since the EC was established, all Commissions have interpreted their obligations under Article 155 to include "general" political leadership. Jenkins's diary entry for August 2, 1977, is as good an expression as any of the Commission's goal-setting role:

> I did a general summing up, of which the main import was that as the harsh reality was that none of the three main governments, France, Germany or Britain, was prepared to support a major Commission initiative, we, combined with trying to get certain urgent, practical things through, had to be prepared to go against them and to blaze a trail to a greater extent than we had done previously, however much this offended people, and that the obvious direction for this was towards monetary union.[12]

As Jenkins's subsequent handling of his major monetary initiative showed and as Delors has demonstrated even more consistently, the function is, in the first place, continuous and, second, best performed by the President, not least because of the President's privileged position as a member of the European Council. The Community calendar does, however, ritualize the process to a certain extent in that every year, in January or February, the Commission lays before Parliament its work program for the following twelve months.

The effectiveness of this general leadership of course varies greatly: Hallstein was very good; Franco Malfatti and Thorn were not. At its worst, strategic goal setting can simply become empty rhetoric that discredits not only the speaker but also the institution to which he belongs. Tugendhat's grasp of the nature and potential of the Commission, outlined in a book he wrote immediately after stepping down as Vice-President at the end of 1984, is in many respects surprisingly flawed; nobody, however, would have quarreled with his description of the consequences of poor leadership of the kind that his President and most of his Commission offered: "The language and actions of the Community and of the member states diverge increasingly, like those of a Victorian mill owner's prayers on a Sunday and his actions during the rest of the week."[13] In other words, if it is to be beneficial, strategic goal setting must be closely linked with the Community's agreed objectives and must be operational. This was the overriding characteristic of Hallstein's leadership. He had clear points of reference in the Treaty of Rome: His task was to translate these aspirations into a realistic but ambitious operational plan and to ensure that the Community kept to its timetable. Hallstein's Commissions were Commissions of the clock, even if, in order to complete particularly troublesome negotiations, the clock had to be stopped for hours or, on certain occasions, even days. As the subsequent discussion will suggest, Delors's leadership has much in common with the Hallstein method.

Policy Formulation. The Commission has a formal right of initiative, not simply in relation to legislation but as far as any policies that can be defined as in the general European interest are concerned. This function of *animateur* (animator) permeates the whole structure and ethos of the institution. Several commentators have underlined the similarities between the early Commission concept and the French Commissariat au Plan, of which Monnet was a distinguished head in the postwar years.[14] The Commission was designed from the beginning to produce ideas, studies, policy papers, and program. It has continued to do so. The output is impossibly large to categorize, as it includes anything from a "think piece" on the more efficient administration of agricultural surpluses to a draft directive to a full-blown policy program such as Cockfield's White Paper of 1985.

This activity is central to the culture of the Commission, which is at its best proactive rather than reactive. This strong bias in favor of policy drafting is not, however, without its dangers. The Commission is quite simply better at proposing than managing. In periods as creative as those of Hallstein or Delors, this fact is easily overlooked. In the future, as the task of consolidating and governing the Community created by the ideas of Delors I and II (the two Commissions presided over by Delors) assumes greater importance, this structural bias will have to be corrected.

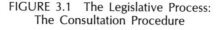

FIGURE 3.1   The Legislative Process:
The Consultation Procedure

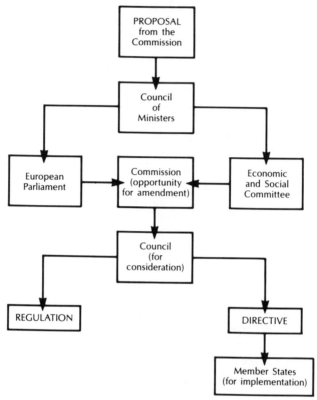

The Drafting of Legislation. The Commission plays the central role in the legislative procedures of the European Community, both under the normal procedures envisaged in the original Treaties and the modified, cooperation procedure approved in the Single European Act. Figures 3.1 and 3.2 underline the point. Even under the normal, consultative procedure, Article 149 requires unanimity on the part of the Council if the latter wishes to amend the Commission proposal. In the cooperation procedure, under which Parliament has a greatly enhanced role, the Commission's position as both intermediary and, in some respects, arbiter between Council and Parliament is even more striking.

The volume of legislation the Community machine has produced over the four decades since the Treaty of Paris is formidable. As Ulrich Everling noted recently in the *Frankfurter Allgemeine Zeitung* in an important article on the Community dimension of German unification, few ordinary citizens of Germany, or indeed of other member states,

FIGURE 3.2 The Legislative Process: The Cooperation Procedure

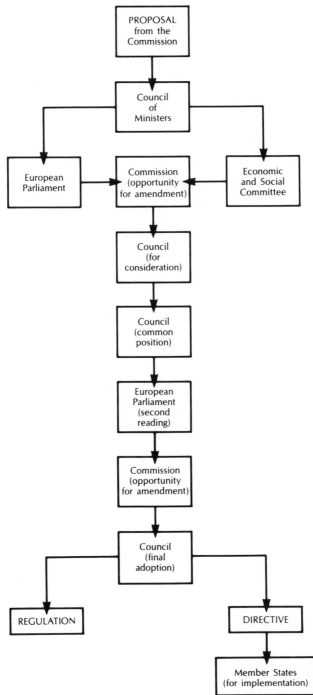

TABLE 3.2   Legislative Output, 1970, 1983, 1987

	1970	1983	1987
Council			
Regulations	249	395	458
Decisions	71	108	125
Directives	25	41	40
Commission			
Regulations	2,426	3,279	3,655
Decisions	435	2,597	4,212
Directives	3	23	23

Source: EC Commission.

are aware of how much of their national law is in fact of Community origin.[15] There have been quieter periods, but the figures in Table 3.2 give some sense of the output of the machine and, more particularly, of the European Commission in its role as initiator of the legislative process.

The Preparation of the Budget. The Community's budget is not remotely comparable to that of federal governments in other Western democracies.[16] Even under the February 1988 agreement, which allowed for an expansion over the period 1988–1992, the agreed ceiling at the end of the process will constitute no more than 1.2 percent of gross national product (GNP). In the United States, federal spending accounts for approximately 25 percent of GNP. Over the Community as a whole, therefore, the macroeconomic impact of the budget is and will remain slight or nonexistent.

That said, the budget has been at the center of Community politics for much of the past fifteen years. Indeed, it was the breakthrough on the budget in February 1988 as much as the coming into effect of the Single European Act and the related progress on the 1992 program that transformed the morale of the institutions. The Commission's responsibilities with regard to the budget are thus a significant part of its overall activity. The procedure is explained in diagrammatic form in Figure 3.3. As with other legislation, the Commission proposes the budget. It is also involved at every subsequent stage of the process, strengthened furthermore by the provision already in force before the Single European Act, that votes in Council on the budget are by qualified majority.

Political Management. The Commission's task as the driving force of European integration involves both political flair and technical expertise. Were the Commission not distinct from the Council, it could not perform this role. Good Commissioners have acquired independent profiles well

FIGURE 3.3 The Budget Process

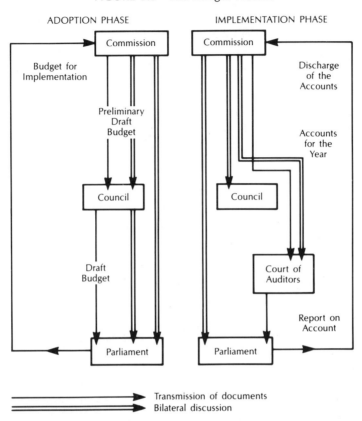

ADOPTION PHASE ⸻ IMPLEMENTATION PHASE

Commission · Commission

Budget for Implementation · Discharge of the Accounts

Preliminary Draft Budget · Accounts for the Year

Council · Council

Draft Budget · Court of Auditors

Parliament · Report on Account · Parliament

⟹ Transmission of documents
⟹ Bilateral discussion

beyond the frontiers of their own particular member state and, on occasion, throughout the Community as a whole. De Gaulle eventually exacted his revenge on Hallstein, the first President of the Commission, but the initial impact of the latter is obvious from a celebrated passage in the General's memoirs: "He had made Brussels, where he resided, into a sort of capital. There he sat, surrounded by all the trappings of sovereignty, directing his colleagues, allocating jobs among them, controlling several thousand officials who were appointed, promoted and remunerated at his discretion, receiving the credentials of foreign ambassadors, laying claim to high honours on the occasion of his official visits."[17] Since Hallstein, other Commissioners, both Presidents and others, have continued to play a supranational political role, appealing to public opinion or important social groups throughout the Community. Davignon's initiatives in forging a new kind of relationship between the

Commission and European big business, including several "national champions," provide one of the best examples before the Delors period.[18]

The delights of supranational politics notwithstanding, even the most ambitious Commissioners have always been exceedingly cautious about going over the heads of member-state governments. It is, after all, in the last resort the Council that decides. To go too far beyond the center of gravity even in Council business subject to qualified majority voting is to court trouble. These political judgments are, in the case of the Commission, reinforced by a still more mundane, practical one. As the previous section showed, the Commission is a small institution relative to its responsibilities. Its own expertise, therefore, has always had to be supplemented.

Against this background, it is hardly surprising that the Commission has over the years developed an elaborate machinery for consultation in the policy formulation phase and for political management when general ideas are translated into firm proposals appropriate for the Council of Ministers or the Parliament. The system is so complex and multilayered, involving both Commissioners and services, that it cannot be adequately described here. In 1971 Noël, the first Secretary General of the Commission, described it well:

> Being based on dialogue, the Community system bears little resemblance to the concept of government in the traditional sense of the word. The Community does not have a single head or a single leader. Decisions are collective and taken only after much confrontation of view points. The Communities have in fact been transformed into a vast convention. They are a meeting place for experts, ambassadors and ministers at hundreds and even thousands of meetings.[19]

The machinery enabling the Commission to canvass views or mobilize the expertise of its member states at the subpolitical levels is particularly extensive and well established. Figure 3.4 tries to capture in diagrammatic form some of the features of this system. On its way to final adoption by the Council, a Commission proposal will typically have been aired in a Commission working group (comprising for the most part national officials), submitted to an advisory committee (which brings together outside experts), passed on formally to COREPER (the Committee of Permanent Representatives) to be discussed in the working group of national officials it sets up, debated or reviewed by COREPER once again, and finally placed before the Council for approval.

Almost inevitably, given the high degree of specialization required to understand much Community business, the same officials from member states may be involved with the Commission at both the pre-proposal

FIGURE 3.4   Bureaucratic Intermingling and
the Commission's Power of Initiative

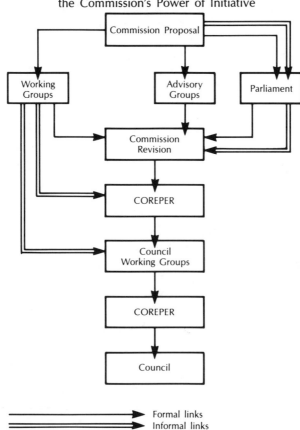

stage and the actual vetting of the formal proposal handed down by COREPER. Even if this is not the case, Commission officials have to deal again and again with the same representatives of the member states. A conflictual model of Commission-Council relations is therefore totally misleading. Of course there are conflicts; that is only to be expected. For a great deal of the time, however, member-state officials work loyally beside Commission officials (and at their expense) in Commission committees, while Commission officials act as thirteenth members of the Council machinery.

It is also inevitable in a system of bureaucratic intermingling of this kind that the borderline between the initiating institution and the decisionmaking institution becomes blurred. Good ideas are not a monopoly of the Commission, and many suggestions flow from member states to the Commission. Equally inevitably, the Commission has on occasion appeared to be more interested in finding a compromise that will satisfy all than in pushing a proposal it believes to be in the general interest of the Community. Contrary to the judgments of many observers in the 1970s, however, there are no grounds for believing that the system is structurally biased against strong leadership. Political management by the Commission is not contradictory to its right of initiative but quite the reverse: It is its essential complement.

The Commission as Guardian of the Treaties

The Commission's responsibilities as guardian of the Treaties are wide-ranging, covering as they do a general obligation to act as the conscience of the Community and very specific duties in relation, for example, to infringement of competition rules by private agents and member governments. The Treaty of Rome also allows the Commission, "within the limits and under conditions laid down by the Council," to collect information and carry out checks, to impose fines on enterprises that in its opinion have distorted competition, and to take member states to the European Court of Justice.[20]

In practice, the Commission has set about establishing its procedures under this general heading with considerable restraint. In the first place, it had (and still has) minimal personnel resources at its disposal. This meant, by definition, that in order to identify infractions of the Treaty, the Commission depended heavily on voluntary notification by member states themselves, by companies who sought in advance clarification of the legality of what they proposed to do, or by other parties who stood to lose if a particular competition-distorting development were allowed to persist. The Commission has at times authorized "dawn raids" to seize documents of companies suspected of practicing cartel arrangements, but because of slender resources such direct actions have been the exception.

A similar approach was adopted in relation to the even more sensitive duty to discipline member states. Strong emphasis was placed on cooperation and agreement rather than confrontation. If possible, the Commission would draw attention to a potential conflict with the Treaty before a member state implemented the legislation or policy in question. If that was not possible, a graduated system was devised to deal with offenders in which resort to the Court of Justice was a final rather than a familiar measure.

The Commission's caution in the early years was only partly due to its lack of resources. Juridical and political considerations were still more important. The Treaty allows member states a significant amount of leeway in adapting Community law to particular national circumstances.

This makes interpretation more onerous and problematical than it would otherwise have been. The real problems were, however, political. A centralized legislative process is one thing, a central enforcement agency quite another. Issues of sovereignty are involved in both instances, but Community law, which is almost invisibly the law of the land, is far easier to tolerate in terms of national sovereignty than having Commission agents roam the member states' territories.

The virtues of this strategy were considerable: Confrontation would have been counterproductive. Education, consensus building, and negotiation were the preconditions of effectiveness. In time, they bore fruit. There was an inexorable growth of activity of all sorts as the Community system took root. These underlying trends need to be borne in mind when one evaluates the real significance of the higher tempo and profile of the Commission in defense of the Treaties in the late 1980s. The Commission has, since 1985, undoubtedly been more systematic than ever before, highlighting the seriousness of the problem through public documentation of its extent and strategically pursuing more significant targets. There have also been some notable scalps. The post-1985 Commission was, however, working within a framework that was already clearly established.[21]

The real questions raised by the developments of the last five years are of another order. In the first place, if the acceptability of Community action has so manifestly increased, can the caution about human resources, which reflected the political judgments of an earlier era, any longer be justified? Second, should not the increased acceptability of Community action be underpinned by more effective accountability?

The Executive Functions of the Commission

The development of the Commission's executive functions over the last thirty years has much in common with the evolution of its role as guardian of the Treaties.[22] Politics has again been more important than precise legal texts in defining where the balance of advantage lay between the various institutions. The Treaties themselves take as well as give as far as the Commission is concerned. In Articles 145 and 155 alike, the presumption is clearly that the Commission will normally be responsible for the implementation of Community policy. Other phrases in both articles—not to mention three decades of practice—caution against the slick identification of the Commission as the executive branch.

In the first place, the executive powers are "conferred" on the Commission by the Council. Second, even in the decidedly more "Commission-friendly" formulation of the Single European Act revision of Article 145, the Council still defines the powers that it confers, "may impose certain requirements in respect to the exercise of these powers," and may even "reserve the right in specific cases to exercise directly implementing powers itself." Third, in some of the most important policy areas for which it is responsible, the Commission, moved both by political considerations and its own lack of resources, has always delegated responsibility for implementation to the member states, who then become individually accountable to the Commission. Both the Council and the member states are thus intimately involved with the Commission in the implementation of Community policies.

Over the years, the feature of this complex system that the Commission has undoubtedly found most irksome is the Council's continuing supervision of its executive function. The debate about "comitology" between the Commission and the Council and among legal experts outside is endless and heated.[23] It arises from the Council's ability under Article 145 to "impose certain requirements in respect to the exercise of these powers." The Council has used its rights to create a number of committees to be associated with the Commission in the exercise of its executive functions. Over the years, the typology of these committees became progressively more complex, covering as it did bodies that were merely advisory and others that had real powers to restrain the Commission. In the Single European Act, and still more in a Council ruling of July 13, 1987, a serious effort was made both to strengthen the presumption that the Commission was responsible for the execution of policy, and to simplify and loosen the continuing hold of the Council in the process, at least in matters concerning the single market. The regulation of 1987 laid down that in those instances where the Council was not prepared to delegate independent powers to the Commission, it should choose between three types of committees: advisory committees, management committees, and regulatory committees.

Advisory committees are self-explanatory. Committees of this type consist of national officials and are chaired by a senior Commission official. So, too, are the management and regulatory committees. The principal differences between the latter two and the former is that in the management and regulatory committees the member states can block a Commission measure.

On a number of occasions since 1987, the continuing prominence of management and regulatory committees in the Community's work and the strong belief (in the Commission, at any rate) that the Council has not given sufficient priority to advisory committees have given rise to Commission protests, including some from the President himself.[24] These criticisms have also been backed up by the Parliament. Once again, however, it is useful to strip away the rhetoric surrounding the matter and examine the reality. In the first place, few in the Commission would deny that their executive responsibilities have been significantly increased even within this irksome framework. The Commission in the early 1990s suffers from too much to do rather than the reverse. Second, even in the "tighter" procedures of the management and regulatory committees, the Commission is not only in the chair but clearly has a strong presumption in its favor. Even if critics can muster a qualified majority in the committee itself, that is not the end of the story, and in the case of management committees, it is not even the end of the measure. In the entirely new context in which the Commission now works, Commission officials have only themselves to blame if they cannot carry member states with them.

The real dangers in the present situation lie elsewhere. As with its duties as guardian of the Treaties, the Commission is paying the price of the political realism of the 1960s and 1970s. It lacks management resources, and those that it has are insufficient for facing the challenges of the new age. There has always been a bias within the Commission in favor of policy formulation as opposed to policy execution. Senior Commission staff are, for the most part, better at drafting directives than they are at implementing them, stronger at planning programs than they are at administering them. Many reports on the institution have made this point. The problems of weak management culture are now, however, hugely compounded by the difficulties that stem from undermanagement. There is a glaring mismatch between what the Commission is asked to do and the resources that it can mobilize for the purpose.

This is true of those policies for which the Commission acts as an executive arm. The increase in the workload of its external services, which reflects not simply ambition but also demand from outside, has now created a situation bordering on crisis. The Commission simply does not have the manpower to staff these posts adequately. Politically, the increasing preference of non-EC states to deal with the Community institutions rather than with the member states in an even wider range of business is presumably irreversible. Even a casual visitor to a non-European capital must, however, be struck by the distribution of European resources. A ten-minute walk in Tokyo from the modest Europe House where the Commission's ambassador is installed, to the priceless piece of real estate that his British colleague presides over, assisted by a staff four or five times as large, illustrates the point rather well.

The problem is also apparent in relation to that still larger segment of Community administration that the Commission delegates. The official line in the Commission is that the latter has deliberately adopted a "private-sector" philosophy with regard to its surveillance functions. Instead, in other words, of mobilizing large resources to keep a constant check on the performance of those implementing policy in the member states, the Commission uses spot checks, exhortation, and more general political pressure through the Council and Parliament.

In the light of successive auditors' reports, this argument seems rather thin.[25] Published annually, these substantial statements by the Court of Auditors provide an increasingly clear picture of how the Community's management system actually works and fails to work. Media comment usually concentrates on the frauds that the reports have uncovered. More significant, however, is the evidence that they give of systemic weakness in the relations between the Commission and the member states. The Commission emerges more often than not as timid in its demands, unclear in its instructions, and amateurish in its surveillance. The member states, for their part, come out if anything in an even worse light. The diversity of their administrative systems, and therefore of the way in which Community business is actually conducted, is a fact of life in a plurinational community such as the EC. Far from trying to compensate for the supranational authority's obvious difficulty in keeping up with twelve different systems, however, many if not all governments appear to practice a policy of minimum disclosure. Basic texts about administrative methods embodied in the statute are communicated; practical modifications are not. The monthly financial statements on revenue collection on behalf of the Community had by 1988 become so useless that the Commission virtually ignored them. Even the annual figures leave many question marks, always assuming that they are actually communicated. By the beginning of 1989, the Italian government had still not told Brussels how much it had collected on the Community's behalf in 1987.

To read these reports and the complementary documentation by the Commission of failures to implement Community legislation[26] is to become aware of one of the principal challenges facing the Commission and the Community in the 1990s: The two must adapt an administrative system developed in a totally different political environment to the realities of a European Community in which most of the important political breakthroughs have already occurred or are more or less assured.

THE DYNAMICS
OF THE NEW COMMUNITY

Much of the analysis of the Commission's functions and organization in the previous section could have been made at almost any point over the past twenty to thirty years. The basic characteristics of the institution have not been transformed; they have evolved. A functionary who had been absent from Brussels for twenty years would return to find much, both good and bad, that was familiar about the institution. By the same token, students can still derive a great deal of insight into the present-day Commission by reading books and articles written fifteen to twenty years ago.

This section advances some explanation of the processes that have transformed the Commission without fundamentally affecting either its constitutional position or its internal organization. The question requires much more exhaustive treatment. But by concentrating on four themes— the inheritance of the past; the transformation of the Community's agenda; developments in the partner institutions, particularly the Council and Parliament; and the "Delors effect"—the analysis should throw some light on the more important elements in the process. It should also provide a framework within which to discuss the reforms of the Commission that are urgently required.

The Inheritance of the Past

This first point need not be labored. The demoralization of the European Community in the 1970s and the first half of the 1980s was real; so, too, is the recovery that followed. The negative features of the period between 1966 and 1985 should not, however, be exaggerated. As subsequent paragraphs will suggest, it was precisely in these years that the new agenda emerged. During the same period, a great deal also happened that vindicated the original design. Anybody who doubts the continuing reality of the integration process even during the bad years should look at the total transformation of the UK's external trade patterns in the 1970s and the early 1980s. At an institutional level, too, progress was real, if for the most part undramatic.

The figures cited in Table 3.2 about the legislative output and judicial actions of the Commission make the point well. The machine ground inexorably on. Even in the bad years, strong Commissioners made a significant impact. Davignon's handling of the steel crisis in the early 1980s is an obvious example. Still more important for the subsequent story was Davignon's success in exploiting opportunities for the Commission offered by the European business world's growing concern about European competitiveness in a global economy dominated by Japan and the United States.[27] In quite a different sphere, however grudging, the Political Directors' recognition that European political cooperation required the full participation of the Commission was already formalized in 1981.[28] The Community's institutional system thus had considerable capacity, though it was half-hidden much of the time.

The Transformation of the Agenda

What, then, was new? In singling out the transformation of the Community's agenda in the 1970s and 1980s as the first and most important change that has occurred, this chapter clearly takes sides in one of the oldest arguments about the European integration process, the argument between the constitutionalists and the functionalists. The constitutionalists' thesis, most ably and vigorously defended by Spinelli, found its clearest expression in the Draft Treaty of European Union that the European Parliament approved by an overwhelming majority in 1984.[29] The precondition for the revival of the Community, the Treaty implied, was a radical reorganization of the Community's constitution in the direction of a much sharper separation of powers and proper political accountability. The question of what the union was to do was important but essentially secondary. In functional terms, indeed, the 1984 Treaty was remarkably cautious.

The functionalist approach, often quite mistakenly identified with a rather crude, mechanistic "spillover" thesis, was based on a fundamentally different insight into the integration process and the role of the member states in it. The Community's institutions would gain in authority vis-à-vis the member states, not by confrontation but by the education of the political classes in the reality of their common interests, through involvement in the integration process itself. The key was a tight link between the supranational institutions and a series of commitments in specific policy areas that those who acceded to the Treaties agreed were best administered in common.[30]

As successive Commission Presidents from Hallstein onward have constantly reminded their fellow Europeans and anybody else ready to listen, the three Communities (Coal and Steel, the Economic Community, and Euratom) were born with a political objective. The definitions of Community business contained in the early Treaties were, however, distinctly mundane, covering as they did trade, agriculture, coal and steel, transport, social policy, and energy policy. The Community's high political destiny was to be fulfilled, initially at least, through "low policy" ventures.[31]

The first explanation of this relatively modest agenda is undoubtedly to be found in political realism. Member states as well established as those of Western Europe would not easily make the qualitative leap to full federation immediately, whatever the political rhetoric of their leaders sometimes suggested. These domestic constraints were, however, reinforced by global realities. The Communities were created in an international system characterized chiefly by superpower rivalry and, in the West, by U.S. hegemony. As a result, high-policy issues, money, foreign policy, and security were the concerns of an alliance system, the principal characteristics of which had already been established before the Community was conceived and were radically different from the integrationist, supranational communities in their basic assumptions about international society. In rhetorical terms, leaders on both sides of the Atlantic constantly emphasized the compatibility between the two systems. In practical terms, however, the NATO–Bretton Woods system defined the limits of European integration as much if not more than crude nationalism. British attachment to NATO and Bretton Woods in place of a strong Community illustrates, by no means uniquely, that transatlantic ties could reinforce nationalism.

The breakup of this relatively simple international order was of vital positive importance for the development of the European union. Medium-sized member states had to come to terms with a world in which U.S. leadership was no longer unquestioned or unquestionable; superpower rivalry eased; new centers of economic and political power, notably in Japan and Germany, emerged; and manufacturing processes and financial markets were globalized.

The initial impact of this multilayered process on the European Community was, however, almost catastrophic, coming as it did so shortly after the fundamental challenge to the EC mounted by de Gaulle. The end of the Bretton Woods system, coupled with the first oil crisis, exposed the limitations of Europe's collective machinery to cope with currency volatility, inflation, and neoprotectionism. No Common Market could long survive a divergence of inflation rates as wide as that which separated Italy from the Federal Republic, or currency volatility that ripped apart the hastily assembled system for closely aligned Community exchange rates and, in doing so, heightened the growing discrepancy between German power and the power of any other Community member state. The apparent easing of East-West tension in the first period of détente undermined the brittle consensus about security policy both within and among Western European nations. The Community institutions had had nothing to do with the shaping of this consensus; they had no defense against its decline. As a result, the Community passed through several years of profound crisis, in the course of which even the achievements of the early years, let alone rhetorical visions of the future, were called into question.

In this perspective, the crisis of the Community in the 1970s and 1980s was not so much due to the limitations on qualified majority voting as to the diminished relevance of the limited Treaty agenda to the real challenges of the day. As Jean-Louis Dewost pointed out in 1980, there was nothing post-Luxembourg to prevent the use of majority voting; the member states did not make wide use of it, however, because their sense of common interest had largely evaporated.[32] By the same token, the recovery of the Community has more to do with the emergence of consensus on a new agenda than with the institutional reforms of the Single European Act as such.

As I stress later, Delors and his colleagues deserve much credit for making this consensus operational in the way that Hallstein did in the 1960s, but the basic elements of the consensus were in place before 1985 and can be found strewn through the conclusions of the European Council since the early 1980s.[33] The most important were:

- the creation of a single market as the only adequate answer to global competition
- the development of flanking policies, including in particular research, development, and competition
- the need to reappraise the bases of the CAP and its place within the overall priorities of the Community
- the advantages of monetary cooperation through and beyond the EMS
- the need for a common foreign policy, including a security dimension
- the importance of environmental issues

Since the passing of the Single European Act, which first encapsulated this new agenda, the forces that gave rise to it have strengthened rather than diminished. The unwinding of U.S. hegemony prompted significant changes in Washington's policy toward the Community, first in the later Reagan years and then more positively and constructively under the Bush administration. The Japanese challenge and globalization of the international economy, which had done so much to prompt the 1992 program, did not go away with its announcement; on the contrary, pressures in both respects increased and thereby helped to keep the 1992 program on track. More dramatically still, the easing of East-West tension, the collapse of communism, and the emergence of a united Germany sharpened the challenge to the Community and its new policies in ways nobody could have foreseen when the Single European Act was drafted. An agenda that to many had seemed highly ambitious increasingly became a practical necessity.

All this helps to explain why, in the words of one senior Commission official, whether it be in EPC, the General Affairs Council, or the Internal Market Council, not to mention in the European Council, Commission officials find themselves pushing at an open door when they exercise the function of initiative. It is also why the demands on the Commission by member states through the Council have grown in importance and number at an exponential rate. What used to be realism is now rather obviously rhetorical; what used to be rhetoric is now urgently realistic.[34]

Changes in the Partner Institutions

The Council

The previous paragraphs should have underlined once again a constant theme of this chapter, namely, the close interdependence of the Commission and its partner institutions. Changes in the latter can therefore have a profound impact on the Commission's own effectiveness. As far as the Council is concerned, three developments should be highlighted: the institutionalization of the European Council, greater use of majority voting and the broader behavioral changes of which it is symptomatic, and the emergence of a more powerful Council Secretariat.

The coincidence between the emergence of the European Council and the earliest indications that the European Community in the new global environment would require a high-policy agenda was not mere chance. Only the heads of government and state had the authority to sanction the change of gear in Community business, which took place gradually and sometimes painfully in the 1970s and 1980s.[35] Nevertheless, the earliest ventures in summitry did not immediately work efficiently or even constructively. Waving a wand on the waters and declaring that the Community would by 1980 achieve economic and monetary union proved in the end to be no more than windy rhetoric; political leadership requires more sustained effort. In 1978 Helmut Schmidt and Valéry Giscard d'Estaing were willing in the context of the global monetary crisis to give European Community affairs, and more particularly the monetary initiative, an extraordinary amount of their time. As a result, the European Council delivered.[36] This success story, however, only served to emphasize that the European Council, like every other element in the Council structure, needed the Commission, especially its President.

Yet the reverse is also true. Far from being a threat to the Commission or its President in their efforts to provide the Community with leadership, the European Council is an indispensable aid. In the first place, the involvement of heads of government and state in Community business politicizes the latter. In the early 1980s, when the most visible consequence of the institutionalization of the European Council was the involvement of Presidents and Prime Ministers in undignified squabbles about milk quotas and sundry other minor items of the Community budget, this did not seem an altogether undiluted blessing. In a long-term perspective, however, the benefits are clear. Without the European Council, it would be very difficult to imagine the Single European Act, let alone the achievement of the Delors package in February 1988, which in psychological terms at any rate was probably the real turning point for Community morale. Moreover, the European Council underwrites de-

cisions once taken. The vulnerability of a political system dependent on
the promises, however solemn, of foreign ministers whose writ can
always be questioned in domestic capitals is apparent. A pledge by a
head of government or state, as Thatcher not infrequently found to her
cost, is by contrast rather hard to wriggle out of. Finally, and by no
means least, the institution of the council has consolidated the primacy
of the President within the Commission and thereby helped to raise
the profile of the Commission as a whole, through the personalization
of hitherto "technocratic" power.

The changes in behavioral patterns within the Community that have
undoubtedly occurred in the past five years are usually rather glibly
linked with the extension of qualified majority voting in the Single
European Act. The importance of this change is beyond question. In
terms of the day-to-day business of the Community, it does matter
whether business on, for example, environmental policy or social policy,
can be taken under articles that allow for qualified majority voting. In
several important respects, however, the majority-voting provisions did
no more than formalize what was becoming a reality, as the overriding
demands of the new agenda made themselves felt in even the most
cautious capitals. It is worth recalling that there would not have been
a Single European Act at all if Italian Prime Minister Craxi had not in
effect resorted to majority voting on the subject of the Intergovernmental
Conference at the Milan meeting of the European Council in June 1985.

The new opportunities for the Commission have been correspondingly
larger than those enshrined in the internal market program. As one
senior figure put it, above all in political, nontechnical business, the
Commission is now almost embarrassed to find itself in the driver's
seat, confronted with governments who in most cases acknowledge the
limitations of their own power and the corresponding necessity for
Community-level action but who are by definition less well placed than
is the Commission to define "the general interest of the Community."
Consensus is, as it should always be, the objective; the definition of
that consensus has, however, in more and more cases shifted from the
lowest common denominator to a higher, if not the highest, common
factor. Hence the impressive insistence of senior Commission figures on
the urgent need for the legitimization of a power they already have
rather than an extension of powers to which they aspire.

The increasing autonomy of the Council vis-à-vis member states who
can neither predict nor organize majorities or even minorities to safeguard
their essential interests, and who have by mutual consent abandoned
the veto, has enhanced the role of the Council Secretariat and, as a
consequence, the importance of the relationship between it and the
Commission. The potential importance of the Secretariat was already

apparent in the 1960s, when, albeit with quite a different agenda, the Community was also robust and ambitious. The present Secretary General, Niels Ersboll, has exploited to an unprecedented degree the opportunities offered by an upgrading of the agenda and radical behavioral change.

The Secretariat is now the principal focus of power brokering in the Community system. Its role is crucial in the interplay between governments, but it is no less important in the new relationship between the Commission and the Council alluded to in the previous paragraph. The presidency nominally and sometimes really plays or attempts to play this role. With the increasing autonomy of both the institutions and the business of the Community, however, the opportunities of individual presidencies, even when they are exercised by larger nations, have significantly diminished. The Secretariat has filled the vacuum. No good presidency can function unless it works closely with Ersboll and his staff.

As a consequence, relations between the Secretariat of the Council and the Commission have also deepened beyond comparison with the regime of the 1970s and early 1980s. Meetings between Ersboll and the Secretary General of the Commission or his deputy, who has special responsibility for liaison with the Council, take place virtually every day, sometimes more than once. The Delors-Ersboll tandem is now, as successive Council Presidents would readily confirm, a fact of life that no government, let alone the presidency, can ignore, particularly in the run up to a General Affairs Council, or, still more, the European Council. As a result of this collaboration, the Commission's legislative programming is now more and more tightly meshed with the Council's own and is furthermore heavily influenced by the latter's sense of what is possible. Above all, each side has contrived to endow the conclusions of the European Council with a quasi-legal status, binding members of the Council themselves and serving as a guideline to both the Commission and subordinate councils.

The Parliament

The Treaties provided for a Parliament but gave it relatively little to do. Even so, shrewd observers soon recognized that the Commission would benefit from an enhancement of Parliament's profile and powers.[37] In the first place, as another supranational institution, it was a natural "ally." In the second place, as the more or less representative body to which the Commission rather than the Council was accountable, steps to make it more representative and its powers vis-à-vis the Commission more extensive and rigorous could only serve to "legitimize" the latter.

The Commission was, therefore, an early champion of parliamentary rights.

The story since the late 1970s, when the Parliament unexpectedly discovered that it could play a determinative role in the budget process and when, more important still, the European Council decided to introduce direct elections, has largely vindicated these early calculations. As Figure 3.2 illustrates, the new cooperative procedures sanctioned by the Single European Act, which augmented the role of Parliament, have at the same time made the position of the Commission even more central. In general, the greater interest in Parliament shown by the media, interest groups, and member-state governments means that the parliamentary platform on which the Commissioners are the most important and regular performers has become increasingly useful to the Commission as an independent launching pad for Commission ideas and initiatives.

All this has meant that the Commission now gives far more time and energy to Parliament than it used to. The shift in gears was perceptible immediately after the first direct elections of 1979 and is nicely caught in Jenkins's diary.[38] As he noted, "we approached the new Parliament with a mixture of respect and apprehension." In the years that followed, the relations between the two institutions have become complex and multilayered. Whereas not long ago Commissioners would regard a visit to Strasbourg during the plenary sessions of the Parliament as a rather minor, sometimes pleasant, but essentially optional commitment (except when their specific business was under discussion), the Commission now moves as a body to Strasbourg in Parliament week and holds its regular weekly meeting there. The demystification or politicization of the "technocratic" Commission has undoubtedly progressed as a result of increased exposure to elected representatives.

The Delors Effect

The prominence I have so far given to the changes in the environment within which the Commission worked is not intended to detract in any way from the relevance of what today most people would regard as the most obvious cause of change in the mid-1980s, namely, the "Delors effect." The situation that Delors and his team inherited was, however, much more favorable beneath the surface than the morale of the institution, let alone public opinion, suggested. There was an increasingly broad consensus about what Europe needed to do to emerge from its sclerosis. Important medicines had already been administered through Community mechanisms, particularly the EMS. Through Davignon, at least, the Commission's potential to influence events had been maintained and indeed strengthened. There is no question that the arrival of Delors had a major and very rapid impact on European Community politics. In order to explain and evaluate this impact, however, I must emphasize that he exploited the potential of a system and an institution that already existed and were already moving in the direction to which he pointed them still more decisively.

His greatest originality was to grasp just how powerful this instrument, devised forty years ago, could be in the totally new context created by the crisis of the global system of the 1970s and early 1980s. He and his colleagues showed the Commission, in other words, how much it could do and in doing so transformed its morale and status. The Delors regime, aided and abetted by Williamson and Ersboll, has also gone some way toward strengthening the long-term capacity of the Commission and the European Council to provide leadership to the Community, first through the consolidation of the presidential system inside the Commission and second by modifications to the working procedures and follow-up of the European Council. Finally, through the enlargement of the Commission's range of responsibilities and his own personal success, Delors has made the institution less remote and more political.

These are formidable achievements. The Delors revolution has, however, raised as many questions as it has settled. The one most commonly asked is, of course, whether the impact of the Commission will be the same when Delors ceases to be President. It is an important question. It is not, however, as important as another: Can the institution itself sustain the consequences of Delors? Is the Commission, conceived as it was in a very different Europe, up to the tasks that, as a result of the new consensus and Delors's exploitation of it, it will have to fulfill in the 1990s?

As far as the achievements of the two Delors Commissions are concerned, it is clearly beyond the scope of this chapter to provide any detailed evaluation.[39] From the perspective of the institution, the first important point to emerge is that Delors vindicated the original design rather than called it into question. His political leadership was a return to basics. Like Jenkins before him, he looked for the "big idea" around which he could mobilize the Community's energies. After some indecision, he identified it as the single market. The most important stages were, however, still to come. The first involved Cockfield still more than Delors: the translation of the general desire for a single market into a detailed operational plan embodied in the White Paper. Thereafter, in 1985, Delors's most important personal contribution was to ensure that this item on which all were agreed became the bridgehead from which the whole Single European Act could be launched.[40]

Once the SEA was in place, the Commission had, for the first time since the 1960s, accepted terms of reference it could use as a basis for real leadership. Appeals to the general interest had been and could still be useful. The Commission's effectiveness is immensely enhanced in a function-oriented Community, however, if the commitments of the member states to specific policy ends are precisely spelled out. Delors explained the point in a reply to questions in the European Parliament in February 1989:

> The Commission has a right of initiative. But a distinction needs to be made according to whether we exercise it within a specific institutional framework or in a more general political context. Within a specific institutional framework, our duties are to give effect to what has formally been decided by the European Council or by an amendment to the Treaty. . . . I should not like these considerations to be overlooked when the Commission's role is being appraised. We might well dream of a Commission that had more powers, but we have to operate within our actual terms of reference.[41]

Since 1986, Delors's leadership has consisted first and foremost in constantly reminding his colleagues in the European Council of what they had signed up to do and spelling out the implications in detail. Making the Single Act work—more succinctly, achieving the goal of 1992—became the central organizing principles of the Commission's internal priority setting and its approach to the Council and Parliament. As I noted earlier, the Community is a people of the book. Delors, Cockfield, Peter Sutherland, and most of the others who have made an impact since 1985 have done so because they understood this and exploited its implications.

The book has been adhered to even when, as has increasingly been the case with Delors II, the Commission has exercised "general" political leadership. The Commission has, it might be said, anticipated "spillover." It has always stressed, however, that the new policies proposed are a necessary result of those already accepted in principle. The "beyond 1992" agenda is not, in this light, a bold flight of fantasy so much as a rational consequence of the 1992 program. As his personal authority has grown, Delors has of course been able to exploit opportunities that had no place in the original script: His foreign policy initiatives in 1989 and, even more dramatically, his handling of the German problem testify to that. It is vitally important, however, to stress that he has crafted his leadership around the built-in strengths of the institution and in doing so has vindicated the original design in a way in which most observers, both academic and political, believed was impossible from the early 1970s onward.

The reassertion of the Commission's leadership role, technically its "rights of initiative," has had a major impact on the Commission itself. In the first instance, morale has been transformed. Second, the range of the institution's responsibilities has grown significantly as the direct and indirect implications of the Single European Act have been brought into the open. Third, the Commission as a whole has become more politicized as the impact of the Commission's policies and responsibilities has broadened. In the days prior to the SEA, apart from a few officials, only the Commissioner for agriculture and, in quite other ways, the Commissioners for trade and development, had responsibilities that gave them constant frontline political exposure. In Delors II, hardly a Commissioner is not in this position. Fourth, the internal workings of the Commission have begun to change as a result of the development of a presidential system.

The first three points require little or no comment. The fourth, by contrast, does. Delors's primacy within the Commission was already clearly apparent during his first four years. At the very beginning, for example, he managed to allocate the portfolios even before the Commission formally took office. Since his first speech of January 1985, it was obvious that the Commission had a leader again. In the early years of the Delors presidency, however, as the outcome of the main strategy remained uncertain, the actual exercise of leadership was punctuated by self-doubt (and threats of resignation) and qualified by the more or less systematic use of an inner group of senior Commissioners composed of Cockfield, Lorenzo Natali, Henning Christophersen, and Frans Andriessen. Furthermore, it had still not taken root through the Secretary General's office in the Commission as a whole.

From February 1988 onward, however, and still more after the formation of the second Commission, the Delors regime has become more and more presidential. The change has many explanations. The most important is, undoubtedly, that as a result of the success of the Single European Act, the growing momentum of the 1992 program, and the achievement of the Delors package, Delors was identified both inside and outside the Commission as "Mr. Europe." Like all Presidents, he had started with advantages: He was now quite simply in another orbit. He could be (and still is) outvoted on specific issues. His position as the principal strategist of the Commission, however, and as a leader who could take over particular policy issues, regardless of who was formally responsible, was undisputed.

The presidential system has been immensely strengthened by the changes that have taken place in the Secretariat General since the end of 1987, when, at almost the exact moment that Delors achieved his major breakthrough in the budget crisis, Williamson took over from Noël.

It was already evident by the time Williamson became Secretary General that the kind of personal dominance that Noël had exercised in his heyday was no longer feasible. Furthermore, as a result of the reorganization of the Commission's work program around the Single European Act, some steps had already been taken to introduce more sophisticated program monitoring and strengthen priority setting. Williamson therefore came at a propitious moment. His personal style and approach were, however, peculiarly well suited to the new situation.

They were modeled, hardly surprisingly, on what he had learned in London, in particular on the role of the Cabinet Office at the hub of British government. There has thus been a much greater emphasis on coordination and information sharing, both on paper and through a growing number of interdepartmental committees. Williamson himself presided over the most important of these committees, including those that dealt with, for example, the G24 assistance to Poland and Hungary during 1989–1990, the German problem, political union, and relations with the Soviet Union. Williamson's impact can also be seen in further improvements to the program-monitoring process and the better-organized establishment of priorities between Commission departments. Elsewhere in his office, relations with the Council have become still closer, facilitated by the changes on the Council side I referred to earlier; the Directorate in charge of parliamentary relations had by 1990 become even bigger than its Council counterpart. Finally, the expansion of the Directorate for Political Affairs has assumed major importance in the light of the European and international upheavals of 1989 and 1990.

Many of these changes meet some of the more important criticisms of the Commission Dirk Spierenberg and others have made. The Williamson period may, however, prove to have had an even greater long-term impact through the close linkages that have been established between his department and the President and his Cabinet. The Secretary General has always, in one sense, been the President's "Director General." In Williamson's case, however, the links have been exploited in quite a new way. Once again, the background is Whitehall. The Cabinet Office is the heart of the whole government machine; it is also an instrument of prime-ministerial leadership. In Brussels, Williamson's office has increasingly become the administrative base of the presidential regime. All the key officials, like Williamson, are the President's staff, nowhere more so than in Foreign Affairs, where Political Director Burghardt, Deputy Chef de Cabinet to Delors in the first Delors Commission, has assumed a role of major importance in the Commission's increasingly assertive forays into foreign policy.

The emergence of the presidential system notwithstanding, the basic impression of continuity with the past remains unaffected. Although Delors has transformed the effectiveness of the Commission, he has only to a small degree altered its structure and organization. Unless, however, these questions are seriously addressed, there must be some doubts about the sustainability of the present momentum and even the durability of the revolution itself. Can an institution designed and developed in another age possibly cope with the political opportunities and the agenda that, thanks to changes in the environment within which the Commission works and Delors's leadership, it now confronts? The achievements of the present Commission are remarkable: They have only highlighted, however, the need for reform.

THE WAY FORWARD:
THE COMMISSION IN THE 1990s

The experience through which the European Commission has passed over the last five years is sufficiently extraordinary to justify, for once, a biblical analogy. Under Delors's leadership, the Commission, like the people of Israel, has seen the waters part before it. There is now rather more than an even chance that it will arrive at the other side (of 1992 rather than the Red Sea), with only a few axles and foot soldiers stuck in the mud. This probable triumph is, however, only the beginning. Ahead lies the desert. To pass through that into the Promised Land, the Commission would benefit greatly from more troops and some mechanization. It would profit even more if, in a not-too-distant future, its leader could come back from the summit not only with a shining face—this it has become accustomed to—but bearing tablets of stone. The age of the prophet or the pioneer is presumably approaching its end: To survive in the New World, the Commission, like the people of Israel, will require legitimacy and efficiency.

Both themes, efficiency and legitimacy, are familiar in the literature about the Commission. The situation in 1990 is, however, in many respects, very different from the one addressed by Ralf Dahrendorf, Spinelli, and many others in the 1970s. The Commission does not require an injection of legitimacy in order to avoid the inexorable progress of bureaucratization at the expense of political leadership. Rather, it needs both legitimacy and bureaucratization in order to sustain the political leadership that it already has.[42]

Lessons from the past have limited utility. The changes in the agenda of the European Community, explored in previous sections, mean that the business of the Commission or other Community institutions is no longer confined to significant but nevertheless relatively marginal questions like agriculture or the management of a common external tariff. In the new age, the Community institutions must address problems of macroeconomic management and social equity, industrial organization, and foreign policy. Where does the Commission, rich in ideas but in management terms rather inconclusively trained by the CAP and the Customs Union, fit in this new Community?

The full answer to these questions could only properly be developed within a comprehensive discussion of the future of the Community institutions as a whole for, as I have repeatedly stressed in this essay, the Commission's performance is inextricably tied up with that of its partner institutions. The question of what kind of Commission is appropriate for the 1990s is, therefore, in the final analysis only a subissue within the broader debate. The discussion that follows concentrates on the Commission, but it is based on some fairly important—and de-batable—assumptions about the general direction union will take.

The first, and most important, is that the quadripartite structure—Commission, Council, Parliament, and Court of Justice—will remain intact. The Council will not give way to a senate: The member states will likely remain the preponderant influence in the Community con-stitution. The Council, furthermore, will, as now, insist on being associated at every stage of the policymaking process, from conception through birth to development and implementation. If these assumptions are correct, the Commission can become ever more powerful as the thirteenth member of the European Community, with all the advantages that stem from its functions as the custodian of the "European interest." It can and should lead to, but it will not in the immediate future be, the sole government of Europe.

The second assumption is a natural corollary of the first. Although the Commission will have to be considerably increased in size simply to perform the functions that it already has, it will not be allowed to become—nor if the quadripartite system persists does it need to become—a bureaucratic mammoth comparable to federal governments elsewhere.

A third assumption based on what has happened over the last ten years is that the range of its responsibilities will continue to grow. There may yet be rearguard actions by national civil servants to devise alternative, intergovernmental structures to develop some of the new policies. The Community method has, however, now established itself so strongly that it is difficult to believe that efforts to halt, let alone reverse, the process of assimilation, which one sees so clearly in the case of the EPC, will be very successful. Given the quadripartite structure, the Commission will not be the only beneficiary of this expansion of Community business. It will, however, have important new responsibilities in policy formulation and management. Two obvious instances are the economic policy dimension of an economic and monetary union and a common foreign policy. As currently constituted, the Commission's services in both areas are skeletal in relation to the need.

Whither, then, the Commission? The overriding questions about the institution's future concern its *capacity* to perform the tasks assigned to it and its *legitimacy*. It would be tempting to start with the efficiency issue and to develop detailed suggestions about where the Commission is understaffed, how it might be better coordinated, and so on. The issue of legitimacy is, however, prior in every sense.

Legitimacy

In the first place, legitimacy is important in itself. The Commission urgently needs to be made more accountable, given the extension of its responsibilities, power, and influence over the recent past. But the issue is prior for other reasons, too. As the recent history of Commission attempts to increase its human resources has demonstrated, management issues will be dealt with piecemeal and, usually, inefficiently if those involved lack a clear picture of what the institution's function within the European polity is. Awareness of how much power has already passed from member states to the Community is limited. Even some of those who are conscious of what has happened would prefer not to admit it, because the implications for personnel policies in member-state governments might be highly embarrassing. Unless and until there is, presumably within the intergovernmental process, a more systematic appreciation and legitimization of what has happened and is happening, there is little hope of any serious reorganization or expansion to make the Commission more efficient.

As far as legitimacy is concerned, the problem in the 1990s is in some respects the reverse of that which prompted previous generations of commentators and actors to call for a reform of the Treaties. The object now is not so much to make the Commission stronger as to legitimize and therefore consolidate the power and influence that it already has. The quadripartite system means that the Commission is not the sole government of Europe, although it is indisputably a major element in it. Its role is political. It is appointed, however, like a bureaucracy in an international organization, and despite improvements in recent years, it is inadequately accountable. The key questions therefore concern the method of appointment, the number of Commissioners (and the related principle of collegiality), and the Commission's openness to scrutiny and selective censure.

The present appointment procedure is quite clearly inappropriate. Given the power that the Commissioners exercise,[43] they must in one way or another be more visibly approved through the democratic processes. Direct elections are, for the time being at any rate, politically unrealistic. Discussion has therefore concentrated on two main possibilities: nomination by the Council, subject to approval by the Parliament, or election by Parliament, subject to approval by the Council. Variants limit both processes to the presidency. It is difficult at this stage to say which will win or which is best. On balance, however, the least unsatisfactory and probably, in terms of the key deciders (the European Council), the most acceptable would be nomination of the prospective President by the European Council, subject to approval by Parliament. With the primarily consensual bias of the Community systems—not only in the Council and the Commission, where politicians of all persuasions are obliged to take common decisions, but also in Parliament—the idea that the Council should put forward two names and leave Parliament to choose would probably cause more problems than it would solve, as it would almost certainly lead to splits along party lines.

An additional advantage of limiting the Council's and Parliament's role to the choice of a President is that it would still further consolidate the presidential system. If this course were taken, the designated President would then presumably have a virtually free hand to choose colleagues, though no sensible President systematically ignores the political-balance wishes of member states.

A more fundamental question raised by this formal recognition of the President's post as an office apart concerns the continuing validity of collegiality. On almost any rational view of the future, collegiality would best be done away with. It is difficult to reconcile with the presidential system; it also makes the individual responsibility of Commissioners harder to pin down. The Community, like every other political body, is not, however, governed solely by reason. Collegiality looks very much like one of those irrational provisions that will survive. The days when Commissioners could in certain circumstances be expected to vote on key issues according to the wishes of their governments are, fortunately, past. There is no indication, though, that any government, however small, is ready to give up a place in the Commission. For reasons I have already mentioned, the system also has some advantages. Nor, as the Delors regime has shown, is collegiality incompatible with a presidential system. A good President may be outvoted on particular issues but can still maintain authority and provide genuine leadership.

The question of number is possibly more open. The British, among the big five, have long argued that one Commissioner per country is quite enough. The original grounds for doing so—that there were not enough good jobs to go around—have since been overtaken by events.

In relation to the range of responsibilities of the Commission, the latter is at the political level a small body compared to its national counterparts. Nevertheless, the advantages of a reduction in numbers are real: It would provide the possibility for a more rational reorganization of the Commission around major "ministries." It would maintain the principle of collegiality but allow the introduction of junior Commissioners. This in turn would make some of the large "ministries" more manageable. Finally, it would pave the way for drastic reform of the cabinet system. In short, the numbers issue is worth a fight.

The issue of better parliamentary scrutiny and the possibility of individual dismissal are even more important. Many improvements could be effected without Treaty revision. Parliament has grown stronger, but it is not by any stretch of the imagination as effective in calling Commissioners to order through searching scrutiny as are some European national legislatures and the U.S. Congress. Parliamentary questions are for the most part anodyne: Scrutiny of Commissioners and officials in both plenary sessions and committees is often superficial. This situation could be remedied without an IGC. As far as the latter is concerned, indeed, the most important contribution it could make in this respect would be a modification of the Parliament's power to dismiss the Commission, so as to allow votes of censure on individual Commissioners.

Over and above these questions of appointment and accountability lies another, which is harder to define but which is in many respects most fundamental of all. It concerns the image of the Commission in the European electorate. If direct elections are ruled out, this problem is by definition very much harder to solve. By one means or another, however, through the IGC and outside, both the reality of Commission power and its limitations need to be spelled out. Thatcher's attack on Brussels "centralists" is, as the present chapter should have demonstrated, manifestly absurd, given the size of the Commission and its dependence on member states for the preparation and fulfillment of its policies. Yet it has struck a chord, as did in some respects even more negatively Helmut Schmidt's frequent attacks on Brussels bureaucrats in the late 1970s. The Commission *is* a remote, vaguely threatening, and unintelligible institution to many European citizens. The measures discussed above may be realistic, but they do not provide any genuine solution to this fundamental defect in the Commission's legitimacy. The parts of the proposed Treaty revision dealing with *subsidiarity* could help. In the final analysis, however, if the Community continues to grow in authority on the basis of the quadripartite system, its citizens need a clear, definitive constitutional document that succinctly explains what the different elements of the quadripartite structure can and cannot do. It would be pleasant to believe that this will result from the new IGC process; it is probably optimistic to imagine that it will.

Efficiency

Under the general heading of efficiency, it is best to consider the issues involved in two subcategories: *internal organization* and *resources*. As far as the internal organization is concerned, most of the options have been canvassed from time to time over the past two decades. By far the most systematic investigation was the Spierenberg Report Jenkins commissioned during his presidency. Many of its proposals are still well worth looking at, but they need to be integrated into a conceptual framework that is somewhat different as a result of recent developments. The Commission now has a much higher profile and a much wider range of responsibilities than it had in Spierenberg's days.

Many commentators have highlighted the fundamental tension between the Commission's exercise of its right of initiative, which casts it in the role of political leadership, and its managerial role. The apparent contradiction between the two has prompted some, including President Delors, to ventilate the idea of hiving off the more managerial functions of the Commission to a series of agencies. In this perspective, the Commission would become an even smaller, high-powered general staff, providing the European Council and its subordinate councils with proposals on strategy and policy. In some quarters at least, the argument has achieved greater credibility through the growing consensus about the need for an "independent" central banking authority. Why not extend the idea to competition policy, agriculture, and so on?

The idea of quasi-independent agencies should not be rejected out of hand. It could be a useful bridge in the difficult discussion about how to reconcile the Community's "autonomy" with shared leadership of the wider European Economic Area, currently under way in the EC-EFTA negotiations. The EFTA states could be associated with the agencies but not with the institutions that in the last resort determine policy. As a general panacea, however, the agency solution is not very credible. At least two objections can be raised. First, the limited empirical research that is available on the implementation of Community policy by the member states suggests that there is a better chance for effective implementation if those responsible downstream are associated at an early stage in the policy formulation and decisionmaking process.[44] Floating executive responsibility off to agencies would obstruct rather than help this development. The other objection is more fundamental. At the moment, when the Commission's lack of accountability is widely regarded (not least by Commission representatives themselves) as problematical, it would be perverse to compound the problem by devolving executive responsibilities to apolitical agencies.

An altogether more promising general strategy would be to move toward a reorganization of the Commission into a number of integrated ministries, in which the vertical lines between the political and civil service levels would be as clearly defined as they are in member-state governments. How many ministries the Commission should have would depend on the outcome of the decision on its size. Even if, in the end, the big five insisted on two Commissioners each, it should be possible to construct sixteen departments plus the presidency. Far better, however, would be twelve major departments with a whole new tier of junior ministers, distributed according to need and not, as of right, per department. Whichever option proves feasible, the most important point is to put an end to the present absurd mismatch between Commissioners' responsibilities and those of Director Generals.

Alongside the issue of agencies versus ministries, the second major theme in the debate concerns coordination. Spierenberg highlighted the issue in his report at the end of the 1970s. His proposal was for the creation of a new style of vice-presidency, involving one member of the Commission only, who would become to all intents and purposes chief operating officer. The evolution of the Delors-Williamson regime points in another direction. Under this option, the growing reality of presidentialism would be acknowledged and the presidency and Secretariat General would be formally charged with coordination.

The principal obstacle to this development at the moment lies not so much in the continuing hankering after autonomy of individual Director Generals as it does in the cabinet system. Both the numbers involved and the overall weight of the cabinet system have grown beyond all reasonable bounds. They are now among the major obstacles to sensible administration inside the Commission. The obvious solution would be to cut the numbers back to two per Cabinet. The Cabinet would then become a source of independent "political" advice and a bridge to the Commissioner's national constituency. Strong Director Generals working within a system coordinated by the Secretary General should be able to provide individual Commissioners with all the material that they need to manage their special portfolios well and, with the Cabinet cut out, to provide the Secretary General with all the material needed to ensure effective coordination and priority setting. The present system, in which the Cabinets have become quasi-autonomous societies subject to their own laws of civility and warfare, is unacceptable on any score.

This reorganization of the Commission would not, however, cope with the most fundamental problem of all, namely, that of *resources*. The Commission, nurtured in another age, is trying to do too much with too few resources. This is true of every aspect of the Commission's activities, whether it is political leadership and policy formulation or guardianship of the Treaties or execution of policy. In the case of policy formulation, which, as I have suggested in previous sections, is the Commission's speciality, the problem is less acute than elsewhere. Even so, in certain areas, numbers and quality are quite manifestly inadequate. The two most obvious examples are general economic policy and foreign policy. DG II, the Directorate General responsible for economic and financial affairs, has over time harbored a number of impressive individuals who have, because of the peculiar advantages of the Commission, had an important influence on policy debate. Recent examples include Padoa Schioppa, the most effective Director General of DG II since 1958, and Michael Emerson, a Director who has been a half-invisible hand behind three of the most important reports on the Community's political economy of the last two decades.[45] Other names might be mentioned. They are, however, the exceptions. Unless and until DG II can acquire the authority that the OECD has in this area, the prospects for an efficient economic and monetary union will be that much less. On the foreign policy side, I have already written at length.[46] In both cases, any solution that does not involve a fairly major transfusion of senior figures, preferably in the main from the member states, is unlikely to be credible in the short term.

The resources question is in terms of crude numbers even more acute in relation to the other principal functions of the Commission. As far as guardianship of Treaty is concerned, the present situation—in which relatively junior officials are, of necessity, almost single-handedly responsible for decisions about major cases under the articles of the Treaty concerned with competition policy and state aids—is indefensible. On the executive side, it is enough to point to the Auditors' reports and to the Commission's own reports on implementation of Community legislation.

The methods devised in the 1950s and 1960s when, by definition, the Commission had to tread softly in dealing with member-state governments, are no longer appropriate in the 1990s. If the Commission is in fact as well as in theory responsible for upholding Community law, and the latter accounts for a significant proportion of national law, it must have resources to carry out its function. Vague promises of goodwill by the member states will not suffice. The case is similar on the executive side. It is obviously important that to the greatest extent possible responsibility for the administration of the Community policy should be delegated. Delegation, however, implies supervision. As matters are at present, the member states are neither ready to supervise themselves nor ready to provide the Commission with the means to supervise them.

These are the issues that urgently require attention. Theoretical diatribes against centralizing tendencies in Brussels are, by contrast, a feeble-minded attempt to pretend that the world is other than it is.

CONCLUSION

The central theme of this chapter has been continuity in the midst of change. The conclusion is simple. Unless the Commission is endowed with both the authority and the means to carry out the functions that, because of a combination of changes in the European and international system and imaginative leadership, it has appropriated to itself, the present renaissance of the European Community could yet prove misleading. Critics of the Commission in the 1970s and early 1980s drew a contrast between its rhetorical claims and reality. In the early 1990s, the problem is quite the reverse. The real threat to rational government in Europe lies not in exaggerated claims by a European Commission that has never been a monster bureaucracy and, under almost any scenario, never will be. Rather, it comes from national governments, who pretend that they still have powers that they have lost and refuse to work toward a rational redistribution of resources to ensure that the responsibilities that they can no longer shoulder alone are effectively performed.

NOTES

1. D. Spierenberg et al., "Proposition de réforme de la Commission des Communautés Européennes et de ses Services" (European Commission, Brussels, 1979, mimeo).

2. Jean-Victor Louis and Denis Waelbroeck, *La Commission au coeur du système intitutionnel des Communautés Européennes* (Brussels, 1989). This contains some useful, post–Single European Act essays and gives good bibliographical information. The best general book in English on the EC system is Neill Nugent, *The Government and Politics of the European Community* (London: Macmillan, 1989). See also David Coombes, *Politics and Bureaucracy in the European Community* (London: George Allen and Unwin, 1970). H. Wallace, W. Wallace, and C. Webb, eds., *Policy-Making in the European Communities* (London and New York: Wiley, 1977), is dated but still useful.

3. For a classical exposition of quadripartism, cf. P. Pescatore, "L'Executif communautaire: justification du quadripartisme institué par les Traités de Paris et de Rome," *Cahiers de droit européen* 4 (1978), pp. 387ff.

4. For Monnet cf. especially J. Monnet, *Mémoires* (Paris: Fayard, 1976). For Schuman, cf. Raymond Poidevin, *Robert Schuman* (Paris: Imprimerie Nationale, 1986).

5. Sabine Pag, "The Relations Between the Commission and National Bureaucracies," in Sabino Cassese, ed., *The European Administration* (Paris: Institut International des Sciences Publiques, 1988).

6. The relevant articles of the Treaty of Rome are 155–163.

7. For the circumstances surrounding two presidential appointments, compare Roy Jenkins, *European Diary, 1977–81* (London: Collins, 1989), pp. 3ff., and Franz-Olivier Giesbert, *Le Président* (Paris: Seuil, 1990), pp. 221–222 (on Delors).

8. S. Holt, *The Common Market* (London, 1968), pp. 41–42.

9. Jenkins, *European Diary*, pp. xiii.

10. On German personnel policies with regard to the EC, cf. Beata Neuss, *Europa mit der linken Hand?* (Munich, 1983). The book also contains useful biographies of all German Commissioners prior to the Delors Commission.

11. Richard Hay, *The European Commission and the Administration of the Community* (Brussels: EC, 1989), p. 31.

12. Jenkins, *European Diary*, p. 135; Peter Ludlow, *The Making of the European Monetary System* (London: Butterworth, 1982), pp. 43ff. has even more information.

13. C. Tugendhat, *Making Sense of Europe* (London: Viking, 1986), p. 81; M. Butler, *Europe: More than a Continent* (London: Heinemann, 1986), makes still better sense of Europe. (Butler was formerly UK Permanent Representative.)

14. Dominique Berlin, "Organisation et fonctionnement de la Commission des Communautés Européennes," in Cassese, *European Administration*, pp. 38–39.

15. Ulrich Everling, "Der Weg nach Deutschland ist Langwierig. Zum Streit über Artikel 23 oder 146/ Die Europäische Gemeinschaft," *Frankfurter Allgemeine Zeitung*, March 15, 1990, pp. 13–14.

16. The Commission has recently produced some rather good literature about the budget and budget reform of 1988. See especially *Community Public Finance* (Brussels: European Commission: 1989).

17. Charles de Gaulle, *Mémoires d'Espoir* (Paris: Plon, 1970).

18. Cf. M. Sharp and C. Shearman, *European Technological Collaboration* (London: Royal Institute of International Affairs, 1987).

19. E. Noël, "The Permanent Representatives Committee and the Deepening of the Communities," *Government and Opposition* 6, 4 (1971), p. 424.

20. Cf. the classical essay by R. Kovar, "La Commission Gardienne des Traités," in *La Commission des CE et l'élargissement de l'Europe* (Brussels: Institute d'Etudes Européennes, 1974), pp. 9–84.

21. For the most recent account of competition policy, see European Commission, *Nineteenth Report on Competition Policy* (July 1990).

22. See, among others, C. Blumann, "La Commission, agent d'exécution du Droit Communautaire," in Louis and Waelbroeck, *La Commission*, pp. 49–70.

23. Cf. note 24. Also, C.-D. Ehlermann, "Compétences d'exécution conférées à la Commission: La nouvelle décision-cadre du Conseil," *Revue du Marché Commun* 316 (April 1988), pp. 232–239.

24. For example, complaints were aired in the debate on institutional reform in the European Parliament, November 21, 1989. *EP Debates*, annex to *Official Journal of the EC*, no. 3–383, p. 60.

25. See, for example, *Official Journal* 1989/C312/01, Annual Report of the Court of Auditors, December 1989.

26. EC COM 90 (1990), Fifth Report of the Commission concerning the implementation of the White Paper (March 1990).

27. Cf. Blumann, "La Commission." Also, P. Ludlow, *Beyond 1992: Europe and Its Western Partners* (Brussels: Center for European Policy Studies, 1989), pp. 27–30.

28. Cf. "Report on Political Cooperation," issued by the Foreign Ministers of the Ten, London, October 1981. Reprinted in A. Pijpers, E. Regelsberger, and W. Wessels, eds., *European Political Cooperation in the 1980s* (Dordrecht: Nijhoff, 1988). See in the same volume an essay by S. Nuttall, "Where the European Commission Comes In," pp. 104–117.

29. F. Capotorti, M. Hilf, F. Jacobs, and J. P. Jacqué, *Le Traité d'Union Européenne* (Brussels: Institute d'Etudes Européennes, 1985).

30. Monnet's *Mémoires* remain the best source for an understanding of the basic philosophy.

31. For this and much that follows, cf. Ludlow, *Beyond 1992*, passim.

32. J.-L. Dewost, "Les Relations entre le Conseil et la Commission dans le processus de décision Communautaire," *Revue du Marché Commun* 238 (June–July 1980), pp. 282ff.

33. J. De Ruyt, *L'acte unique européen: Commentaire* (Brussels: Editions de l'Université de Bruxelles, 1987), contains much useful information on the origins of the Single Act.

34. On realism (old-style) versus rhetoric (also old-style), cf. Tugendhat, *Making Sense*, pp. 15–127.

35. On the European Council, cf. S. Bulmer and W. Wessels, *The European Council* (London: Macmillan, 1987).

36. Cf. Ludlow, *The Making of the EMS*.

37. See, for example, G. Vedel, "La responsabilité politique de la Commission," in *La Commission des CE*, pp. 235–244. Cf. also, E. Noël, pp. 131–145 in same volume.

38. Jenkins, *European Diary*, p. 375.

39. Much relevant material can be found in Peter Ludlow, ed., *The Annual Review of the European Communities, 1990* (London: Brassey's, 1990).

40. Cf. Ludlow, *Beyond 1992;* De Ruyt, *L'acte unique européen*. For an entertaining account of the relaunching of Europe, see D. Buchan and N. Colchester, *Europe Relaunched* (London: Hutchinson, 1990).

41. *EC Bulletin, Supplement* (February 1989), p. 60.

42. For Spinelli, see in particular A. Spinelli, *The Eurocrats* (Baltimore: Johns Hopkins University Press, 1966). For Dahrendorf, see the articles entitled "über Brüssel hinaus" and "Ein Neues Ziel für Europa" and written under the pseudonym Wieland (while Dahrendorf was still a Commissioner) in *Die Zeit*, July 9 and 16, 1971. Coombes, *Politics and Bureaucracy*, is still well worth reading, especially chapter 12 on "Political Leadership and Political Union."

43. Cf. J.-V. Louis, "La Désignation de la Commission et de ses problèmes," in Louis and Waelbroeck, *La Commission*, pp. 9–23.

44. Cf. H. Siedentopf and J. Ziller, eds., *L'Europe des administrations?* (Maastricht: European Institute of Public Administration, 1988), and C. Azzi, ed., *L'Application du Droit Communautaire par les etats membres* (Maastricht: European Institute of Public Administration, 1985).

45. Commission of the EC, *The Role of Public Finance in European Integration* (The MacDougall Report), 1977. T. Padoa Schioppa, et al., *Efficiency, Stability and Equity: A Strategy for the Evolution of the Economic System of the EC* (London: Oxford University Press, 1987). Commission of the EC, "The Economics of 1992," *European Economy* 35 (1988).

46. H. Froment-Meurice and P. Ludlow, "Towards a European Foreign Policy," in *Governing Europe*, vol. 2 (Brussels: Center for European Policy Studies, 1990).

4

The EC Council: The Community's Decisionmaking Center

Wolfgang Wessels

Over the last quarter of a century the weight of European Community decisionmaking has grown considerably. Community legislation has expanded greatly in scope, especially since the coming into force of the Single European Act in 1987. The legal acts of the EC touch central issues of economic, environmental, and social policy. Thus Community legislation has replaced that of national political systems to a considerable degree. The EC not only takes binding decisions for its member states and its citizens but also adopts policies vis-à-vis other states or international organizations. Over the years, the EC has become a major actor in crucial economic areas and even in world politics.

Given the salience of this political system, it is of paramount importance for politicians and for political scientists to know who takes the binding decisions and in what form. The perennial question of "authoritative allocation of values" becomes of specific interest.[1] This is an intriguing question, as the Community cannot be easily classified, analyzed, and assessed by using traditional categories and notions of political and legal science.

The Rome Treaties of 1957—the constitutional framework of the EC—established a Council as the ultimate locus of Community decisionmaking on all major issues, whether budgetary, legislative, or treaty-making. The Council is formally composed of one representative of each member government. Although the terminology is confusing, the Council of the EC is institutionally distinct from the European Council, an institutionalized summit of heads of state and government, established in 1974 and later codified in Article 2 of the Single European Act. The European Council is still outside the legal and institutional checks and balances

of the Rome Treaties. Thus its activities and acts, in contrast to those
of the organs of the EC, are not subject to juridical control by the EC
Court of Justice. Discussion of the Council here will refer to the Council
as established in 1957 (often referred to as the Council of Ministers),
rather than to the European Council.

The Council is a legal fiction insofar as there is not *one* Council
composed of one group of ministers but a large number of sectorally
organized councils—twenty-three as of 1989. In that year, councils existed
for issues ranging from development, education, energy, environment,
and Euratom to telecommunication, tourism, transport, and women's
issues. The most important are the General Council of the (Foreign)
Ministers and the Agricultural Council. Except for defense and some
odd departments such as ministries for religion or intra-German affairs,
each national ministry deals with one or more councils at the European
level that can be considered "its" council or councils.

An analysis of the policies of the Council will lead us to a deeper
understanding of the specific qualities and dynamics of the Community
and also to insights into the Western European political system in general.
The Council's history and performance can only be explained by looking
at the evolution of its national and international environment; at the
same time, the Council itself is a major force in the political system of
the European Community and the broader West European system. In
this argument the EC system, with the Council at its peak, is perceived
as closely linked with the substantial postwar changes in West European
states and their position in the international system—a perspective often
ignored in debates focused narrowly on European integration.

I begin this chapter by considering the Council as an institutional
reaction to a basic dilemma facing European states: how to cope with
interdependence among them while ensuring the economic performance
and providing the social services that contemporary European electorates
demand. In the second section I examine the evolution of the Council
over time, providing specific information, in quantitative form, about
the time lags in the legislative process and relationships among the
Council, Commission, and European Parliament. In the concluding section
I assess the Council's performance.

THE EC COUNCIL:
NATIONAL REACTIONS TO A BASIC DILEMMA

When they established the European Community in 1957, the member
states sought to ensure more effective common policymaking. The
converse of these ambitions, however, was the loss of national autonomy
that increased integration and cooperation entailed. As time has passed,

this basic dilemma has increased: The higher the interdependence among European countries, the stronger the propensity to move to Community rather than national policy; but this propensity reacts adversely on national autonomy.

As interdependence rises, whether the result of market forces or government policy, the propensity to move to Community activity increases, as common or coordinated actions become more effective. Because its own policies both cope with and contribute to rising interdependence, the Council can be seen as both a product and a shaper of the dynamics of the West European welfare and service states in situations of *increasing* interdependence and a *decreasing* stability of global regimes.

The institutional evolution of the EC is thus connected with the post–World War II history of West European states, which is characterized by a combination of participatory mass democracy, capitalistic market economy, and the development of a welfare and service state.[2] Politically, these changes are closely linked to trends toward extensive and intensive participation of interest groups[3] and a significant increase in functions and numbers of bureaucracies.[4] In the history of the national state,[5] we have entered a new phase of a "cooperative state,"[6] or the "industrial state."[7] This new European state is not a reborn version of those European nation-states that died in the two world wars but a qualitatively new entity with some major new attributes. For the EC Council, these changes in the state mean that substantial opposition to strong supranational European bodies does not come only from outdated elements of the traditional state in the defense of "anachronistic" sovereignty. Basic constraints and major dynamics of the Council's evolution and performance are also to be identified in principal structures and functions of this "modern" West European state. The Council is thus more than a classical intergovernmental conference of diplomats: Rather, as I show in this chapter, it indicates the enlargement of the scope of modern West European states, which puts diplomats into a marginal position even for policy decisions taken outside the traditional national framework.

The dilemma of West European governments is that successful economic performance is a major prerequisite for the stability of these welfare and service states. Governments in power see their electoral fate as being directly linked with the state of their economy and a sufficient performance of state services. To achieve this goal, West European economies have to be open to an international and European division of labor. With economic interpenetration, however, interdependencies increase and the (at least de facto) autonomy of national systems decreases. During the 1960s and especially the 1970s, looking for help from outside Europe, from international regimes that could solve or set rules for the management of the interdependent welfare states, became less and less useful. The capacity of the United States to guarantee appropriate regimes has been sharply reduced.[8] The uncertainties and along with them the demand for common European responses have thus grown constantly over the last decades.

The problem has become even larger for West European politicians in the last years: With rising expectations, the modern West European states are made more and more responsible for a performance that is less and less within the reach of their autonomous actions. The "hard core of the welfare state"[9] is broken by the very dynamic of its own internal logic. Thus not only are de facto interdependencies important—this phenomenon always existed within what are called "world economies"[10]—but the changed political sensibilities of Western democracies have accentuated the consequences of economic interpenetration. The EC as such has further increased this market-led interdependence by its own instruments; with the transfer of competencies throughout the history of the EC, the legal autonomy of political action by the national states has decreased and the economic interpenetration has increased. These basic trends in Western Europe have led to an EC "core area which has progressively drawn other economies and societies and therefore governments to it."[11]

This policy-led interdependence will increase even more in the near future. With the establishment of the internal market and with the planned economic and monetary union, the dilemma will again become sharper.[12] The instruments in the hands of national governments or central banks will either be transferred to the European level or become even less effective than in the 1980s.

In this situation governments realize that a doctrine of "naive sovereignty," that is, to keep all policy instruments in their own jurisdiction, is counterproductive: The real effect of their own instruments on the economic and political realities is zero or—as Mitterrand learned in his first years from 1981 to 1983—even negative. The Community and especially the Council offer access and influence where decisions with real effects are made. Member governments move from a position of "decisionmaker"[13] to that of a "co-decisionmaker."[14]

To sum up this argument, European integration *is*, contrary to some other statements, "a thread woven into the fabric" of the European society—at least in the 1990s.[15] The Community and its institutions are based on more than just the "political will" of heads of governments or just legal treaty properties (as important as they might be). They are reactions to persistent fundamental patterns of West European political and social developments. These fundamentals have not basically been changed but have been strengthened by the collapse of the Soviet empire in Eastern Europe. Thus we do not need to revise this argument after 1989.

From a micropolitical view, the sovereignties transferred to the Community must be managed in a way that will reduce the influence-autonomy dilemma. The Council serves to increase the calculability of common or coordinated activities for member governments. In the tension between the need for investment in common or coordinated policies and the strong preference to keep ultimate sovereignty, the Council is the major control mechanism through which states give up autonomy for well-guaranteed access and influence. This feature is more than a "pooled sovereignty,"[16] as this notion only implies close horizontal cooperation and common management of competencies and instruments still in the hands of the national states. The concept of pooled sovereignty is useful for certain aspects of the EC system such as in the coordination of foreign policies of the EC members in the so-called European political cooperation.[17] But the transfer of real powers to the EC and their extensive use by the Council (which in its decisionmaking and interaction style points at an amalgamation of national systems) make actual practice closer to a system of cooperative federalism such as that in the United States and the Federal Republic of Germany. In this sense the Council is not an "interstate body" (as Keohane and Hoffmann perceive it in Chapter 1) but a body at the supranational level. Along with the Commission[18] and the European Parliament,[19] the EC Council is involved in a complex decisionmaking system.

Even more important, the Court of Justice[20] is involved in the control of decision implementation. Thus the EC system has a state quality of its own that leads to a political game of two levels, both of which have sovereignty, though to different degrees.

Some would argue that the propensities to integrate might be different among member states according to their national history and to their weight. Community history shows, however, that the benefits of participation are increasingly regarded as outweighing the reluctance to give up autonomy. Even countries like the UK and Denmark, which show no enthusiasm for European integration as such, play the EC game fully and quite often more seriously than countries with strong federalist currents. And neutral EFTA countries apply for membership—some, like the Austrians, in order to get rid of a few of their autonomous but ineffective policies.[21] By looking more closely at the participation tendencies, decisionmaking, and interaction styles of the Council, we can identify West European states' general patterns of reaction to this basic dilemma.

Though highly important, the academic work on the Council is rather limited. The major book dates from the mid-1970s.[22] Though specific aspects—especially the presidency,[23] the Committee of Permanent Representatives,[24] and in a related way the European Council[25]—have been subjects of research, the Council itself has not been analyzed in depth over the past decade.

The political debate, however, has always been quite lively. One school of thought, represented mainly by the traditional federalists,[26] has seen the Council in its present form as major obstacle to any progress toward some kind of federal system. For them, the Council is the body representing narrow national interests that are no longer in tune with the necessities of Europe in an interdependent world. An alternative school perceives the Council as the major body representing and defending legitimate national interest.[27] For them, the Council, a "natural" prolongation of sovereign national states, is the only acceptable actor in the international arena. Its intergovernmental features are regarded as a necessary protection against supranational bodies who have no legitimacy, or at least less legitimacy than do historically grown national governments. A veto power for each government in the Council is thus regarded as the most important safeguard for the real "social legitimacy."[28]

In the Community this debate has gained in momentum over the last few years. With the Single European Act, the first major revision and enlargement of the EC Treaties, and especially its program for the internal market, decisionmaking by the Council has increased considerably. With German unification, the activities to move forward toward a political union were further promoted, especially by the European Council sessions in Dublin and the Intergovernmental Conference beginning in December 1990.

Given the increasing importance of the Council, its performance will be a crucial issue for the future of (Western) Europe. Three major criteria can be identified for assessing the future role of the Council:[29]

- the efficiency of decisionmaking (especially increasing its speed against what has been characterized as *"lourdeur institutionnel,"* or institutional drag[30])
- the effectiveness of its decisions at the level of legal and administrative implementation[31] and the actual impact on economic and political realities
- its legitimacy, meaning the acceptance of Council decisions by EC citizens.[32]

THE EVOLUTION OF THE COUNCIL

Participation: Patterns of Growth and Differentiation

The dynamics of the Council are already observable when we look at the number of actors participating and at the frequency of their meetings. The Council is formally composed of one representative of each member government. One member of the EC Commission partic-

TABLE 4.1   Number of Meetings of the Council Between 1967 and 1987

Sectorally Delimited Council	1967	1970	1975	1980	1985	1987
Agriculture	8	15	15	15	14	16
General and foreign affairs	7	12	16	13	14	12
Economy and finance	1	1	8	9	7	8
Labor and social affairs	1	3	2	2	2	2
Transport	1	3	2	2	3	4
Technology/industry	1	1	—	—	1	5
Euratom	1	2	—	—	—	—
Budget	—	—	3	5	5	6
Energy	—	1	—	2	3	2
Education	—	—	1	1	1	1
Environment	—	—	3	2	3	4
Development cooperation	—	—	2	1	2	3
Research	—	—	2	—	2	3
Fisheries	—	—	—	7	3	3
Health	—	—	—	—	—	1
Consumer protection and information	—	—	—	—	1	3
Internal Market	—	—	—	—	—	6
Miscellaneous	—	3	2	4	8	2
Total	20	41	56	63	69	81

Source: Annual Reports of the General Secretariat of the Council of the EC.

ipates with specific rights. Also present are up to 100 civil servants: up to six from each member state and a respective number of functionaries of the Commission and of the Secretariat of the Council. The conference-style composition reduces the confidentiality of the deliberations. Ministers sometimes feel "controlled" by civil servants from other national ministries. This situation explains the tendency of ministers to have informal lunch or weekend meetings without civil servants in which many of the real deals are struck.

As indicated at the beginning of this chapter, the Council actually operates as over twenty sectorally delimited councils. In 1987, one or another of these councils had eighty meetings, involving 120 days' work per year, in Brussels or in Luxembourg. Thus the Council is in session for two or three days per normal week. As Table 4.1 shows, the number of Council meetings has increased steadily for the last twenty years. This indicator, therefore, provides no evidence for the view that the Community went through its own "dark ages" after 1966, as Keohane and Hoffmann suggest in Chapter 1. The number of national politicians and civil servants involved in the Council has increased throughout the lifetime of the EC.

The foreign ministers (in the "general" Council) and the ministers in the Agricultural Council meet at least once per month, with informal sessions at least once per presidency. The frequency of the meetings of the foreign ministers is even higher than these statistics indicate, as they also come together in the framework of European Political Cooperation[33] and at the sessions of the European Council.[34] Bilateral contacts and meetings on other occasions, for example, through NATO or the UN, could be added to these numbers. This intensity of contact generates the often-quoted remark that participants get to see their EC homologues as often as they meet their national cabinet colleagues. Most other ministers meet officially at least once per half-year presidency and often once for an informal weekend session, normally in a castle within the electoral district of the minister holding the presidency.

Of special importance are the sessions of the European Council in which the French President and the heads of the other eleven governments as well as the President of the EC Commission, the foreign ministers, and one other member of the Commission meet at least twice per year.[35] The European Council has so far never acted in a legal sense as Council. Although this body is in formal terms not part of the EC Treaties, the European Council has a major impact on EC decisionmaking.[36]

The chair of the Council rotates in half-year presidencies among the member countries in alphabetical order. The role of the chair has been enlarged considerably over the years to what might be called a "neutral broker"[37] between diverging interests.[38] The presidency is assisted by a Secretariat General of the Council, the head of which intentionally maintains a low profile but is known to be highly instrumental for achieving consensus.

The Council's work is prepared and to a high degree even completed by a complex administrative substructure, COREPER. Below this administrative body on a senior level there are around 180 working groups of national civil servants who negotiate in detail each paragraph of the proposals put forward by the Commission. In a rough estimation, 80 percent of the Council's acts are decided on a professional bureaucratic level. Some documents—the so-called A points on the Council's agenda—can even pass the Council without political debate. In the national capitals of member states, this work is prepared by highly differentiated administrative and political procedures that vary among the member states according to the respective constitutional architecture and political constellations.[39]

Each Council is at the top of a pyramid: European-wide interest groups, national and Commission administrations, and, increasingly, committees of the EP form an equivalent to what is known in the United States as an "iron triangle." These lobbies and national and community civil servants are in intensive contact; some working groups and committees meet weekly[40] and have developed a broad transnational understanding. With the acceleration of the Council's activities, all other actors—lobbies and national ministerial departments—have also speeded up their work.

The horizontal differentiation of the Council in terms of ministries involved is thus matched by an equivalent vertical differentiation in the administrative setup. The overall effect is an ever-increasing involvement of national decisionmakers—ministers and civil servants—in terms of number and frequency. This picture confirms two elements of my basic hypothesis: The Council has along with the evolution of the welfare and service states considerably enlarged the scope of its activities, and this has meant access to the EC by a growing number of national decisionmakers, who use their channels intensively. The Council and its subgroups are not mainly a meeting place for some European specialists but for the ministers and high civil servants alike. Council business is taken very seriously.

Decisionmaking

The procedures of decisionmaking in the Community, with the Council at its center, have increased in number and complexity. The Single European Act has added two new variations (the "cooperation" and the "assent procedure") that are less examples of clearly designed rules than the result of intensive bargaining giving some (yet not too much) power to the European Parliament. Complex procedures are of course subject to conflictual interpretations caused by the attempt of each body to keep or increase its influence. The budgetary procedure is thus a history of legal and political battles between the EP and the Council.[41] The Court of Justice as a constitutional court decides on some controversial issues; the involved bodies themselves have reached so-called interinstitutional agreements on how to interpret the rules.

Of specific interest for achieving the internal market as well as for demonstrating some patterns of the decisionmaking style is the new cooperation procedure installed by the SEA.[42] Prior to the Single European Act, most Community legislation was adopted according to the consultation procedure, outlined in Figure 3.1 in Chapter 3. According to this procedure, the Commission proposed legislation to the Council; Parliament gave its opinion, but the Council made the final decision. As explained in the earlier chapters, the Luxembourg compromise of 1966, although not legally binding, ensured that in most cases the Council acted by unanimity, even when applying articles that permitted majority voting on the basis of the original EC Treaty. The new cooperation procedure, as shown in Figure 3.2 in Chapter 3, is more complex.

It applies only to some ten articles of the EEC Treaty, but they include important areas, notably most of the legislative harmonization necessary for the completion of the single market, as well as decisions on research programs and the structural funds. In those cases the legislative procedure is based on the following steps:

1. The Commission elaborates its proposal after consulting informally advisory expert groups of national civil servants, lobbies, and technical experts.
2. The European Parliament, after intensive deliberations in committees, parliamentary parties, and the plenary adopts its opinion in a "first reading" (possibly delayed to obtain concessions).
3. The Council defines a "common position," which can be and sometimes is taken by qualified majority voting.
4. The second reading of the European Parliament takes place within a three-month deadline in which the parliamentarians (MEPs) may adopt one of the following three options:

   • explicitly approve the text, or by remaining silent approve it tacitly, in which case the Council "shall definitely adopt the act in question in accordance with the common position" (Article 149)
   • reject the text by an absolute majority (presently at least 260 MEPs), in which case the proposal will fail unless the Council unanimously agrees within three months to overrule the Parliament
   • again by an absolute majority propose amendments that, if supported by the Commission, are incorporated into the revised proposal, which the Council can modify only by unanimity. Any amendments by the EP not supported by the Commission require unanimity to be adopted by the Council, whereas the revised proposal of the Commission, incorporating those of the Parliament's amendments that it approves, necessitates only a qualified majority.

In spite of the complexity and the two readings in the Council, the cooperation procedure needs less time than the consultation procedure that involves only one reading per body. The major difference is that in all cooperation procedures majority voting is possible, whereas this is only partly the case in consultation procedures (for example, as in Article 43 of the EEC Treaty). Tables 4.2 and 4.3 indicate the differences. Even clearer are figures for individual cases. On average, after the SEA the Council has taken decisions four times as fast as before. Thus in

TABLE 4.2 Time Lags in Case of Cooperation Procedure (in days)

	tl 1[a]	*tl 2*[b]	*tl 3*[c]	*tl 4*[d]	*tl 0*[e]	*Total Number of Cases*
1987	326	256	66	38	686	7
1988	349	136	89	36	610	47
1989	292	89	80	46	507	42
Average	322	160	78	40	600	

[a]Time lag EP 1 (from Commission proposal to EP 1st reading).
[b]Time lag Council 1 (from EP 1st reading to Council common position).
[c]Time lag EP 2 (from Council common position to EP 2nd reading).
[d]Time lag Council 2 (from EP 2nd reading to Council adoption).
[e]Total time lag (from Commission proposal to Council adoption).

Source: This table was prepared by Thomas Sloot in the framework of a study in preparation for the Institut für Europäische Politik on the decisionmaking of the EC after the introduction of the SEA (used by permission). The data base contains all proposals concerned under Article 149 of the EEC Treaty and all those included in the White Paper by the Commission.

TABLE 4.3 Time Lags in Case of Consultation Procedure (only in internal market affairs) (in days)

	tl 1[a]	*tl 2*[a]	*tl 0*[b]	*Total Number of Cases*
1987	319	630	885	21
1988	299	106	745	13
1989	374	637	988	21
Average	323	505	891	

[a]Time lag here means the number of days from the position of the EP to the decision by the Council.
[b]Total time lag.

Source: See Table 4.2.

the cooperation procedure as in other procedures, the Council has increasingly to take into account the activities of the European Parliament.

As to the difference between time lag 1 and time lag 2, the time the EP and the Council need for their respective first readings without set time limits, the EP shows a good record. By a major adaptation of its internal working rules it has developed a complex but smoothly working procedure to deal with Commission proposals in terms of the majorities needed; an informal but rather persistent and well-functioning "grand coalition" has been formed between the Socialists and the European

TABLE 4.4   Average Number of Parliament's Amendments Made in the First Reading and Their Acceptance by Commission and Council[a]

	Average Number per Proposal Made in First Reading by EP	Accepted in the Revised Proposal of the Commission[b]	Accepted by the Council in First Reading[b]
Before 1985	7.5	—	—
1985	10.4	5.6 (53)	—
1986	0	0	—
1987	10.2	7.4 (73)	2.4 (24)
1988	16.4	9.7 (59)	6.3 (38)
1989	14.4	7.4 (51)	5.4 (38)
Total	13.4	8.2 (60)	5.4 (33)

[a]These calculations are based on 151 "first readings" of the EP, 146 revised proposals of the Commission, and 89 common positions of the Council.
[b]Figures in parentheses are percentages.

Source: See Table 4.2.

People's party (the Christian Democrats) mastering the necessary absolute majority. As in the budgetary procedure,[43] the EP is able to develop consistent and efficient procedures if and insofar as it has real powers.

The Council apparently needs less time (time lag 2) than the EP, though this statistic is misleading; in nearly all cases working groups of the Council start their work right after the Commission has put forward its proposal—the Council normally does not wait for the opinions of the EP. Sometimes the Council has even agreed upon a common "orientation" and merely as a formality waited for the opinion of the EP, a procedure that the latter of course heavily criticizes.

This observation leads to a closer look at the impact of the European Parliament on the Council's decisions. Rather crude statistical material seems to indicate that the EP has gained considerable influence on the EC's decisionmaking. Table 4.4 shows that 60 percent of the European Parliament's amendments of the first reading were accepted by the Commission, 33 percent by the Council. During the second reading the European Parliament dealt with 115 common positions of the Council, 47 of which it approved and 67 it amended (Table 4.5). Nearly half of those amendments (49 percent) were accepted by the Commission, but only 14 percent by the Council. Only in one case did the Parliament reject a common position of the Council in the second reading. This "Benzene directive" was, however, not of major importance, as the substance was integrated into another legislative text. The reluctance of

TABLE 4.5   Opinion of Parliament at the Second Reading

	Rejection	*Amendments*	*Approval*	*Total*
1987		4	3	7
1988	1	20	26	47
1989		43	18	61
Total	1	67	47	115

Source: See Table 4.2.

the EP completely to reject a text is due to a basic pro-integration propensity by a broad majority of the EP that prefers to have an imperfect decision taken by the Council than no agreement at all. In case of rejection, one member country could block any progress when entering a coalition with the absolute majority of the EP. Thus in the "television directive" (1989) the EP refrained from the rejection that a majority would have liked, so as not to let Denmark kill the directive entirely.

This quantitative record of the EP's influence is, however, rather misleading: Case studies[44] indicate that, except for some rare cases, the impact of the EP on the crucial issues of the Council's deliberations is rather limited. In terms of our basic arguments this finding would support the view that member governments still keep the ultimate control on major Community decisions, though they are prepared to have the European Parliament involved.

Patterns of Interaction

Within this complex set of rules, the behavioral patterns of the Council's decisionmaking vary across policy sectors, though some general observations can be made.

Vital decisions for the future of the Community are normally taken by the European Council.[45] It is especially in this body that broad "package deals"[46] among member countries are concluded. Different benefits and costs of member countries and converging preferences[47] are mixed into a positive-sum game that makes each member country interested in pursuing common or coordinated policies and giving up some of its autonomy for a higher impact on problem solving. These deals normally include the enlargement of the EC's scope of activities, the creation or strengthening of specific Community instruments, and adaptations of EC institutions. The Single European Act was a masterpiece among such package deals. The procedural dynamics of the Council in the last years as described above can only be understood by taking into account the overall agreement put down in the SEA and the subsequent

Delors package by which the European Council, in February 1988, agreed upon the financial implications of the SEA.

The strong de facto role of the European Council does not reduce the Council of Ministers to a body of secondary importance. In legal terms, the European Council does not take any binding decisions for the EC. The agreements at the top are put into the normal EC procedures and then passed by the Council. Even more important, in many areas the Council makes decisions de facto as well as de jure.

The interaction styles in the Council show several rather persistent characteristics. Normally a quite open exchange of positions—sometimes put into diplomatic formulas—prevails. A basically cooperative spirit is mixed with a stubborn defense of what is regarded as a national interest: The participants regard the decisionmaking not as a zero-sum game with either clear winners or clear losers, but each country perceives some profits from common agreements; thus some kind of compromise formula has to be found at the end of the day. Nightlong sessions, especially by the agricultural ministers, are part of the media-induced dramatics of the meetings: Ministers can demonstrate that they are fighting for the interests of their countries even into the late hours and then, at the same time, explain to their national electorate that it was their personal contribution that led to the compromise formula for the sake of European integration. Patterns of national political cultures[48] and personal styles intermingle. Given these differences in national and partisan background, the procedures of the Council are highly efficient. The group pressure to internalize basic interaction norms is quite considerable—even more so after the admission of Greece, Spain, and Portugal: The bigger the club, the less acceptable are exceptions to common rules. The interplay between ministers rushing in from their capitals with some high civil servants is helped by the presidency, the Council Secretariat, and the Permanent Representatives, who best know the explicit and implicit rules and the respective margin of maneuver.

A specific feature of the Council's interaction style is the way in which binding decisions are achieved. Since the Single European Act, the voting frequency has increased quite considerably[49] within and outside those areas directly affected by the SEA. Already in 1986—as a kind of anticipatory effect—ninety-three decisions were taken by majority vote (sixty-one in agriculture and fishery, eighteen in trade, three in budgetary affairs, and eleven in other areas). In 1987 thirty-four cases of majority votes were reported for the first term and sixty-two for the second term. In 1988 there were seventy-eight cases, a small downswing to be explained by fewer votes in agriculture and more decisions related to the Delors package, which needed unanimity. In 1989 a total of sixty-one majority votes were taken. The progressive reduction of majority voting might be explained in at least two ways: One argument stresses that after solving "easier" issues for the internal market, the more difficult problems are now tackled facing more national opposition. This argument is not convincing, as some "tough" decisions have been passed by majority votes (e.g., the television directive). Another more convincing argument perceives a learning process by which member governments in minority positions realize that they might gain in at least some minor points if they agree to the total package. The German agreement to the television directive is an example of that kind of tactical maneuvering. This argument leads us more deeply into the behavioral pattern of reaching a decision in the Council.

Many participants at Council sessions say they have never observed a "real" vote[50] in the sense of raising hands. The vote is taken in two forms. One is by silence: The President concludes a debate by ascertaining whether anyone wants to speak again and, if no one does, states: "Thus we decided in this way." Of the sixty-one cases in 1989, seventeen decisions were taken in this implicit way, and another twenty-six were even passed as A points. Thus around two-thirds of all majority votes were taken in silence. The second vote is with a positive confirmation: The President looks around the table and states: "I see that the conditions for a decision are fulfilled." Eighteen decisions in 1989 were reached by this statement of the chair.

The anticipatory effect on the behavior of member governments is more important than these figures indicate. The possible threat to pass to majority voting has apparently mobilized the internal procedures in the national capitals as well as in Brussels, which explains the significant increase in the speed of decisionmaking: Governments have to be flexible and open to proposals by the Commission and the President.

The interaction style within the Council is also coined by participation of the President whose role has been reinforced by the revision of the internal procedures from July 29, 1987. The presidency has developed quite Byzantine ways of finding a compromise formula. One method is the so-called confession, by which the President contacts each government bilaterally to confidentially get a final negotiation position; the President can then roughly identify the space of compromise where decisions can be made. Each President wants to show a good record in passing as much legislation as possible; thus the chair pushes its partners, especially at the end of its term, to accept compromises that might otherwise have needed a longer period. The President's energy can quite often mobilize additional national resources.

The Commission also plays an active role; it can change its proposals during all stages of the Council's and Parliament's deliberations and does so actively to get to a consensus as soon as possible. Against the position of the Commission the Council can only decide by unanimity, which it does when it wants to get a point through. In some bizarre cases there were even agreements by unanimity but with more abstentions (which do not count as negative votes) than positive votes necessary for a majority vote.

To look for variations between sectors[51] leads to further insights into the Council's interaction style. Councils that have to operate under time constraints normally invest a large time budget (including long night sessions) in achieving a consensus. The Agricultural Council when fixing the agricultural prices in spring, the Budgetary Council in the yearly budgetary process in autumn, or the Trade Council in trade disputes with the United States or in view of GATT agreements normally keep their deadline, though sometimes the clock is "stopped." When distributional effects among the EC members are at stake, especially in the Budgetary Council and Agricultural Council, the internal bargaining is more time-consuming than fixing a position vis-à-vis a third country with minor internal effects. A typical pattern to deal with these distributional effects is to make incremental adaptations to former decisions.

The overall political climate is also important: The SEA has led to a constructive and open attitude by all governments, whereas the budgetary disputes in the first half of the 1980s had blocked or at least slowed down the work of sectorally delimited councils, as listed in Table 4.1. Positive and negative spillover thus affects the interaction style of the Council. In general the interaction style is clearly dominated by bargaining among member states, with the active participation of the President. Thus the Commission is an important and active co-player, especially influential when using interest convergences of member states. The European Parliament is usually outside this interaction network.

AN ASSESSMENT OF
THE COUNCIL'S PERFORMANCE

This picture of the EC decisionmaking and the Council's interaction style signals that the EC members have moved upward along the trade-off curve between loss of autonomy and gain in influence. In the Council the member governments as a group keep ultimate control of EC decisions; at the same time, for the sake of achieving positions efficiently they accept being subject to majority votes. This change since the SEA marks a new era in the evolution of Western Europe.

A characterization of these evolutions as "pooling of national sovereignties"[52] is only of limited use: In most cases the Council legally uses those competences already transferred to the Community.[53] Beyond the legal criteria, the horizontal and vertical differentiation as well as the dynamics of the decisionmaking and the interaction style of the Council would make it more appropriate to characterize this evolution as an "amalgamation"[54] of the national system *into* a new common system with its own competencies, institutions, and procedures. The central features of this process lead neither to a federation in the traditional notion nor to an extensive use of intergovernmentalism. The mixture of the two systems, clearly documented in the dynamics of the Council, is close to what is known as cooperative federalism.[55] Understanding the nature of cooperative federalism may also help us get a better assessment of the Council in terms of efficiency, effectiveness, and legitimacy.

One of the major criticisms vis-à-vis the Council is that this body is inefficient; in particular, the speed of its decisionmaking is said to be deplorable. Yet the overall time taken by EC institutions in general as well as by the Council is not disproportionate to that needed to pass national legislation, especially in systems with two chambers. Within this general pattern there might be some areas, like fiscal harmonization, where no progress is achieved. As the possibility of electing a new government does not exist on the Community level, the possibilities of effective blockages over a longer period are generally higher than in national political systems, where the electoral possibility for change is inherent. The necessity for large majorities for "normal" legislative acts and for unanimity in all constitutional acts might set higher thresholds than in national systems, but it reflects a basic trend in West European political systems to establish a consensus. With the exception of the UK, the conventional political wisdom in most West European countries urges governments to get a broad agreement on major political acts,[56] even if the constitutional rules might allow for a narrower margin of majority. Over the more than forty years of EC history, the necessity for consensus might have slowed down the decisionmaking process, but it has ultimately not prevented the EC from making considerable progress in all major dimensions, especially by using the package-deal method. A requirement to establish a consensus or at least large majorities might reduce speed but would increase the stability of agreements and mutual confidence. The Council might not be a legislative machinery smoothly transferring input into output; but particularly since the SEA, the Council has achieved a high degree of efficiency, without reducing—at least so far—the acceptability of the decisions.

Council-member governments are quite often blamed for failing to implement common decisions. The proper application by national or regional administrations is an even larger difficulty.[57] An intensively discussed problem in Council effectiveness is the role of the implementation committees, in which national civil servants are supposed to "help" or to "control" the application of the legislation by the Commission. Though the Council has decided to install committees, which in comparison with other forums give the national civil servants the largest say vis-à-vis the Commission, the practice of these committees shows that both national and Community civil servants cooperate to a high degree.

A major critical remark concerning effectiveness points to the quality of the Council's output. It is argued that the Community's acts are a typical product of a "joint decision trap,"[58] which typically occurs if two levels of governments (as in federal systems) have to cooperate and the lower one controls the outcome. In the case of the EC the argument runs as follows: Because of the way decisions are made by member governments in the Council, the EC does not tackle its problems effectively in terms of its own goals, distributional effects among countries dominating in the bargaining style of the Council. As shown in the case of the Common Agricultural Policy, the Council—so the argument goes— is not solving problems in the most economic way but is satisfying the immediate political needs of member governments. Thus the real problems are even further increased. The medium-term consequence is an ever-increasing overload of the political bodies of the EC. This thesis has some merits, as indeed the cost-benefit analyses of member countries do dominate the Council's deliberations. Yet this argument also has shortcomings: Without the broad access and strong influence of national decisionmakers no decision on the Community level would be taken at all; that is, the effectiveness would be zero.

A further yardstick for assessing the Council is the issue of its democratic legitimacy. Measuring the Council's performance against classical notions of how binding decisions should be reached in and for democratic societies indicates that it has substantial shortcomings. If the Council is perceived as a legislative chamber, then there is a significant lack of transparency. Its rules of confidentiality are not compatible with democratic standards. It is even impossible to get an official statistic about the voting patterns of member states. Furthermore, the horizontal and vertical differentiation in and below COREPER creates an administrative network that diffuses responsibility.[59] Neither the political leadership nor parliaments can really control how decisions are prepared on this level. One effective though not necessarily democratic watch mechanism is the network of well-informed lobbies. This assessment from a traditional democratic perspective must be partly corrected by putting the activities of the directly elected European Parliament and the Court of Justice into the picture. Both guarantee at least a certain democratic and legal control.[60]

This record can, however, be judged according to other interpretations of legitimacy. The amalgamation process working within and by the Council has led to a broad and diffuse acceptance by the European citizen, as documented by regular opinion polls. The strong pressure for consensus even in cases in which the Council can take decisions by qualified majorities has led to a rather surprising stability of a political system that takes binding decisions on central issues of national systems.

Overall, the dynamics of the Council's evolution are part of a long-term evolution of Western Europe into a new, amalgamated system of "open states." The Council does not meet ideal standards of efficiency, effectiveness, and legitimacy, but neither do national governments. The European Community political system is complex and often confusing. Yet it has been strengthened by the Single European Act. In considering the changes that have taken place and that continue to occur, there is little reason to be pessimistic.

NOTES

1. See David Easton, "Political Science," in *International Encyclopedia of the Social Sciences*, vol. 12 (Glencoe, 1968), pp. 282–298; see also Max Weber's notion of "Politik als Monopol legitimierter Geweltsamkeit" in Max Weber, *Politik als Beruf* (Düsseldorf: Droste Verlag, 1986), p. 37.

2. See Peter Flora, "On the History and Current Problems of the Welfare State," in J. N. Eisenstadt and Ora Ahimeir, eds., *The Welfare State and Its Aftermath* (London: Barnes and Noble, 1985).

3. See Gerhard Lehmbruch and Philippe C. Schmitter, eds., *Patterns of Corporatist Policy Making* (Beverly Hills, Calif.: Sage, 1982).

4. See Gérard Timsit, *Théorie de l'administration* (Paris: Economica, 1986); and Renate Mayntz, *Soziologie der öffentlichen Verwaltung*, 3d ed. (Heidelberg: C. F. Müller, 1985).

5. See Stein Rokkan, "Dimensions of State Formation and Nation Building: A Possible Paradigm for Research on Variations Within Europe," in Charles Tilly, ed., *The Formation of National States in Europe* (Princeton: Princeton University Press, 1975).

6. See Joachim Jens Hesse, "Aufgaben einer Stattslehre heute," in Thomas Ellwein et al., eds., *Jahrbuch zur Staats- und Verwaltungswissenschaft*, vol. 1 (Baden-Baden: Nomos, 1987).

7. See Ernst Forsthoff, *Der Staat der Industriegesellschaft, dargestellt am Beispiel der Bundesrepublik Deutschland* (Munich: C. H. Beck, 1971).

8. See Robert O. Keohane, *After Hegemony: Cooperation and Discord in the World Political Economy* (Princeton: Princeton University Press, 1984); and Paul Kennedy, *The Rise and Fall of the Great Powers: Economic Change and Military Conflict from 1500 to 2000* (New York: Random House, 1987).

9. See Karl Kaiser, "Interdependenz und Autonomie: Die Bundesrepublik und Grossbritannien in ihrer multilateralen Umwelt," in Karl Kaiser and Roger

Morgan, eds., *Strukturwandlungen der Aussenpolitik in Grossbritannien und der Bundesrepublic* (Munich: Oldenbourg, 1970).

10. See Fernand Braudel, *L'identité de la France. Les Hommes et les choses* (Paris: Arthaud-Flammarion, 1986).

11. See William Wallace, *The Transformation of Western Europe* (London: Frances Pinter, 1990).

12. See, for example, the debate about the "magic triangle" between fixed exchange rate, national autonomy in monetary policies, and the free movement of capital. See for this the report by Tommaso Padoa Schioppa et al., *Efficiency, Stability and Equity* (Brussels: EC, 1987).

13. See Robert D. Putnam and Nicholas Bayne, *Hanging Together: The Seven-Power Summits* (London: Heinemann Education Books, 1984).

14. See Wolfgang Wessels, *Der offene Staat, Modelle Zwischenstaatlicher Verwaltungsstränge* (Bonn: Europa Union Verlag, forthcoming).

15. See Alan S. Milward, *The Reconstruction of Western Europe, 1945–1951,* (London: Methuen, 1984): "the process of integration is neither a thread woven into the fabric of Europe's political destiny nor one woven into the destiny of all highly developed capitalist nation states" (p. 493).

16. See, in this volume, Chapter 1 by Robert O. Keohane and Stanley Hoffmann.

17. See Alfred Pijpers, Elfriede Regelsberger, and Wolfgang Wessels, eds., *European Political Cooperation in the 1980s: Towards a Foreign Policy for Western Europe?* (The Hague: Nijhoff, 1988).

18. See, in this volume, Chapter 3 by Peter Ludlow.

19. See Otto Schmuck and Wolfgang Wessels, eds., *Das Europäische Parlament im dynamischen Integrationsprozess: Auf der Suche nach einem zeitgemässen Leitbild* (Bonn: Europa Union Verlag, 1989).

20. See, in this volume, Chapter 6 by G. Federico Mancini.

21. See Heinrich Schneider, *Alleingang nach Brüssel, Österreichs EG-Politik* (Bonn: Europa Union Verlag, 1990).

22. See Christoph Sasse et al., *Decision-Making in the European Community* (Paris: Presses Universitaires de France, 1977).

23. See Geoffrey Edwards and Helen Wallace, *The Council of Ministers of the European Community and the President-in-Office* (London: Federal Trust of Education and Research, 1977); Colm O'Nuallain, ed., *The Presidency of the European Council of Ministers: Impacts and Implications for National Governments* (London: Institute of Public Administration, 1985); and Guy de Bassompierre, *Changing the Guard in Brussels: An Insider's View of the EC Presidency* (Washington, D.C.: Center for Strategic and International Studies, and New York: Praeger, 1988).

24. See Fiona Hayes-Renshaw et al., "The Permanent Representation of the Member States of the European Communities," *Journal of Common Market Studies,* 28, 2 (December 1989).

25. See Simon Bulmer and Wolfgang Wessels, *The European Council: Decision-Making in European Politics* (London, 1987); and Wolfgang Wessels, "The European Council: A Denaturing of the Community or Indispensable Decision-Making Body?" in Jean Marc Hohscheit and Wolfgang Wessels, eds., *The European Council,*

1974–1986: Evaluation and Prospects (Maastricht: European Institute of Public Administration, 1988).

26. See Lucio Levi, "Recent Developments in Federalist Theory," *The Federalist*, 29, 2 (1987), pp. 97–136.

27. See Margaret Thatcher, speech at the opening ceremony of the Thirty-Ninth Academic Year of the College of Europe, Bruges, September 20, 1988 (Brussels: British Embassy Press Service, 1988).

28. See Joseph H. H. Weiler, "Europäisches Parlament, Europäische Integration, Demokratie und Legitimität," in Schmuck and Wessels, *Das Europäische Parlament*.

29. See Wolfgang Wessels and Christian Engels, eds., *The Institutions After the Single European Act* (Bonn: Europa Union Verlag, 1991).

30. See Samuel Krislov et al., "The Political Organs and the Decision-Making Process in the United States and the European Community," in M. Cappelletti et al., eds. *Integration Through Law: Europe and the American Federal Experience*, vol. 1, book 2. (New York: De Gruyter, 1986).

31. See Heinrich Siedentopf and Jacques Ziller, eds., *Making European Policies Work: The Implementation of Community Legislation in the Member States*, vol. 1, *Comparative Synthesis*, and vol. 2, *National Reports* (Beverly Hills, Calif.: Sage, for the European Institute of Public Administration, 1988).

32. See Eberhard Grabitz et al., *Direktwahl und Demokratisierung, Eine Funktionsbilanz des Europäischen Parlaments nach der ersten Wahlperiode* (Bonne: Europa Union Verlag, 1988); and Weiler, "Europäisches Parlament."

33. See Pijpers et al., *European Political Cooperation*.

34. See Wessels, "European Council."

35. See Bulmer and Wessels, *European Council*, and Bassompierre, *Changing the Guard*.

36. See Wessels, "European Council."

37. For the use of this term, see Joel D. Aberbach et al., *Bureaucrats and Politicians in Western Democracies* (Cambridge: Harvard University Press, 1981).

38. See Bassompierre, *Changing the Guard*, and Wessels, *Der offene Staat*.

39. See Sasse et al., *Decision-Making*, and O'Nuallain, *Presidency*.

40. See Wessels, *Der offene Staat*.

41. See Thomas Läfer, *Die Organe der EG, Rechtsetzung und Haushaltsverfahren zwischen Kooperation und Konflikt* (Bonn: Europa Union Verlag, 1990).

42. Works on this new procedure are increasing rapidly; see especially Richard Corbett and Otto Schmuck, "The New Procedures of the European Community After the Single European Act: Efficiency and Legitimacy in the Light of Experience," in Wessels and Engels, *Institutions After the Single European Act*.

43. See Läfer, *Die Organe der EG*.

44. See Grabitz et al., *Direktwahl und Demokratisierung*, and Christine Borrmann and Christian Engel, *Die Verwirklichung des Binnenmarktzieles 1992 durch eine engere Zusammenarbeit zwischen dem EG-Ministerrat, dem Europäischen Parlament und der EG-Kommission* (Bonn: Europa Union Verlag, forthcoming).

45. See Wessels, "European Council."

46. See Helen Wallace, "Negotiations and Coalition Formation in the European Community," *Government and Opposition*, 20, 4 (1985).

47. See Chapter 1 in this volume.

48. See Michael Butler, *Europe: More than a Continent* (London: Heinemann, 1986).

49. See Werner Ungerer, "Die neuen Verfahren nach der Einheitlichen Europäischen Akte: Eine Bilanz aus Ratsperspektive," *Integration* 3 (1989): 95–106.

50. The minutes of the Council meetings are confidential and normally do not indicate this procedure.

51. See generally Helen Wallace, William Wallace, and Carole Webb, eds., *Policy-Making in the European Communities*, 2d ed. (London: Wiley, 1983).

52. See Chapter 1 in this volume.

53. In some cases the Council also issues positions "as Council and the ministers assembled in the Council"; this formula and the cooperation among the member countries in the EPC (see Pijpers et al., *European Political Cooperation*) would better justify the notion of "pooling of sovereignties."

54. This term is borrowed from K. W. Deutsch et al., *Political Community and the North Atlantic Area* (Princeton: Princeton University Press, 1957).

55. See Wolfgang Wessels, *Alternative Strategies for Institution Reforms*, European University Institute Working Paper 85/1984 (Florence: European University Institute, 1984); Fritz W. Scharpf, *The Joint-Decision Trap: Lessons from German Federalism and European Integration* (Berlin, 1989); and Sabine Pag, "The Relations Between the Commission and National Bureaucracies," in Sabino Cassese, ed., *The European Administration* (Paris: Institute International des Sciences Publiques, 1988).

56. See Yves Meny, *Government and Politics in Western Europe, Britain, France, Italy, West Germany* (Oxford: Oxford University Press, 1990).

57. See Siedentopf and Ziller, *Making European Policies Work.*

58. See Scharpf, *Joint-Decision Trap.*

59. Ibid.

60. See Chapters 5 and 6 in this volume.

5

Sovereignty and Accountability in the European Community

Shirley Williams

This chapter addresses four questions. First, what sovereign powers have national governments lost to the European Community since it was first established? Second, how far has the transfer of power to the Community been accompanied by public accountability for the exercise of those powers? Third, what is the "democratic deficit," defined as the gap between the powers transferred to the Community and the efficacy of European Parliamentary oversight and control? Fourth, what steps could be taken to increase the power and influence of the European Parliament, and how can the political will to take those steps be evoked?

This chapter concludes that the loss of accountability to national parliaments has not been compensated by increased accountability to the European Parliament. The "comitology," the structure of advisory, regulatory, and management committees staffed by national civil servants, is answerable to national governments, not to the Community institutions; European Parliamentary scrutiny is largely excluded from both policy-making and implementation. The best approach to closing the "democratic deficit" would be to create in each member country a committee on Community affairs on which both MEPs and national deputies serve, and to extend and strengthen the European Parliament's co-decision-making powers.

THE LOSS OF SOVEREIGN NATIONAL POWER

The European Coal and Steel Community, established in 1951, and its successor, the European Economic Community, established by the Treaty of Rome in 1957, required a pooling of sovereignty in certain specific areas among those nation-states that became members. Apart from coal and steel, until 1985 the most important areas within the Community's jurisdiction where practical progress was made in implementing common policies were agriculture and the removal of internal tariffs on goods.

Although the Community's authority was limited to certain areas, within them important principles were established, not least the doctrine of direct effect and the supremacy of Community law over national law.[1]

But the issue of whether sovereignty had been transferred to a supranational body, the Community, or was "pooled," that is, collectively held by an association of states that reaches decisions on specified matters by a qualified majority, was muddied by the Luxembourg compromise reached in 1966 among certain member states outside the framework of the Treaties and never accepted as legitimate by some of the other member states. The Luxembourg compromise was a recognition of the right of a member to exercise a veto where a Community proposal affected an issue it regarded as being of fundamental national importance. It had no constitutional validity. It simply acknowledged that the major Community countries could not be compelled to accept and implement decisions they regarded as contrary to vital national interests.

Despite its dubious legitimacy, the Luxembourg compromise had a significant influence on the development of the Community between 1966 and 1984.[2] Two of the three new members who joined the Community in the 1970s, Britain and Denmark, were strong supporters of unanimity, and hence of the Luxembourg compromise, not least because they often found themselves in a minority on proposals that would extend the Community's competence. Decisions were no longer made by qualified majorities but by an exhausting attempt to achieve a consensus. On many issues, no consensus could be reached. The only way out of a series of stalemates that threatened the Community's momentum and credibility was the striking of political deals between governments at the highest level, deals made outside the Community's framework. The significance of the deals was such that heads of government became involved; the European Council emerged as the seat of strategic decisionmaking for the Community. The heads of government arrogated to themselves the pace, direction, and form of the Community's development.

The Community was a strange hybrid, its decisionmaking intergovernmental, its normative law supranational within its own areas of competence.[3] Sovereignty was pooled, but any member, relying on the Luxembourg accord, could block the extension of the *acquis communautaire* to new areas or its deepening in areas within the Community's jurisdiction;

the laborious and slow progress before 1985 in achieving a single market illustrates the point.

Several factors combined to bring pressure on the Commission and the Council to take dramatic action to break out of the stalemate and stagnation that characterized the Community's decisionmaking processes in the 1970s and early 1980s. The globalization of the market and increasing competition from other trading blocs threatened the Community's economic position. The recession of 1979–1984 had slowed the modest momentum toward the single market, modest because the process of harmonizing regulations, requiring unanimous support or at least acquiescence, was increasingly cumbersome. Consequently, the Community was associated with inertia, a complex and intricate regulatory pattern, and an inability to innovate, at a time when other trading blocs, the United States in particular, were rapidly deregulating. Charges of Eurosclerosis damaged the Community's image as a market worth investing in and as the inspiration for a renewal of Western Europe.

The institution most committed to the objective of European union, the European Parliament, had been urging with increasing passion, culminating in the Draft Treaty of European Union of February 14, 1984,[4] that a decisive move toward qualified voting and the pooling of sovereignty needed to be made if the Community was to regain momentum.

In June 1985, at the Milan summit, the European Council responded to these pressures, but not in the way the European Parliament had hoped. The Council resolved to complete the internal market by the end of 1992, and to do so by accepting weighted majority voting over a wide range of the directives needed for completion. Second, and as important, the Commission built upon the 1979 verdict of the European Court in the Cassis de Dijon case,[5] a verdict that established the principle of "mutual recognition," that products lawfully sold in one member country can be lawfully sold in all, providing they do not violate Community guidelines. "Mutual recognition" acts as a fail-safe mechanism for the single market; where new directives cannot be agreed upon, products and services will nonetheless be able to be traded.

The European Council's political commitment to a date for completion of the internal market had remarkable consequences. It led to "dynamic adjustment processes in the economic sphere whose political repercussions have all the force of a self-fulfilling prophecy."[6] Firms both inside and outside the Community made their decisions on the basis of the expectation of a single market. An extensive network of lobbyists and lawyers developed around the Community's institutions, most of them representing business interests and therefore pressing for business objectives, in particular deregulation. It is not surprising that the Single

European Act, which introduced qualified majority voting, at least as regards the directives needed to complete the single internal market, was supported by a government like that of Britain, whose defense of national sovereignty was rivaled only by its enthusiasm for deregulation.[7]

For the European Parliament, the Single European Act proved to be paradoxical. On the one hand, some enhancement of the European Parliament's powers was reluctantly conceded. On the other hand, the dynamic of the timetable for achieving a single market in a Community of countries with very disparate living standards and working conditions, coupled with the mutual-recognition doctrine, made it extremely difficult for the European Parliament to insist upon the upward harmonization of social and environmental standards, while effectively depriving the national parliaments of richer member states of the means to protect their existing high standards.

THE TRANSFER OF POWER

Governments do not sacrifice their powers absolutely. That is why sovereignty has been pooled rather than transferred. In practice, if not in theory, governments retain the right to leave the Community. Governments are represented on the Council of Ministers, and, at the level of heads of government, on the European Council, which meets twice a year. It is the Council of Ministers that decides whether to adopt a Commission proposal and whether to concur with amendments proposed by the European Parliament. More important, the European Council, despite the Single European Act, continues to be the arbiter of the Community's development and destiny.

It is not the European Council and the Council of Ministers that ensure the representation of national governments' opinions. At multiple levels of decisionmaking prior to or below the ministerial level, national civil servants are involved in the Community's decisionmaking processes, a system known in Brussels as comitology. Hundreds sit on the expert committees that advise the Commission on its proposals. Many more serve on the regulatory and management committees that work on the detailed implementation of Community directives, before they are finally passed over to national governments to administer. So governments have many opportunities to shape directives and to influence their execution; by the time the process is complete, few directives remain unaffected by national interests and the exercise of national influence through the Council, COREPER, or the subordinate committees largely staffed by national civil servants.[8]

For national parliaments, the loss of powers is without such compensation. They have little or no input into Commission proposals, certainly none formally. Their scrutiny of the process of framing and agreeing on a directive is often limited to hearing a report of what the Council has decided, which can be criticized but cannot be undone. Occasionally, popular discontent with Commission proposals (as on the harmonization of standards for beer or milk a decade ago) erupts into parliamentary pressure on ministers that can make them reconsider. But this is rare. Most national parliaments have until recently lacked effective mechanisms linking them to the European Parliament. They have been suspicious of attempts by the European Parliament to demand greater powers and have been unwilling to work closely with it in establishing a joint structure of parliamentary accountability. Their loss has *not* been Strasbourg's gain.

National parliamentary scrutiny, given the weakness of links to the European Parliament, has been largely ineffective. If I may take the example of the British Parliament, both Houses have committees to scrutinize Community legislation and can recommend that a proposal be debated by the House. Such debates are usually held outside prime parliamentary time and arouse only limited interest, as ministers rarely commit themselves before Council meetings and will therefore promise only to take parliamentary views into account. Ministers make a parliamentary statement after important Council meetings, and the Prime Minister invariably makes a statement (twice a year) after European Councils, but Parliament can only question and criticize after the event; the decisions cannot be reopened.

From time to time, ministers are questioned about the positions they will take at Council meetings. Commission proposals themselves are not within the jurisdiction of national parliaments, and Council proceedings are conducted in closed sessions, even at the final "legislative" stage where decisions on proposals are taken. It is therefore very difficult to get a handle on one's own government's policies. There is no senior minister in the House of Commons with specific responsibility for Community affairs, so debates are answered by the foreign secretary, or by the minister responsible for the subject under debate, for example, agriculture.[9]

One national parliament, however, has managed to retain significant leverage over the Council by dint of closely controlling its own national representatives at Council meetings. That country is Denmark. The Danes have a parliamentary committee on European Community legislation that is in near-permanent session. The committee extracts statements on the government's position prior to Council meetings, insists on being consulted as negotiations proceed, and holds its minister accountable for what happened. In practice, this strengthens the negotiating hand of the Danes but makes them rather uncomfortable partners. It also, on occasion, slows down proceedings. Danish insistence on accountability

---

occasion, slows down proceedings. Danish insistence on accountability to the national parliament works for the Danes, but, if extended to the other eleven, would make the Community unworkable. Danish practice flies in the face of Kant's categorical imperative.

Given the weakness of national parliaments as instruments to ensure the accountability of the Council and the Commission, can the European Parliament redress the balance? It has, after all, been directly elected since 1979. The 518 members of the European Parliament do not sit as national delegations but as members of Community-wide parties, and about a quarter of their official work is taken up by party meetings and party committees of one kind or another. Like the national civil servants on Commission committees, they interact constantly across national and language differences. Their friendships and their networks of interest and influence weave the fabric of parliamentary Europe.

The European Parliament has limited but not inconsiderable powers over expenditure in the Community's budget. But it has no authority to raise revenues, one of the fundamental prerogatives of parliaments in a democracy. The Community's "own" resources, first agricultural levies and then a share of value-added tax, derive from intergovernmental agreements, not from a decision of the European Parliament.

The European Parliament uses its budgetary powers to some effect; its approval is required for "noncompulsory" expenditure, which includes the now doubled expenditure on structural funds, as well as administrative costs and new activities like Community research programs or the protection of the environment. The limits on agricultural expenditure (which is a "compulsory expenditure") and the increase in the EC's own resources, both results of the acceptance of the 1987 Delors package, will increase the area of budget expenditure over which the European Parliament can exercise detailed control. But the use of the constitutional requirement that the total budget be adopted by the European Parliament to bring in Parliament's own interpretations and amendments has been curbed by the European Court of Justice's annulment of the decision by the President of Parliament on the 1986 budget, following a Council appeal.[10] The balance of power on controlling expenditure has therefore not been finally established.

When it comes to initiating proposals or influencing them, the EP's input remains marginal, though individual Commissioners or "cabinet" staff may privately consult influential members of the European Parliament before tabling the proposals. Committees of experts, some 550 of them in 1987, over 70 percent composed of national civil servants in a nonofficial capacity, are the architects and builders of Commission policy, not members of the European Parliament. Once proposals have been formulated by the Commission, in consultation with committees of experts, there is another process of official scrutiny to be gone through. The guardian of the gateway through which Commission proposals pass before reaching the Council is COREPER, which meets for two or more days a week. Working groups under COREPER meet to consider every aspect of the Commission's proposals. COREPER makes some decisions on details that never reach the Council. Other decisions are formally adopted by the Council without discussion, on COREPER'S advice. The major decisions taken by the Council are themselves influenced by civil-service advice to ministers at, and before, each Council meeting, though ministers, and certainly heads of government, quite often make decisions on their own. After the decision, the process of implementation is discussed by some 250 regulation, management, and consultation committees before the legislation is finally administered at the national level by the national bureaucracy. European Parliamentary scrutiny is entirely excluded from the implementation process, and very largely from the policymaking process, too.

The European Parliament is well aware of the importance of this bureaucratic structure in enhancing the influence of national governments and weakening that of the Commission and of Parliament itself. In its Resolution on European Union, Parliament complained: "despite the improvements which have occurred through the extension of majority voting in the Council, and the use of the co-operation procedure since adoption of the Single European Act, the Community's decision-making systems still lack efficiency and suffer from the dilatoriness of the Council in its legislative role and from regular interventions by the numerous committees of national civil servants in the Commission's executive tasks."[11]

Despite its limited influence, the European Parliament does derive its authority from the people. The Council and the Commission do not: Their authority is derived from the member states, each represented on every Council, and each of whom appoints one or two Commissioners to the seventeen-member Commission.

The Commission's position is ambivalent. Commissioners swear, on appointment, that "they shall neither seek, nor take, instructions from any Government or from any other body."[12] They must be loyal to the Community as a whole. In this sense, the Commission embodies the concept of collective decisionmaking within the Community. The Commission is constitutionally accountable to the European Parliament, which has the right to demand the Commission's resignation en bloc. In practice, however, this right is a deterrent that cannot be exercised without threatening the destruction of the Community itself. Each Commissioner is protected from the wrath of the European Parliament by the consequences for all.

Furthermore, each Commissioner knows that his or her individual reappointment will be decided not by the Council as a whole nor by the European Parliament but by the decision of the national government that appointed him or her in the first place. Some Commissioners are motivated by the Community spirit the Merger Act enjoins upon them and act with remarkable determination and independence. Others have been appointed toward the end of their careers as a reward for a lifetime of public service. A third group looks to their national governments for the advancement of their careers, and these Commissioners may become instruments for their own governments' policies toward the Community. Whatever the Treaties say, Commissioners are effectively answerable to their President, their colleagues, and their governments rather than to the European Parliament.

THE DEMOCRATIC DEFICIT

Neither the European Parliament nor the national parliaments would claim to be effective in scrutinizing the Council of Ministers and in shaping European legislation, despite the recent improvements in the European Parliament's role following the Single European Act. The "democratic deficit" is the gap between the powers transferred to the Community level and the control of the elected Parliament over them, a gap filled by national civil servants operating as European experts or as members of regulation and management committees, and to some extent by organized lobbies, mainly representing business. These civil servants are acquiring a detailed knowledge of the Community, which complements their knowledge of their own country's administration. National government ministers whose portfolios fall within the area of Community competence—finance, agriculture, foreign affairs, trade and industry, and more recently transport and the environment—are gaining a similar insight. But most national politicians, leading members of the opposition and backbenchers alike, have no role in the Community. The national civil servants they scrutinize are building a knowledge and an influence over large areas of policy they cannot begin to match. "The 'losers,'" writes Wolfgang Wessels, "are the parliamentarians and parties; their patterns of interaction have not developed resources and forms comparable to those of national bureaucrats and (governmental) politicians."[13] One of the unforeseen consequences of the Community, therefore, beyond the transfer of sovereignty in specified areas, is the weakening of national parliaments vis-à-vis their own executives, even in those areas that lie outside Community competence at the present time.

The European Parliament has tried to get a greater purchase on the Community decisionmaking proceedings, from which it is so largely excluded. Its own committees shadow the major areas of Community involvement; on occasion the chairs of relevant European Parliament committees have taken part in Council meetings. Council members, and of course Commissioners, are invited to appear before the European Parliament to answer questions, and since 1973 there have been two regular, oral question times at each parliamentary session, one for the President of the Council, the other for the Commission.

The European Parliament might more effectively question the Commission and the President of the Council, and national parliaments might exercise more effective scrutiny over their own minister at the Council, if they knew what went on. However, the Council of Ministers meets in camera, even when it is discussing Commission proposals and reaching a common position on them—a process that might be described as legislative debate, as distinct from the multiple deal-making that characterizes the twice-yearly meetings of the European Council. Even the minutes of Council meetings are not made public. The absence of public debate reduces media interest in Council meetings; there is an anodyne press statement after most Council meetings but little opportunity for media questioning of the participants. Each minister tells his or her own national media what he or she wants them to hear. Hence the only well-informed commentary on Council meetings comes from a number of internationally published newspapers and journals with small but influential readerships, such as the *Financial Times*, the *Wall Street Journal*, the *International Herald Tribune*, and the *Economist*, to mention only the major English-language publications. These have multiple sources in different countries and can therefore piece together what actually happened. Even the best national newspapers rely almost entirely on national government sources for their European stories, as does television, though occasionally a foreign head of government may be interviewed.

The absence of nationally known politicians (other than government spokespersons) from the Community decisionmaking process has reduced media interest in both the European Parliament and even the Community. The politics of rhetoric at the national level remains more compelling than the confusing procedural manipulations in Strasbourg. In societies where politics and the media are mutually dependent in the business of attracting public attention, one consequence has been a low level of public participation, exemplified by poor voting turnouts in European elections. With the exception of a few famous politicians on the point of retirement (like Spinelli and Brandt), the European Parliament has attracted few well-known national politicians (though unquestionably able and gifted ones), because its powers have been so limited and its coverage so slight. Name recognition of members of the European Parliament is low, and access to them is difficult. Indeed, the respect in which the European Parliament is held is exemplified by its geographical isolation in Strasbourg, far away from the executive it is meant to scrutinize and remote from the main arteries of Europe's transport system.

The Single European Act

The Single European Act, ratified in 1987, grudgingly conferred some additional functions on the European Parliament, among them the power of assent to the accession of new members and to trade and cooperation agreements under Article 238 of the Rome Treaty, and a cooperation procedure involving the European Parliament in decisions taken by qualified majorities in specified areas, such as the completion of the internal market. These new functions fell far short of the European Parliament's demands, expressed in its 1984 Draft Treaty for European Union,[14] for joint decisionmaking in all Community legislation. Indeed, the European Parliament denounced the European Act, saying "it in no way represents the real reforms our people need."[15] The Act was a constitutional prerequisite if the internal market was to be completed according to the Council's timetable, and the completion of the internal market was the main objective of the business lobby and of those European governments responsive to business interests. The functions conferred on Parliament seemed little more than sops to calm the clamor from European-minded MEPs, fired by the heady rhetoric of Spinelli's vision of European union.

But from these sops, the European Parliament is piecing together substantial extra influence on decisionmaking, more than the Council ever conceived. In its first reading of a Commission proposal, the European Parliament gives its opinion, as it was able to do before the Single European Act. Parliament's opinion is taken into account by the Council in reaching a common position. That common position is then submitted to Parliament for a second reading, which has to take place within a maximum of three months. The European Parliament can then accept, reject, or amend the common opinion. If Parliament rejects it, a unanimous vote of the Council is required to override the rejection. If Parliament amends the common position and the Commission agrees with those amendments, only a qualified majority of the Council is required to endorse them. But if the Commission disagrees with the European Parliament, a unanimous vote of the Council is required to override the Commission and adopt the amendments.

The European Parliament is already learning how to use its new functions to gain as much influence as possible over the Community's decisionmaking processes. The threat of rejection is used to get pledges that Parliament's amendments will be accepted. In 1980, before the Single European Act, the European Court of Justice struck down legislation approved by the Council on the grounds that the European Parliament had not been consulted. So the European Parliament, building on that verdict, now threatens to delay giving its opinion in order to get changes to common positions. It recently used that threat effectively in its battle with the Council to raise the environmental standards controlling emissions from small cars; and in December 1989 the European Council meeting at Strasbourg was unable to take final decisions on the first stage of monetary union because the European Parliament had not yet expressed its opinion on the measures the Commission had proposed.

Changed Circumstances, New Powers

The European Parliament is trying to build on its joint decisionmaking powers with regard to accession and cooperation agreements by insisting on participating in the negotiations themselves and in the preparation of negotiating briefs. In 1985 the joint decisionmaking powers conceded to the European Parliament in respect to Article 238 must have seemed of marginal importance. No new countries were seeking to join the Community, following the major expansion involved in incorporating Spain, Portugal, and, earlier, Greece within the Community. Pressure for association agreements was modest because the Community was mired in a long period of inactivity. But now the concession of joint decisionmaking powers to the European Parliament looks very different.

The new drive toward completing the internal market has alerted the Community's closest trading partners. The European Free Trade Area, for one, is seeking to upgrade further its existing association agreement and to establish an institutional dialogue with the Community (although the Commission has firmly discouraged any notion that EFTA might be involved in Community decisionmaking procedures). Austria has formally applied for Community membership and Sweden has declared its intention to do so; others are actively discussing whether to apply at a later date. Turkey, linked through NATO to most of the Community's members in a common defense strategy, is another candidate for membership.

Following the political upheavals of 1989, a queue of countries in Central and Eastern Europe is seeking some kind of association and even some assurance that they may accede to the Community at a later date, raising huge and difficult questions about the Community's identity and cohesion. The European Parliament's joint decisionmaking powers in respect to new members and association agreements have therefore become much more significant. Indeed, the European Parliament's insistence on being consulted before negotiating briefs are drawn up and during the course of negotiations could pave the way for parliamentary participation in European political cooperation and in the framing of its most delicate component, the Community's policies toward Eastern Europe and the Soviet Union.

The manifestation of "people power" in Eastern Europe has other consequences for the European Parliament. In short order, the Eastern European countries have held free multiparty elections and set up the institutions of democracy. The Commission requires that these basic conditions are met before it provides Community aid. Yet the Community itself offers no model to these emerging democracies of an effective, accountable democratic structure. Indeed, demonstrating all too clearly the frustration of its own attempts to enhance its powers, the European Parliament somewhat paradoxically resolved in 1989 that it would not agree to the accession of any new member until those powers have been conceded.[16]

The whole cloth that the EP is trying to make is woven out of sparse fragments. Jealous of its own prerogatives, the Council made sure that the Single European Act was limited, as far as qualified majority voting is concerned, to the completion of the internal market. However, the internal market has its own momentum. As barriers to the movement of goods and services are removed, the anomaly of differences in taxes is highlighted. And taxes are Parliament's business.

Raising revenue lies at the very heart of a legislature's power in a democracy. It was the raising of taxes that drove monarchs into dependence on their parliaments and unrepresented colonists to revolution. The Community escaped from dependence on Parliament by way of its own resources, gleaned first from agricultural levies and then, at one remove, from a small proportion of nationally raised value-added tax. Decisions on the level of value-added tax are made by national parliaments. But now the logic of the internal market is driving the Commission toward fiscal and economic harmonization, raising the issues both of sovereignty and of democratic accountability in one of the most sensitive areas. The Delors Committee Report is blunt: "The success of the internal market performance hinges to a decisive extent on a much closer coordination of national economic policies, as well as on more effective Community policies. This implies that in essence a number of steps towards economic and monetary union will already have to be taken in the course of establishing a single market in Europe."[17]

Fine civil servant that he was, Arthur Cockfield (later Lord Cockfield) had perceived this necessity when he first became Commissioner for the internal market in 1984. The achievement of the single market "is not the ultimate goal," he wrote in his 1985 White Paper; "at best it is the precursor"—to, of course, "the ever closer union among the peoples of Europe." His painstaking and detailed blueprint for 1992 included proposals for harmonizing excise taxes and establishing two broad bands, a low and a high one, for value-added tax. Each band allowed limited flexibility for national VAT rates, within the same kinds of constraints that apply to state taxes in the United States. Cockfield, however, was no politician. His proposals set off a firestorm of controversy about Community interference with national prerogatives. The Commission backed down, bowing to national demands to retain both zero rates and very high rates. But of course Cockfield was right. Widely divergent rates of value-added tax and excise are not compatible with a single internal market. Some reconciliation of national differences in taxation has been achieved by the Commission, but it has fallen well short of fiscal harmonization. Such harmonization is inescapable if the Community is to have a genuine single market, though in the short run the refunding of national taxes to suppliers through a Community clearinghouse may provide a basis for compromise. In other words, a single market implies economic and monetary union. It is the logical next step.

The Community also faces another fiscal problem. By 1992, its resources will be insufficient to meet the growing demands on its budget, let alone to finance unexpected needs like those of Eastern Europe. The convergence of these two needs, for greater revenue and tax harmonization, brings the issue of democratic accountability to a head. For control over the national budget is the most important of the formal powers remaining with national parliaments. If a substantial part of those powers is transferred to the Community level, so that the Commission, with the agreement of the Council, raises its own revenue by levying taxes directly on Community citizens, but not on the member states, to whom will it be accountable? The democratic answer must be to the European Parliament. Will the European Parliament then gain the power of joint decisionmaking over the raising of Community revenue? The cooperation procedure might be held to operate in this area, as fiscal harmonization is a spillover from the process of establishing an internal market, but the cooperation procedure is weaker than national parliamentary powers and weaker than joint decisionmaking. The issue of public accountability is likely to come to a crunch on this matter.

The other areas of competence that arouse intense concern among European Parliamentarians are the environment and social policy. This concern is a further by-product of the drive to set up a single market and of the acceptance of "mutual recognition" rather than harmonization as a way to do so. Given the great inequalities of living standards among Community countries, and the widely different national criteria for working conditions, health and safety, worker representation, and environmental protection, there is a real danger that the regulatory structure of the richer countries will be undermined or bypassed rather than becoming the model to which the poorer countries aspire. That is why MEPs so relentlessly pursue their demand that qualified majority voting should apply to environmental and social policies.

So far the European Parliament has had only limited success. Social policy and environmental policy are now subject to the cooperation procedure. But voting still requires unanimity; any member can block proposals for action. In an effort to avoid the veto, the European Parliament pressed for a decision by a majority on the Community Charter of Fundamental Social Rights (the "Social Charter") and got it. On a proposal from the Commission, the charter was adopted at the Strasbourg Council of Ministers in December 1989 by eleven to one.[18] But the charter has no legislative force. It does not extend the Community's jurisdiction to social policy. It is a declaration of principle to which future directives on working conditions, health and safety, employment, and training will be expected to conform.

The Commission, which certainly wants the Community to be more than just a single market, a "businessman's Europe," is sympathetic to Parliament's objective. Jacques Delors, President of the Commission and an ex-member of the Community's Economic and Social Committee (which brings together representatives of the "social partners," industry and the trade unions) has identified himself closely with the Social Charter. On a momentous occasion at the British Trade Union Congress annual conference, he expounded it to such effect that the congress, long divided on the issue of Community membership, gave him a standing ovation. (It was a green light on the Labour party's road to Damascus, for Labour in the same year reversed its policy of negotiating its way out of the Community.)

The Social Charter, however, is more than a means of gaining the support of labor for the Commission—and indeed for a process of deregulation that, without the Social Charter, is deeply unattractive to organized labor. It is a platform on which that consummate politician and longtime member of the French Socialist party, Jacques Delors, can stand. For Delors's career is not planned to end with the Commission presidency, but with the presidency of the French Republic. As a potential national leader, Delors knows his record as Commission President will be taken into account in France; it must therefore be a record acceptable to French voters and to members of his own party. Deregulation without social provision for its consequences will not be well received by his party or its counterparts throughout Europe. Hence Delors's emphasis on "the European model," the social market or welfare capitalism, as distinct from the U.S. model of market capitalism.

That Delors is a political actor with ambitions to reenter the national democratic process helps to shape Community policy. He is virtually unique. Commissioners, like MEPs, have often been politicians, but usually politicians compensated for a disappointment, like loss of office, or rewarded for years of service. Few have had national political careers ahead of them. Jenkins was one such, but because he was rethinking his party allegiance at the time, his period of office as Commission President was not influenced by his future position in his then party. In Britain, Edward Heath and now Michael Heseltine have put the Community at the top of their own personal political agendas but have not moved from the national stage to the European Parliament. Better to be a past or future member of the European Council than chair of a largely powerless EP committee.

A People's Europe

This attenuated political scene does not convey the anger, the passion, the commitment, and the partisanship that constitute the lifeblood of politics. Nor does it facilitate the expression of popular opinion. Strasbourg, and of course Brussels, are accessible to professional lobbyists— many, incidentally, from the United States and Japan—with company credit cards in their pockets. But Strasbourg is inaccessible to Greek peasants, Portuguese fishermen, Spanish factory workers, and Scottish bank clerks. MEPs' advice centers in their own constituencies attract nothing like the number of constituents national members get, for bread-and-butter issues like housing, social security, schools, garbage collection, and parking, all of them outside the Community's jurisdiction, fill constituency mailbags. The occasional inquiry from a firm or a trade union is usually referred to their own national organizations, well represented in the Economic and Social Committee.

But without citizen participation, Citizens' Europe languishes. For all the high-pressure public relations on Europe 1992, the man and woman in the European street feel uninvolved. The proposals that might have touched them, such as the abolition of frontier controls, the right of residence anywhere in the Community, and the right to vote in other members' national elections as well as in European elections, have been bogged down in wrangling among member states.

Frontier controls, themselves symbolic of the goal of a single internal market, are most unlikely to be gone by 1992, even within the Schengen group (Germany, France, the Netherlands, Belgium, and Luxembourg), who agreed to remove frontiers between one another. The unwillingness of member states to harmonize VAT or excise within narrow bands makes the removal of frontier controls impracticable, quite apart from issues of terrorism and drug trafficking. Instead of visible proof to every Community citizen that a single market has been achieved, there will be visible proof of a two-speed market, the Schengen core and the periphery. Yet the British and others are not just being perverse. There are acute political problems in imposing VAT on zero-rated essentials like food and children's clothes. And there are real difficulties in policing terrorism and drug trafficking without frontier controls, especially in a country whose citizens do not carry identity cards or papers and would resent being made to do so.

The foundations of a European identity might be laid in the schools, but many member states fiercely defend their own turf when it comes to education, which is not within the Community's jurisdiction. School curricula still recount national histories and national geographies. Attempts to create a European core curriculum have run into resistance in several member states.

As the influential French writer Alain Minc has recently emphasized, to build financial Europe is not the same as building Europe. The Community's institutions have been almost wholly concentrated on economic and financial issues and, within these areas, on issues of interest to business rather than to labor. The Social Charter was an attempt to balance the emphasis on competitiveness and growth with concern for working conditions and worker participation, and with the establishment of certain basic social rights, including the right to a minimum income. The political will to make the Social Charter more than a rhetorical statement is not yet evident; indeed the charter is politically highly divisive not only *among* the member states but also *within* certain member states. Other issues that most closely engage individuals and families, like health, housing, social services, and school education, remain firmly within national jurisdiction.

The rare Community programs in these areas that member states agree to, such as Commett and Erasmus, two scientific and educational exchange programs, are more favorable for the Community's image than all the work to remove economic and technical barriers: Witness the thousands of students now studying in Community countries outside their own borders. The enrollment of hundreds of Irish students in Northern Irish universities is but one striking instance of the way Community programs can help to heal old wounds.

There is a growing sense of Europeanness. It shows up in the movement of people across Europe's frontiers for pleasure or for work. The density and frequency of interchange is creating a European "footprint" (to borrow a term from television), most marked in the core of the countries along the Rhine and around the golden triangle of Paris-Bonn-Milan. This European footprint overlaps other footprints, close historical associations between EC members and non-EC states. It is still discernible in Central Europe and beyond, as far east as Riga and Kiev. This "Europe" is a Europe that shares historical memories, dreams of a common civilization, and is drawn toward the nucleus of the Community (to shift the metaphor) like electrons in an atom. The Community's effect on this Europe is profound. But if the nucleus itself is not structured as a fully accountable democracy, the fragments it attracts may not be— or become—so either.

REDRESSING THE DEMOCRATIC DEFICIT

We return to the question of how democratic accountability in the Community can be strengthened. Of the three institutions engaged in policymaking (I exclude the European Court of Justice, though the Court's verdicts have unquestionably affected policymaking procedures), links between the Commission and the European Parliament, and between the Commission and the Council, are strong. The weak link is the relationship between the Council and the European Parliament. However, before turning to that relationship, let me consider one or two ways in which the link between the Commission and the European Parliament might be strengthened.

There seems no good reason why Commissioners nominated by national governments should not be subject to a confirmation process in the European Parliament. Confirmation would give each Commissioner independent authority, would underline the Commission's accountability to the European Parliament, and would make much more convincing each Commissioner's commitment to the Community rather than to his or her national government. Parliament should also be able to petition for the dismissal of a Commissioner, though the procedure should be sufficiently difficult to inhibit its use other than in exceptional circumstances.

Much harder would be the transformation of the comitology from a corpus of largely national civil servants to a corpus of European ones. So long as implementation remains the responsibility of national governments, committees concerned with implementation and regulation should be composed mainly, though not entirely, of national civil servants. But that argument does not hold good for expert advisory committees. These committees should be much more reflective of the "European interest." Some of their members could be drawn from the ranks of independent experts, on the payroll of neither a national government nor the Community itself. They should not be answerable to COREPER. Because its members represent the nation-states, COREPER should become the bureaucratic arm of the Council, not of the Commission as well.

The European Parliament cannot be effective as the body to which the Commission is accountable if it holds its sessions in a place inconveniently far removed from Brussels. The sheer logistical burden of a Parliament whose members and staff have to move every month between three different capitals hampers everything it does. The lack of any sense of urgency among national governments about this absurd situation exemplifies the contempt with which they regard the European Parliament. If it is to do its job better, the EP must move to Brussels.

Neither the EP nor the national parliaments can scrutinize the Council effectively while it meets in secret. It is reasonable for the Council to meet in secret when it is behaving like a summit meeting or a cabinet, working out deals and reaching accommodations. But when the Council moves into its legislative mode, debating and even voting on Community proposals, after the EP has submitted its amendments, it should act in the open, as any democratic legislative body does. When European union is achieved, the Council might evolve into an upper house, a Bundesrat of the Community, a development of its legislative rather than its executive mode; then it would have to operate openly.

THE EUROPEAN PARLIAMENT AND THE NATIONAL PARLIAMENTS

The key objective of the EP is joint decisionmaking over the whole of Community legislation. Apart from resistance by the Council of Ministers, there is one obvious threat to that objective: conflict between the EP and national governments. Constitutionally, joint decisionmaking over the raising of revenue is a sine qua non of accountability, and, as already discussed, fiscal harmonization cannot be long postponed. But taxation and revenue-raising powers lie at the heart of the power of national parliaments, too. So an institutional link between the EP and the national parliaments is essential, and is one way to strengthen parliamentary accountability, at European and national levels, vis-à-vis the Council of Ministers.

One way of achieving that institutional link would be to have in each national parliament a committee chaired by a cabinet minister for Europe, to scrutinize and debate all substantial Community proposals. The country's MEPs would serve on this committee alongside national members of parliament. Some member countries are already doing this. There would be problems in scheduling so the timetables of both the EP and the national parliaments would have to be adjusted to allow for regular and frequent meetings of these joint committees. The committees could summon national ministers, national civil servants, and Commission members or staff to give evidence.

The frequent association of MEPs with national parliamentarians would enable each to feed information to the other. Legislators would be in a similar position to ministers in the Council, who bridge national and Community agendas and whose influence is thereby greatly strengthened. The work of these committees would be complemented from time to time by "assizes"—meetings between committees of the European Parliament and corresponding committees of national parliaments to discuss a particular issue, agricultural policy or transportation policy, for example. In this way, MEPs and members of national parliaments would be brought together not only in the context of their common representation of the people of one member state but also in the context of their shared responsibilities for certain functions of government.

To achieve greater democratic accountability in the Community will be difficult; the present situation, unsatisfactory though it is, makes life easy for the Council of Ministers. It will require from national parliaments recognition of the world as it is, that power is inevitably moving to Brussels and that a deal with MEPs is a prerequisite of national parliaments' exercising some control over their ministers. It requires from the European Parliament the political will to be tough, to fight for its constitutional position as the Dutch or British parliaments did centuries ago. It should insist on joint decisionmaking on revenue-raising matters, including setting harmonized tax bands. It should press for the right of European Parliament committee chairs to be included when Councils discuss their subject. And it should refuse to sanction any further derogations from a single voting system for the European Parliament.

A single voting system would pave the way to much closer cooperation among European political parties. It is not inconceivable that national political parties might consult each other as to the order of names on the party lists, thereby ensuring that politicians respected in the Community outside their own countries would be elected to the European Parliament (there are several European prophets without honor in their own countries but much honored elsewhere). A common voting system would also simplify the Byzantine complexity of twelve national systems, albeit eleven have some form of proportional representation.

Ever since its Draft Treaty for European Union of February 1984, the European Parliament has reiterated its concerns about the democratic deficit, the inadequacies of the Treaties even as amended by the Single European Act, and the slow progress toward a Citizens' Europe. It has emphasized, in the report of its Committee on International Affairs, the reforms it regards as key: joint decisionmaking with the Council over all areas where the Community has legislative competence; systematic

majority voting in the Council; the Commission's right to exercise
executive powers independently of the comitology of national civil
servants; the confirmation of the European Commission and its President
by the European Parliament; the right to initiate legislative proposals;
the right of inquiry; and the requirement that the European Parliament
ratify any constitutional decisions, international agreements, and conventions that require ratification by member states.[19]

The European Parliament hopes to increase its powers in the wake
of an intergovernmental consensus behind economic and monetary union,
as it did through the Single European Act in the wake of intergovernmental
consensus on the timetable for the internal market. At the Madrid
European Council in December 1989, the EP was rebuffed; no steps
were taken to widen the agenda of the 1990 Intergovernmental Conference.

Showing greater political astuteness than in the past, the European
Parliament in its approach to the 1990 Intergovernmental Conference
sought to mobilize the national parliaments on its side to support the
widening of the IGC agenda. The European Parliament demonstrated
that it recognized the role of the national parliaments in the future
constitutional structure of the Community by inviting them to collaborate
in drawing up a draft constitution for a European union.

These efforts bore fruit. Mitterrand, in a speech to the European
Parliament in November 1989, and Jacques Delors, President of the
Commission, in his speech there on January 17, 1990, referred to the
need for national parliaments to be consulted about the IGC and to be
brought into partnership with the European Parliament. At the special
Dublin summit on April 28, 1990, the European Council endorsed a
Franco-German proposal for an intergovernmental conference on political
reform parallel to that on European monetary union. Paradoxically, it
was not the years of pressure by the EP that moved the Community's
two most significant members. It was the need to anchor a united
Germany firmly into a Community structure that was, and was to be
seen to be, democratic.

Achieving a consensus on political union would have been difficult
in any case, as member states have very different objectives, ranging
from full-blown federalism to a modest increase in the European Parliament's powers of scrutiny. But the task has been made much more
arduous by the eruption of the crisis in the Persian Gulf. The Gulf War
illuminated, like a conflagration, every crack and fissure between the
Community's members on foreign policy matters. On one side of a fault
line that runs along the Rhine are countries who see themselves as
playing a world, or at least an Atlantic, role, however diminished by
their relative economic decline that role may be. On the other side are

those who have eschewed military action other than for their own defense and who feel uneasy about heroic political postures. The different responses of a France, a Britain, an Italy, and a Germany to the Gulf War suggest that political cooperation on foreign policy will be very hard to realize and that the convergence of interests between the member states has a long way to go before it will be feasible. On the other hand, concern for establishing some system of security and order, probably based on CSCE, in Eastern Europe and the disintegrating Soviet Union may propel the Community countries toward a common strategy.

The other factors that drive the Community closer to political union remain, regardless of the Gulf War. These are German unification and the progress toward monetary and economic union. Monetary and economic union may be a slower process than the 1989 Delors Report envisaged, first, because Britain will now be within rather than outside that process, second, because John Major's hard Ecu proposal, and the probable lengthening of the second, transitional stage of monetary union, are both attracting increasing support. The process does, however, offer the European Parliament another opportunity to extend its own limited powers and to strengthen democratic accountability.

Mikhail Gorbachev once spoke of a "common European house." If the Community is to retain its identity within this amorphous European house, it will have to define that identity, what distinguishes the Community from the European countries around it. The Community is identified by its decisionmaking institutions in which sovereignty is pooled. That distinguishes it from EFTA or any other close association of countries. But if the Community is to be what it claims to be, the hub of Europe and the democratic model for Europeans, then its decisionmaking institutions must become truly accountable, not to Europe's governments or its bureaucrats, but to its people.

NOTES

An earlier version of this chapter was published in *The Political Quarterly* 61, 3 (1990): 299–317. Used with permission.

1. Case 26/62, *Van Gend en Loos* v. *Nederlandse administratie der belastingen* (1963), European Court Reports (ECR) 1; case 6/64, *Costa* v. *Enel* (1964), ECR 585; case 41/74, *Van Duyn* v. *Home Office* (1974), ECR 1337. For a detailed discussion, see Chapter 6, by G. Federico Mancini, in this volume.

2. Joseph H. H. Weiler, "The Community System: The Dual Character of Supranationalism," *Yearbook of European Law* (1981), p. 267.

3. Ibid.

4. *Bulletin of the European Communities* 17, 2 (1984).

5. Case 120/78, *Rewe-Zentral AG* v. *Bundesmonopolverwaltung für Branntwein* (*Cassis de Dijon*) (1979), ECR 649.

6. Fritz W. Scharpf, *The Joint-Decision Trap: Lessons from German Federalism and European Integration* (Berlin, 1989), postscript.

7. Renaud Dehousse, *1992 and Beyond: The Institutional Dimension of the Internal Market Challenge*. Legal Issues of European Integration, European Institute, University of Amsterdam (Boston: Law and Taxation Publishers, 1989).

8. Wolfgang Wessels, *The Community Bureaucracy at the Crossroads*, College of Europe, new series 42 (Brussels: De Tempel, 1985).

9. Several member countries have now appointed Ministers for Community Affairs.

10. Case 34/86, *Council* v. *European Parliament* (1986), ECR 2155.

11. Resolution on European Union, February 16, 1989, *Official Journal of the European Communities (OJ)*, 1989 (89/C 69).

12. Treaty establishing a Single Council and a Single Commission of the Communities, 1965, Article 10.

13. Wessels, *Community Bureaucracy.*

14. *Bulletin of the European Communities* 17, 2 (1984).

15. Resolution of January 16, 1986, *OJ*, 1986 (86/C 36).

16. Resolution on European Union.

17. Delors Committee Report on Economic and Monetary Union (Brussels: European Commission, April 1989).

18. *European Community News*, no. 41/89, December 11, 1989.

19. The Martin Report (see European Parliament Resolution of November 27, 1989), *OJ*.

6

The Making of a Constitution for Europe

G. Federico Mancini

For educated observers of European affairs, whether friends or foes of a strong Community, the magnitude of the contribution made by the Court of Justice to the integration of Europe has almost become a byword. It is unnecessary to quote the friends, which in any event, because they tend to be enthusiastic, would be somewhat embarrassing for a member of the Court. Far more interesting are the enemies or the less-than-lukewarm supporters of a united Europe. In Britain politicians who openly criticize judges are frowned upon; Thatcher, a barrister, is aware of this rule and cannot therefore be quoted, though her private reactions to judgments encroaching on British sovereign rights and interests are easy to visualize. But that old, unredeemed Gaullist, the former Prime Minister Michel Debré, is eminently quotable: "I accuse the Court of Justice," he said as late as 1979, "of morbid megalomania," by which, of course, he meant insufficient deference to the sovereign rights and interests of France.

If one were asked to synthesize the direction in which the case law produced in Luxembourg has moved since 1957, one would have to say that it coincides with the making of a constitution for Europe. Unlike the United States, the EC was born as a peculiar form of international organization. Its peculiarity resided in the unique institutional structure and the unprecedented law-making and judicial powers it was given. But these features—admittedly reminiscent of a federal state—should not overshadow two essential facts: First, whereas the U.S. Declaration of Independence speaks of *"one people"* dissolving the bonds that connected them with *"another people,"* the preamble of the Rome Treaty recites that the contracting parties are "determined to lay the foundations of an ever closer union among the *peoples* of Europe."[1] Second and more important, the instrument giving rise to the Community was a traditional multilateral *treaty*.

Treaties are basically different from constitutions. In many countries (and "many" includes even some of the founding states of the EC) they do not enjoy the status of higher law. The interpretation of treaties is subject to canons unlike all others (such as, for example, the presumption that states do not lose their sovereignty). As a rule, treaties devise systems of checks and balances whose main function is to keep under control the powers of the organization they set up. In the case of the Rome Treaty, these differences are emphasized by two highly significant characteristics. The Treaty does not safeguard the fundamental rights of the individuals affected by its application nor does it recognize, even in an embryonic form, a constitutional right to European citizenship. Europe cannot confer citizenship; this remains the prerogative of the member states. By the same token, individual citizens of a member state are entitled to move from their state to another member state exclusively by virtue of their being workers, self-employed persons, or providers of services, that is, as units of a factor of production.

The main endeavor of the Court of Justice has precisely been to remove or reduce the differences just mentioned. In other words, the Court has sought to "constitutionalize" the Treaty, to fashion a constitutional framework for a quasi-federal structure in Europe. Whether this effort was always inspired by a clear and consistent philosophy is arguable, but that is not really important. What really matters are its achievements—and they are patent to all.

To be sure, the Court has been helped by favorable circumstances. The combination of being, as it were, out of sight and out of mind by virtue of its location in the fairy-tale Grand Duchy of Luxembourg and the benign neglect of the media has certainly contributed to its ability to create a sense of belonging on the part of its independent-minded members and, where necessary, to convert them into confirmed Europeans.[2] Furthermore, the judges and advocates general have usually been middle-aged, and at least half of them have been academics. As a group, therefore, they have never met the three conditions of Lord Diplock's famous verdict: "By training, temperament and age judges are too averse to change to be entrusted with the development of rules of conduct for a brave new world."[3]

Nevertheless, these circumstances do not explain the whole story. The Court would have been far less successful had it not been assisted by two mighty allies: the national courts and the Commission. The institutional position of the former will be clarified below. It is sufficient to mention here that by referring to Luxembourg sensitive questions of interpretation of Community law, the national courts have been indirectly responsible for the boldest judgments the Court has made. Moreover, by adhering to these judgments in deciding the cases before them, and therefore by lending them the credibility national judges usually enjoy in their own countries, they have rendered the case law of the Court both effective and respected throughout the Community.

As to the Commission, the founding fathers and especially Jean Monnet conceived it as a sort of "Platonic embodiment of Communitarian spirit, with Gallic élan, self-confidence and expertise."[4] As the executive-political branch of the Community, the Commission may not have always lived up to those expectations, but as "watchdog of the Treaty," that is, both as the prosecutor of member-state infractions and as an amicus curiae on cases referred by the national courts, it has undoubtedly played a positive role. In other words, the Commission has led the Court— particularly by assuaging the concern some of the judges may have felt regarding the acceptability of their rulings[5]—on the path toward further integration and increased Community power.

On the other hand, the Parliament and the Council are not natural allies of the Court. The Parliament evinced great sympathy for the Court in the 1960s and 1970s, but then its function was simply that of a debating forum. More recently, however, the Parliament has been involved in a permanent trial of strength with the Council: The stake is a new allocation of power in the budgetary and legislative areas. The Court is a victim of this (in itself entirely legitimate) turbulence. The reason is obvious. Luxembourg is more and more encumbered by increasingly political and emotion-loaded intra-Community controversies: hence a visibility and an exposure to scrutiny by the media that are in sharp contrast with the conditions under which progress was made in the past.

The Council, the Community legislative body, is bound not to be an ally of the Court. Although formally an institution with supranational characteristics like the others, it was drawn by its very composition— a gathering of national ministers—into resembling an intergovernmental roundtable often characterized by all the warmth of a love match in a snake pit. In other words, its members regularly speak, and no doubt think, in terms of negotiating with their partners much as they would do in any other international context.[6] The observation that "decisionally, the Community is closer to the United Nations than it is to the United States" is therefore particularly telling.[7]

This situation is heightened by the weight acquired in the area of lawmaking by COREPER and its many subcommittees. Although a minister may occasionally be expected to deal with a given problem in a supranational spirit, it would be naive to expect an ambassador or a

national bureaucrat, with whatever leanings, to assist willfully in the
process of the wasting away of member-state power, thereby blighting
his own career.

CONSTITUTIONALIZING THE TREATY

I noted above that, unlike federal constitutions, the treaties creating
international organizations do not usually enjoy higher-law status with
regard to the laws of the contracting powers. Article 6 of the U.S.
Constitution reads: "The laws of the United States . . . shall be the
supreme law of the land; and the judges in every state shall be bound
thereby; any thing in the constitution or laws of any state to the contrary
notwithstanding." In the same vein, Section 109 of the Australian
Constitution provides that "when a law of a State is inconsistent with
a law of the Commonwealth the latter shall prevail and the former shall
be . . . invalid," and the German Fundamental Law stipulates just as
clearly that *Bundesrecht bricht Landesrecht* (federal law outweighs state
law). On the contrary, the Rome Treaty, while including some hortatory
provisions to the same effect (Article 5), fails to state squarely whether
Community law is preeminent vis-à-vis prior and subsequent member-
state law.

The now undisputed existence of a supremacy clause in the Community
framework is therefore a product of judicial creativity. In *Costa* v. *Enel*,[8]
a case that arose in the early 1960s before a *giudice conciliatore* (local
magistrate) in Milan, a shareholder of a nationalized power company
challenged as being contrary to the Treaty the Italian law nationalizing
the electric industry. The Italian government claimed before the Court
of Justice that the Court had no business to deal with the matter: The
magistrate, it said, should apply the nationalization law as the most
current indication of parliamentary intention and could not avail himself
of the reference procedure provided for by the Treaty. But the Court
ruled that "by creating a Community of unlimited duration, having its
own institutions, its own personality . . . and, more particularly, real
powers stemming from a limitation of sovereignty or a transfer of powers
from the States to the Community, the Member States have limited their
sovereign rights . . . and have thus created a body of law which binds
both their nationals and themselves."[9]

Is this line of reasoning entirely cogent? Some legal writers doubt it,
and a few have regarded *Costa* v. *Enel* as an example of judicial activism
"running wild."[10] Yet the Court's supremacy doctrine was accepted by
the judiciaries and the administrations of both the original and the new
member states, with the exception of some grumblings by the French
Conseil d'Etat, the Italian Corte Costituzionale, and a couple of English

law lords. Lord Denning, a majestic but irritable elderly gentleman, was caught intimating that "once a bill is passed by Parliament, that will dispose of all this discussion about the Treaty."[11] A few years later, however, Lord Diplock admitted that even subsequent acts of Parliament must be interpreted in line with Community law, no matter how far-fetched the interpretation.[12] Diplock and many other national judges before him obviously realized that the alternative to the supremacy clause would have been a rapid erosion of the Community; and this was a possibility that nobody really envisaged, not even the most intransigent custodians of national sovereignty. Actually, the "or else" argument, though not fully spelled out, was used by the Court, and it was this argument, much more than the one I have quoted, that led to a ready reception of the doctrine in *Costa* v. *Enel.*

But the recognition of Community preeminence was not only an indispensable development, it was also a logical development. It is self-evident that in a federal or quasi-federal context the issue of supremacy will arise only if federal norms are to apply directly, that is, to bear upon the federation's citizens without any need of intervention by the member states.[13] Article 189 of the Rome Treaty identifies a category of Community norms that do not require national implementing measures but are binding on the states and their citizens as soon as they enter into force: The founders called them "regulations" and provided them principally for those areas where the Treaty itself merely defines the thrust of Community policy and leaves its elaboration to later decisions of the Council and the Commission. One year before *Costa* v. *Enel,* however, the Court had enormously extended the Community power to deal directly with the public by ruling in *Van Gend en Loos*[14] that even Treaty provisions may be relied upon by private individuals if they expressly grant them rights and impose on the member states an obligation so precise and unconditional that it can be fulfilled without the necessity of further measures.

Costa v. *Enel* may therefore be regarded as a sequel to *Van Gend en Loos.* It is not the only sequel, however. Eleven years after *Van Gend en Loos,* the Court took in *Van Duyn* v. *Home Office*[15] a further step forward by attributing direct effect to provisions of directives not transposed into the laws of the member states within the prescribed time limit, so long as they met the conditions laid down in *Van Gend en Loos.* In order to appreciate fully the scope of this development it should be borne in mind that whereas the principal subjects governed by regulations are agriculture, transport, customs, and the social security of migrant workers, Community authorities resort to directives when they intend to harmonize national laws on such matters as taxes, banking, equality of the sexes, protection of the environment, employment contracts, and organization of companies—plain cooking compared to haute cuisine, in other words. The hope of seeing Europe grow institutionally in matters of social relationships and in terms of quality of life rests to a large extent on the adoption and the implementation of directives.[16]

Making directives immediately enforceable, however, poses a formidable problem. Unlike regulations and the Treaty provisions dealt with by *Van Gend en Loos*, directives resemble international treaties, insofar as they are binding *only* on the states and *only* as to the result to be achieved. It is understandable, therefore, that, whereas the *Van Gend en Loos* doctrine established itself within a relatively short time, its extension to directives met with bitter opposition in many quarters. For example, the French Conseil d'Etat and the German Bundesfinanzhof bluntly refused to abide by it and Hjalte Rasmussen, in a most un-Danish fit of temper, went so far as to condemn it as a case of "revolting judicial behaviour."[17]

Understandable criticism is not necessarily justifiable. It is mistaken to believe that in attributing direct effect to directives not yet complied with by the member states, the Court was only guided by political considerations, such as the intention of bypassing the states in a strategic area of lawmaking.[18] Noncompliance with directives is the most typical and most frequent form of member-state infraction; moreover, the Community authorities often turn a blind eye to it and, even when the Commission institutes proceedings against the defaulting state under Article 169 of the Treaty, the Court cannot impose any penalty on the offender. This gives the directives a dangerously elastic quality: Italy, Greece, or Belgium may agree to accept the enactment of a directive with which it is uncomfortable knowing that the price to pay for possible failure to transpose it is nonexistent or minimal.

Given these circumstances, it is sometimes submitted that the *Van Duyn* doctrine was essentially concerned with assuring respect for the rule of law. The Court's main purpose, in other words, was "to ensure that neither level of government can rely upon its malfeasance—the Member State's failure to comply, the Community's failure or even inability to enforce compliance," with a view to frustrating the legitimate expectation of the Community citizens on whom the directive confers rights. Indeed, "if a Court is forced to condone wholesale violation of a norm, that norm can be longer be termed law"; and nobody will deny that "directives are intended to have the force of law under the Treaty."[19]

In arriving at its judgment in *Van Duyn*, the Court may also have considered that by reducing the advantages member states derived from noncompliance, its judgment would have strengthened the "federal" reach of the Community power to legislate, and it may even have welcomed such a consequence. But does that warrant the revolt staged by the Conseil d'Etat or the Bundesfinanzhof? I doubt it; and so did the German Constitutional Court, which sharply scolded the Bundesfinanzhof for its rejection of the *Van Duyn* doctrine.[20] This went a long way toward restoring whatever legitimacy the Court of Justice had lost in the eyes of some observers following *Van Duyn*. The wound, one might say, is healed and the scars it has left are scarcely visible.

Supremacy and direct effect are usually regarded as two of the three principal doctrines encapsulating the judicial constitutionalization of the Treaty. The third notion is preemption, which may be dealt with very briefly. A familiar notion to U.S. lawyers, preemption plays a decisive role in the allocation of power, and it is an essential complement of the supremacy doctrine because it determines "whether a whole policy area has been actually or potentially occupied by the central authority so as to influence the intervention of the States in that area."[21] The Court of Justice discovered this problem at a rather early stage and has tended to solve it in an increasingly trenchant way.

It may be useful to give two illustrations indicative of this attitude. Under the common agricultural policy, the Community has adopted for most products a Community-wide marketing system; the Court has taken the view that the very existence of such a system precludes member states from legislating within the field covered by it.[22] Even more telling are the recent British fishery cases involving conservation measures in the North Sea. After lengthy consideration of the way in which powers to adopt these rules had been transferred to the Community, the Court held that member states were no longer at liberty to enact conservation laws, even though no Community measures had been taken.[23]

Let us now turn to a different but no less important achievement of the Court's case law. An essential feature of all federal systems is the judicial review of legislation. Striving as it did to endow the Community with a constitutional framework for a quasi-federal structure, the Court was bound to come to grips with this "conundrum to democracies," as Mauro Cappelletti has aptly called it.[24] Under Article 173 of the Treaty, the Court has the power to review the legality of acts of the Council and the Commission in actions brought by those institutions, by the member states, and even, albeit within certain limited circumstances, by "natural and legal persons." But this is tantamount to solving only a part—indeed the smaller part—of the problem. As Oliver Wendell Holmes said: "I do not think the United States would come to an end if the Supreme Court lost its power to declare an Act of Congress void, but the Union would be imperiled if the courts could not make that declaration as to the laws of the several states."[25] The Treaty does not empower the Court to review member-states' laws apart from the obvious exception of review under Article 169, which does not provide for the annulment of such laws. It does, however, provide for a machinery that, although overtly conceived for a different function (securing the uniform application of Community law throughout the member states), has been utilized by the Court in such a way as to enable it to monitor national laws for incompatibility with the Treaty and with secondary legislation. Under Article 177 of the Treaty, the Court of Justice is given jurisdiction to rule, on a reference from courts and tribunals of the member states, on any question of interpretation and validity of Community law raised before them; lower courts *may* request the Court of Justice to give a preliminary ruling, whereas courts of last resort *must* send the matter to Luxembourg.

How effective is the preliminary rulings procedure? In comparing it with a full-fledged dual system of federal courts as can be found in the United States, some learned writers have described it as legally frailer but politically more faithful to the federal ethos.[26] Although the latter opinion is disputable, the former is no doubt correct, for the Community system of review, much more than the U.S. one, requires the cooperation and goodwill of the state courts. The reason is twofold: Under Article 177, litigants do not have *locus standi* to appeal national judicial decisions to the Court of Justice, and the Court lacks coercive powers to enforce its judgments.[27]

The Court's first preoccupation was therefore to win that cooperation and that goodwill. The early results were frustrating. It took almost four years before the first reference made by a national judicial body (the Gerechtshof in The Hague) was received at the Court, and legend has it that on that day there was abundant popping of champagne corks in the deliberation room. As time went by, however, requests for a preliminary ruling began to arrive in increasing numbers; nowadays they amount to 150 a year on average. More importantly, most national courts—about 95 percent according to a recent survey—accept the rulings requested by other courts when they have to decide a similar case. In short, the interpretations given at Luxembourg have acquired a binding authority and, at least to some extent, have been attributed precedential value.

Why did this happen? The only reason I can see, much as expounding it may sound awkward, is the cleverness of my predecessors. If what makes a judge "good" is his awareness of the constraints on judicial decisionmaking and the knowledge that rulings must be convincing in order to evoke obedience, the Luxembourg judges of the 1960s and 1970s were obviously *very* good. In other words, knowing that the Court had almost no powers that were not traceable to its institutional standing and the persuasiveness of its judgments, they made the most of these assets.[28] Thus they developed a style that may be drab and repetitive but explains as well as declares the law, and they showed unlimited patience vis-à-vis the national judges, reformulating questions couched in imprecise terms or extracting from the documents concerning the main proceedings the elements of Community law that needed to be interpreted with regard to the subject matter of the dispute.

It was by following this courteously didactic method that the Luxembourg judges won the confidence of their colleagues from Palermo to Edinburgh and from Bordeaux to Berlin, and it was by winning their confidence that they were able to transform the procedure of Article 177 into a tool whereby private individuals may challenge their national legislation for incompatibility with Community law. It bears repeating that under Article 177 national judges can *only* request the Court of Justice to interpret a Community measure. The Court never told them they were entitled to overstep that bound; in fact, whenever they did so—for example, whenever they asked if national rule A is in violation of Community regulation B or directive C—the Court answered that its only power is to explain what B or C actually means. But having paid this lip service to the language of the Treaty and having clarified the meaning of the relevant Community measure, the Court usually went on to indicate to what extent a *certain type* of national legislation can be regarded as compatible with that measure.[29] The national judge is thus led by the hand as far as the door; crossing the threshold is the judge's job, but now a job no harder than child's play.

COMMUNITY CITIZENSHIP
AND HUMAN RIGHTS

Let us now return to the issues of Community citizenship and the human rights of the Community citizens. As I pointed out at the beginning of the chapter, the Treaty guarantees labor mobility and the right of the migrant worker and his family to share, on a par with the national workers, the social benefits of the host country, including housing, medical care, education, and social security rights. But this system, although a remarkable advance by comparison with the time when the migration of workers was handled by the authorities of the host state, does not entail any recognition of a common citizenship status. Individuals may be said to derive their transnational rights from their constitutional position as nationals of a member state and from their functional status as workers.[30]

In recent times, however, an evolution has been clearly detectable. Since 1979 the European Parliament has been elected by popular vote, and on the cover of passports issued by the member states the words "European Community" are printed above the name of the issuing country. College students are granted scholarships enabling them to get credit in any other EC country. Even more significantly, the Council has adopted directives under which the right to stay or settle in another member state and enjoy the same privileges as its nationals would be conferred on *all* Europeans, whether workers or not.[31] The Court has of course been aware that certain progressive forces are trying to give rise to a form, albeit still imperfect, of European citizenship and recently, seizing the opportunity offered, it legitimized their efforts with one of its shrewdest judgments.[32]

In June 1982, Ian William Cowan, a United Kingdom national, was paying a visit to his son in Paris. At the exit of a metro station he was thrashed by a gang of rowdies, and the assault caused him severe physical damage, for which he asked compensation under Article 706/15 of the French Code of Criminal Procedure. As far as foreigners are concerned, however, this provision requires the victim of an assault to hold a residence permit or to be the national of a country that has entered into a reciprocal agreement with France. As he met neither condition, Cowan was not indemnified. He therefore brought the case before the Commission d'Indemnisation des Victimes d'Infractions (Compensation Board for Victims of Crime), a body attached to the Paris Tribunal de Grande Instance. The board stayed the proceedings and asked the Court to rule on the interpretation of the principle of nondiscrimination as set out in Article 7 of the Treaty in order that it could assess whether the French measure was compatible with Community law.

The Court stressed that under Article 7 the principle of nondiscrimination applies not only to goods and workers moving throughout the common market but also to the movement of services and noted that the latter includes both the freedom to provide and the freedom to receive a service anywhere in the Community. A corollary of this finding is that a person who goes to another country in order to receive such a service must be guaranteed protection on the same basis as the nationals of that country and the aliens residing there. A tourist is by definition a recipient of services; hence, when a state grants protection against the risk of assault and, if the risk materializes, financial compensation, the tourist is obviously entitled to both. Cowan was probably a tourist, and this is why the Court insisted on that notion. However, since leaving one's country without resorting to services provided in the host country (means of transportation, hotels, restaurants, etc.) is impossible, it is safe to conclude that the Cowan judgment does not fall much behind the words of Justice Jackson's concurring opinion in *Edwards*

v. *California:* "It is a privilege of citizenship of the United States, protected from state abridgment, to enter any state of the Union, either for temporary sojourn or for the establishment of permanent residence therein."[33]

Human rights is the next area for consideration. In the same way that they ignored the issue of citizenship, the framers of the Rome Treaty did not envisage the need to protect human rights. Presumably, they knew that bills of rights are in the long run a powerful vehicle of integration and in 1957, when the European climate was already tinged with skepticism and in any event was no longer virginal, they were not eager to see the integration process speeded up by a central authority empowered to safeguard the civil liberties of the Community citizens first in Brussels and later, perhaps, in the six countries concerned.[34] But there is a further possibility: The Treaty founders may have thought that the scope of Community law was essentially limited to economic issues and, as such, did not involve human rights problems. If this is the reason why they omitted to guarantee those rights, no U.S. observer should be shocked by their attitude: In arguing for the ratification of the Constitution despite the absence of a bill of rights, Alexander Hamilton and James Madison took the view that the limited powers of the federal government made such a bill unnecessary.[35] Indeed, it is well known that the U.S. Supreme Court did not issue any important opinion in the area of free speech until well into this century.

Europe, however, experienced a quicker development. As Community law came to govern diverse and sometimes unforeseen facets of human activity, it encroached upon a whole gamut of old and new rights with both an economic and a strictly "civil" content. Thus, a problem that in 1957 might have appeared to be of practical insignificance turned ten years later into one of the most controversial questions of Community law, so much so that it ended by taking on the character of a major judicial conflict. On October 18, 1967, the Constitutional Court of the Federal Republic of Germany indicated, albeit in a hypothetical fashion, that the Community order, lacking any protection for human rights, had no lawful democratic basis. The transfer of powers from Germany to the Community could therefore not deprive German citizens of the protection accorded to them by their constitution; it followed that Community law had to be examined at the national level to ensure that it was compatible with internal constitutional provisions.[36]

It was a brutal blow jeopardizing not only the supremacy but the very independence of Community law. Something had to be done, and the Court did it, both for fear that its hard-won conquests might vanish and because of its own growing awareness that a "democratic deficit" had become apparent in the management of the Community. Thus, initially in dicta and finally in a judgment of 1974 (*Nold* v. *Commission*), the Luxembourg judges declared that "fundamental rights form an integral part of the general principles of law," the observance of which it ensures. But what book would they have to consult for the identification and the protection of such rights? *Nold* answered this question too: "The Court is bound to draw inspiration from constitutional traditions common to the Member States. . . . International treaties for the protection of human rights on which the Member States have collaborated . . . can supply guidelines which should be followed within the framework of Community law."[37]

There were to be two sources in other words: common constitutional values and human rights conventions. In the fifteen years following *Nold*, the Court extracted from both of them but increasingly from the second one whatever elements could contribute to the preservation of minimum human rights standards in the legislative output and the administrative practice of Brussels. More specifically, and disregarding rights of a purely economic nature, the Court concerned itself with procedural and substantive due process,[38] respect for private life,[39] lawyers' business secrecy,[40] the fact that criminal-law provisions cannot be made retroactive,[41] the principle of review by courts,[42] the inviolability of domicile, and the right not to incriminate oneself.[43] Some of these rights, it should be noted, were dealt with in cases brought by companies complaining about antitrust searches and inquiries made by Commission officials under Article 85 of the Treaty.

How should one assess this case law? According to Cappelletti, watching "those thirteen little men unknown to most of the 320 million Community citizens, devoid of political power, charisma and popular legitimation" who claim "for themselves the . . . capacity to do what the framers did not even think of doing, and what the political branches of the Community do not even try to undertake," is a fascinating spectacle.[44] Though perhaps guilty of artistic license, Cappelletti may not be mistaken. Reading an unwritten bill of rights into Community law is indeed the most striking contribution the Court has made to the development of a constitution for Europe. This statement, however, should be qualified in two respects. First, as said above, that contribution was forced on the Court from outside, by the German and, later, the Italian Constitutional Courts.[45] Second, the Court's effort to safeguard the fundamental rights of the Community citizens stopped at the threshold of national legislation.

So far, in other words, Europe has not experienced anything resembling *Gitlow* v. *New York*, the judgment in which the U.S. Supreme Court held that the limitations laid down in the U.S. Bill of Rights are not only applicable to the federal government but extend to the laws and administrative practices of the individual states.[46] In *Cinéthèque* v. *Fédération Nationale des Cinémas Français*, the Court of Justice made it clear that "it has no power to examine the compatibility" with its human rights catalog of laws concerning areas that fall "within the jurisdiction of the national legislator."[47] For a self-inflicted restriction, this is rather severe. It is, however, compensated in that, in terms of respect for human rights, no member state is comparable with Manuel Noriega's Panama or, for that matter, Huey Long's Louisiana. Moreover, one can safely assume that because Community law penetrates directly the legal systems of the member states, national courts interpreting the laws of their own state in the light of a fundamental freedom are unlikely to remain below the standards set at Luxembourg.[48]

CONCLUSION

The foregoing survey—which is incomplete, as it has not dealt with the case law of the Court in such crucial matters as the movement of goods and the international posture of the Community—should leave no doubt as to the degree of activism the Court displayed in fostering the integration of Europe and forging a European identity. Judicial activism, however, is not necessarily a good thing. Judges are usually incompetent as lawmakers, and their inventiveness is incompatible with the values of certainty and predictability; it is indeed unfair, because the findings of inventive courts catch the litigants by surprise.[49] Worse still, as Judge Thijmen Koopmans has put it, courts "are not designed to be a reflex of a democratic society."[50] If this is true, adventurous enterprises of the kind described above are only acceptable under very particular conditions. Listing such conditions would serve no purpose, but those prevailing in Europe during the Gaullist revolt and the dark age of stagnation that followed it should certainly be counted among them: Above all, there were the inexistence of a body both representative and genuinely legislative and the obdurate reluctance of the member states to fully implement the Treaty they themselves had framed.

In these circumstances, does it have any meaning to raise the problem of the Court's activism? Things are changing: Under the Single European Act the Parliament can exert a considerable influence on the lawmaking process, the Commission is headed by a dedicated European who also happens to be a consummate politician, hundreds of directives are being enacted, and we are witnessing a heated debate on whether an integrated Europe should be a giant consumer's union with goods, services, and capital flowing unhindered or a political entity directing economic change into socially beneficial channels.

Some observers argue in the light of these changes that the time has come for the Court to reconsider its philosophy. When democracy advances and politics asserts its claims, judges are bound to take a pace back. The reason for their being in the van has waned, and if they insist on remaining there, they risk becoming so embroiled in the passions of the day as to imperil their most precious resource, their independence.

These remarks contain more than a kernel of truth, and the Court itself seems to have grasped this. *Cinéthèque* might indeed signal the opening of a new trend in its jurisprudence, and a similar attitude is detectable in *Comitology*, a judgment that refused to equalize the juris-dictional status of Parliament to that of the Commission and the Council by giving it standing to bring an action under Article 173.[51] Accepting a measure of self-restraint, however, does not mean embarking on a course of strict constructionism. The Court is likely to extend the area of problems it feels should be solved by the political institutions, but in other areas it will undoubtedly go on feeling that it can, or rather must, exercise guidance.

There are essentially two such areas. The first includes a number of issues the Council is obliged or empowered to regulate under the Treaty but did not regulate on purpose, so as to avoid for as long as possible their adjustment to Community criteria. State aids to industry are a case in point. Deciding whether they are compatible with the common market falls to the Commission, but the surveillance power of its officials is seriously impaired by the lack of rules imposing on the states a timely and accurate notification of the subsidies they grant.[52] Sooner or later, therefore, such rules will have to be written by the Court.

The second area is a result of the Single Act. The words of Article 8a ("The internal market shall comprise an area without internal frontiers in which the free movement of goods, persons, services and capital is ensured") have by now rung all over the world. Only specialists, however, know that they are accompanied by manifold derogations, sometimes in the form of joint declarations appended to the SEA, which deprive them of much of their scope and effectiveness. The binding force and the meaning of such declarations are often uncertain. What should one make, for example, of the most incisive one, which stipulates that "setting the date of 31 December 1992 does not create an automatic legal effect"? Is this a formal rule governing the decisions of a court of law? And if it is, does it mean that Article 8a is incapable of instituting legal obligations, or can it be read in a less disruptive way?[53]

The Court still has ample room to mold the destiny of the Community both by writing new rules and by cutting a number of Gordian knots. The most difficult challenge will be to reconcile this prospect with the necessity of a retreat from the daring of old—or, one might say, with

the need for a little rest, all the more pleasant for being so richly
deserved. But, of course, one always expects judges to know how to
conceal a contradiction.

NOTES

This chapter is based on an address that was delivered at the Center for
European Studies, Harvard University, November 2, 1989. An earlier version of
this chapter was published in *Common Market Law Review* 26 (1989): 595–614.
Used with permission.

1. See F. Jacobs and K. Karst, "The 'Federal' Legal Order: The U.S.A. and
Europe Compared: Juridical Perspective," in M. Cappelletti et al., eds., *Integration
Through Law*, vol. 1, book 1, (New York: De Gruyter, 1986), p. 171.

2. See E. Stein, "Lawyers, Judges and the Making of a Transnational Constitution," *American Journal of International Law* 75 (1981), 1.

3. Diplock, "The Courts as Legislators," in B. W. Harvey, ed., *The Lawyer
and Justice* 1978, p. 280.

4. S. Krislov, C.-D. Ehlermann, and J. Weiler, "The Political Organs and the
Decision-Making Process in the United States and the European Community,"
in Cappelletti et al., *Integration Through Law*, cit., vol. 1, book 2, p. 18.

5. See Stein, "Lawyers, Judges," cit., n. 2.

6. See Jacobs and Karst, "The 'Federal' Legal Order," cit., n. 1, p. 186.

7. M. Cappelletti, M. Seccombe, and J. Weiler, "A General Introduction," in
Cappelletti et al., *Integration Through Law*, cit., n. 1, p. 29.

8. Case 6/64, *Costa v. Enel*, preliminary ruling of July 15, 1964, European
Court Reports (ECR) 585. This line of case law found its apogee in case 106/
77, *Simmenthal v. Commission*, preliminary ruling of March 9, 1978, ECR 629.
In a more recent ruling on a point of law referred to them by the House of
Lords, the Luxembourg judges made a further step forward on the same road:
National law, they said, must not prevent interim protection being given to
Community law rights even when the existence of such rights has yet to be
ascertained by the European Court (case C-213/89, *The Queen v. Secretary of
State for Transport ex parte Factortame*, preliminary ruling of June 19, 1990, not
yet reported). In some quarters in Britain this judgment was received with
grumblings and at times anger. Lord Denning, who in 1974 had described the
Treaty of Rome as "an incoming tide" flowing "into the estuaries and up the
rivers" of Britain, proposed to amend this dictum in the following way: "No
longer is European law an incoming tide. . . . It is now like a tidal wave bringing
down our sea walls and flowing inland over our fields and houses—to the
dismay of all" (Introduction in G. Smith, *The European Court of Justice: Judges
or Policy Makers?* [London: Bruges Group, 1990]).

9. *Costa v. Enel.*

10. H. Rasmussen, *On Law and Policy in the European Court of Justice: A
Comparative Study in Judicial Policy Making* (Dordrecht: Martinus Nijhoff, 1986).

11. *Felixstowe Dock and Ry Co.* v. *British Transport Docks Board* (1976), 2 *Common Market Law Reports*, 655.

12. *Garland* v. *British Rail Engineering* (1982), 2 *All England Law Reports*, 402.

13. D. J. Elazar and I. Greilsammer, "Federal Democracy: The USA and Europe Compared—A Political Science Perspective," in Cappelletti et al., *Integration Through Law*, cit., vol. 1, book 1, p. 103.

14. Case 26/62, *Van Gend en Loos* v. *Nederlandse administratie der belastingen,* judgment of February 5, 1963, ECR 1.

15. Case 41/74, *Van Duyn* v. *Home Office,* judgment of December 4, 1974, ECR 1337.

16. For a further elaboration of this idea, see my article on "The Incorporation of Community Law into the Domestic Laws of the Member States of the European Communities," in Unidroit, ed., *International Uniform Law in Practice* (Rome: Unidroit and Oceana, 1988), p. 23.

17. Rasmussen, *On Law and Policy*, n. 10, p. 12.

18. This and the following remarks are drawn from Cappelletti et al., "A General Introduction," cit., n. 7, pp. 38ff.

19. Ibid., p. 39.

20. *Bundesverfassungsgericht*, 28vR 687/85, judgment of April 8, 1987, Entscheidungen des Bundesverfassungsgericht, 1987, 223.

21. Cappelletti et al., "A General Introduction," cit., n. 7, p. 32.

22. Jacobs and Karst, "The 'Federal' Legal Order," cit., n. 1, p. 238.

23. Case 804/79, *Commission* v. *United Kingdom,* judgment of May 5, 1981, ECR 1045. See T. Koopmans, "Federalism, the European Community and the Case Law of the Court of Justice," in K. Lenaerts, ed., *Two Hundred Years of U.S. Constitution and Thirty Years of EEC Treaty: Outlook for a Comparison* (Brussels: Kluwer, Stoy Scientia, 1988), 25.

24. See M. Cappelletti, *The Judicial Process in Comparative Perspective* (Oxford: Clarendon Press, 1989), 149.

25. O. W. Holmes, Jr., "Law and the Court," in *Collected Legal Papers* (New York: Peter Smith, 1952), 291, 295–296.

26. Cappelletti et al., "A General Introduction," cit., n. 7, p. 23.

27. Cappelletti, *Judicial Process*, cit., n. 24, p. 367.

28. Ibid., n. 24, p. 371.

29. See Koopmans, "Federalism, the European Community," cit., n. 23, pp. 30ff.

30. Cappelletti et al., "A General Introduction," cit., n. 7, p. 48. See also M. Garth, "Migrant Workers and Rights of Mobility in the European Community and the United States: A Study of Law, Community and Citizenship in the Welfare State," in Cappelletti et al., *Integration Through Law*, cit., n. 1, vol. 1, book 3, pp. 103ff.

31. See Council Directive no. 366/90, of June 28, 1990, on the right of residence for students, *Official Journal of the European Communities (OJ)* 1990, L 180, p. 30; Council Directive no. 365/90, of June 28, 1990, on the right of residence for employees and self-employed persons who have ceased their occupational activity, *OJ* 1990, L 180, p. 28; Council Directive no. 364/90, of

June 28, 1990, on the right of residence, *OJ* 1990, L 180, p. 26. Furthermore, the Commission has proposed a directive on voting rights for Community nationals in local elections in their member states of residence, *OJ* 1988, C 246, p. 4.

32. Case 186/87, *Cowan* v. *Trésor Public*, preliminary ruling of February 2, 1989, ECR 195.

33. *Edwards* v. *California*, 314 U.S. (1941), p. 183.

34. I have developed this theme at some length in my speech to the Special International Conference on Procedural Law on the occasion of the Ninth Centenary of the University of Bologna (September 22–24, 1988), to be published in the proceedings of the Conference under the title "Safeguarding Human Rights: The Rôle of the Court of Justice of the European Communities." See therein for further references.

35. Cappelletti, *Judicial Process*, cit., n. 24, p. 171.

36. *Bundesverfassungsgericht*, order of October 18, 1967 Entscheidungen des Bundesverfassungsgericht, 1967, 223.

37. Case 4/73, *Nold* v. *Commission*, judgment of May 14, 1974, ECR 491, para. 13.

38. Case 98/79, *Pecastaing* v. *Belgian State*, judgment of March 5, 1980, ECR 691; case 209/78, *Van Landewyck* v. *Commission*, judgment of October 29, 1980, ECR 3125; joined cases 100-103/80, *Musique diffusion française SA* v. *Commission* ("Pioneer"), judgment of June 7, 1983 ECR 1825.

39. Case 136/79, *Panasonic (National) UK Limited* v. *Commission*, judgment of June 26, 1980, ECR 2033; case 145/83 *Stanley Adams* v. *Commission*, judgment of November 7, 1985, ECR 3539.

40. Case 155/79, *AM & S Europe* v. *Commission*, judgment of May 18, 1982, ECR 1575.

41. Case 63/83, *Regina* v. *Kirk*, preliminary ruling of July 10, 1984, ECR 2689.

42. Case 141/84, *de Compte* v. *European Parliament*, judgment of June 20, 1985, ECR 1951; case 222/84, *Johnston* v. *Chief Constable of the Royal Ulster Constabulary*, judgment of May 15, 1986, ECR 1651; case 222/86, *Unectef* v. *Heylens*, preliminary ruling of October 15, 1987, ECR 4097.

43. Joined cases 46/87 and 227/88, judgment of September 21, 1989, *Hoechst AG* v. *Commission*, ECR 2859; joined cases 97, 98, and 99/87, judgment of October 17, 1989, *Dow Chemical Iberica SA et al.* v. *Commission*, ECR 3165; case 85/87, judgment of October 17, 1989, *Dow Benelux NV* v. *Commission*, ECR 3137; case 27/88, judgment of October 18, 1989, *Solvay & Cie* v. *Commission*, ECR 3355; case 374/87, judgment of October 18, 1989, *Orkem* v. *Commission*, ECR 3283.

44. Cappelletti, *Judicial Process*, cit., n. 24, p. 174.

45. *Corte costituzionale*, judgment of December 27, 1973, no. 183, in *Giurisprudenza costituzionale*, 1973, 2401.

46. *Gitlow* v. *New York*, 268, U.S. (1925), 652.

47. Joined cases 60 and 61/84, *Cinéthèque* v. *Fédération Nationale des Cinémas Français*, preliminary ruling of July 11, 1985, ECR 2605, para. 26. This judgment

has been criticized by J. Weiler in "The European Court at a Crossroads: Community Human Rights and Member State Action," in F. Capotorti et al., *Du droit international au droit de l'intégration* (Baden-Baden: Nomos, 1987), 821ff. However, in case 5/88, *Wachauf* v. *Federal Republic of Germany,* judgment of July 13, 1989, ECR 2609, at point 19, the Court refined this case law by holding that national implementing measures of a Community provision incorporating the protection of a human right must give effect to this provision in such a way as not to disregard that right.

48. J. A. Frowein, "Fundamental Human Rights as a Vehicle of Legal Integration in Europe," in Cappelletti et al., *Integration Through Law,* cit., n. 1, vol. 1, book 3, p. 302.

49. See generally Cappelletti, *Judicial Process,* cit., n. 24, pp. 35ff.

50. T. Koopmans, "The Roots of Judicial Activism," in F. Matscher and H. Petzold, eds., *Protecting Human Rights: The European Dimension,* (Cologne: Carl Heymans, 1988), p. 321.

51. Case 302/87, *Parliament* v. *Council* ("Comitology") judgment of September 27, 1988, ECR 5615. More recently, however, the Court held that the Parliament should have the right to challenge Council and Commission decisions, but *only* in order to safeguard its prerogatives (for example, taking part in the legislative process) and, hence, to ensure the institutional balance created by the Treaty, of which such prerogatives are an element (case C-70/88, *European Parliament* v. *Council* ("Chernobyl"), judgment of May 22, 1990, not yet reported). In the essay quoted in n. 8 above, G. Smith wrote that this "abrupt *volte face* can only be described as one of (the Court's) most blatantly policy based judgments ever." Actually, *volte face* is too strong a term. In *Chernobyl* the *locus standi* of the Parliament is not grounded on Article 173, and it does not cover the whole gamut of rights for which the Parliament had requested (and had not obtained) protection in *Comitology.*

52. See generally J. Pelkmans, "The Institutional Economics of European Integration," in Cappelletti et al., *Integration Through Law,* cit., n. 1, vol. 1, book 1, pp. 373ff.

53. See A. S. Toth, "The Legal Status of the Declarations annexed to the Single European Act," in 23 *Common Market Law Review* (1986), 803ff.

Acronyms and Abbreviations

CAP	Common Agricultural Policy
COREPER	Committee of Permanent Representatives
CSCE	Conference on Security and Cooperation in Europe
DG	Directorate General
EC	European Community
ECSC	European Coal and Steel Community
Ecu	European currency unit
EFTA	European Free Trade Area
EMS	European Monetary System
EMU	economic and monetary union
EPC	European political cooperation
ESPRIT	European Strategic Programme for Research and Development in Information Technology
Euratom	European Atomic Energy Community
EUREKA	European Programme for High Technology Research and Development
GATT	General Agreement on Tariffs and Trade
GNP	gross national product
IGC	Intergovernmental Conference
MEP	member of European Parliament
MP	member of [British] Parliament
NATO	North Atlantic Treaty Organization
OECD	Organization for Economic Cooperation and Development
RACE	Research and Development in Advanced Communications
SEA	Single European Act
UNICE	Union des Confederations de l'Industrie et des Employeurs d'Europe
VAT	value-added tax

About the Book

The New European Community is the first systematic, book-length discussion of the major political institutions of the European Community (EC) after the transformation of the 1987 Single European Act, itself a surprise and a mystery whose effects are unraveled here.

Professors Keohane and Hoffmann open the volume by placing the evolution of the new European Community into broad, theoretical perspective. Their expert contributors—including highly regarded international scholars, a judge of the European Court of Justice, and a long-term British politician—present engaging overviews of the process at work in major EC events and institutions. The centerpiece of the volume, Peter Ludlow's chapter on the European Commission, lays out all of the systems and actors in the emerging EC and shows their direct connection with problems of Community development and integration.

Filled with examples, illustrations, anecdotes, and valuable data, *The New European Community* will be indispensable for all students and scholars of international relations and European studies as well as for those in business and government who want to understand the European Community before and beyond 1992.

About the
Editors and Contributors

Stanley Hoffmann is Douglas Dillon Professor of the Civilization of France, and Chairman of the Center for European Studies, Harvard University, Cambridge, Massachusetts.

Robert O. Keohane is Stanfield Professor of International Peace, and Chair of the Department of Government, Harvard University, Cambridge, Massachusetts.

Peter Ludlow is Director of the Centre for European Policy Studies in Brussels.

G. Federico Mancini is a Judge of the European Court of Justice, Luxembourg.

Andrew Moravcsik is a member of the faculty, Department of Government, Harvard University, Cambridge, Massachusetts.

Wolfgang Wessels is a research fellow at the Institut für Europäische Politik in Bonn.

Shirley Williams, who was a founder of the British Social Democratic party, is a member of the faculty, John F. Kennedy School of Government, Harvard University, Cambridge, Massachusetts.

Index